INTERPRETIVE VOICES

INTERPRETIVE VOICES
Responding to Patients

Edited by
Debbie Bandler Bellman
and Jean Arundale

KARNAC

First edition published in 2015 by
Karnac Books Ltd
118 Finchley Road
London NW3 5HT

British Library Cataloguing in Publication Data

A C.I.P. for this book is available from the British Library

ISBN-13: 978-1-78220-037-6

Typeset by V Publishing Solutions Pvt Ltd., Chennai, India

Printed in Great Britain

www.karnacbooks.com

For today's and tomorrow's analytic voices

CONTENTS

ACKNOWLEDGEMENTS

We are very grateful to the many who have helped with this book. Especial thanks go to our contributors, for all their hard work and keenness to write, and without whom this volume would not exist. We have welcomed the chance to publish again with Karnac, and are indebted to our editorial contacts, Roderick Tweedy, the Project Manager Kate Pearce, and all others on Karnac's production team.

Our gratitude goes also to our colleagues, supervisors, and analysts, whose analytic voices have all made invaluable contributions to the development of our own.

To our patients, we say thank you for guiding us in how to listen and speak in ways that are interpretively meaningful. In order to preserve the confidentiality of patients, we have left out any identifying details and disguised all clinical illustrations.

Last but not least, we would like to thank our families and important others for their ongoing support and encouragement.

ABOUT THE EDITORS AND CONTRIBUTORS

Simon Archer is a psychoanalyst in private practice in York. He trained first as a fine artist and worked as an art therapist before training as a psychotherapist with the British Association of Psychotherapists (now the British Psychotherapy Foundation). Later he trained with the Institute of Psychoanalysis. He is a Full Member of the British Psychoanalytic Association and a Fellow of the British Psychoanalytical Society. He has a particular interest in shame and the part it plays in mental structure and emotional functioning, and has published a number of papers on the subject.

Jean Arundale is a training and supervising analyst for the British Psychoanalytic Association (BPA) and the British Psychotherapy Foundation. In the BPA, she served for five years as Chair of the Scientific Committee and a member of the Board. She is primarily in private practice but also works part-time as a consultant psychotherapist in the NHS, heading a psychodynamic psychotherapy service at Guy's Hospital. She has presented papers at University College London and European Psychoanalytical Federation conferences, and has taught, published, and edited variously in the field of psychoanalysis.

Debbie Bandler Bellman is a psychoanalyst and a child and adolescent psychotherapist, in private practice. As a Full Member of the BPA and member of the BPA Board, she was Honorary Secretary for five years and currently is Chair of the Scientific Committee. She also serves on the BPA Training Committee and teaches on its psychoanalysis training. In the field of child psychotherapy she is a training analyst of the Association of Child Psychotherapists and a supervisor for the British Psychotherapy Foundation's child and adolescent psychotherapy training. She has published a number of psychoanalytic papers, is a past editor of the *Journal of Child Psychotherapy*, and with Jean Arundale co-edited *Transference and Countertransference: A Unifying Focus of Psychoanalysis*, published by Karnac, 2011.

Lesley Caldwell is a member of the British Psychoanalytic Association (BPA), in private practice in London. She serves as a BPA representative on the International Psychoanalytical Association's Committee for Women and Psychoanalysis. She is Honorary Professor in the Psychoanalysis Unit at University College London, where she organises the Interdisciplinary programme and teaches and supervises on the master's and doctoral programmes. With Helen Taylor Robinson she is joint general editor of the *Collected Works of Donald Winnicott* (to be published by Oxford University Press, 2015).

Sara Collins is a training and supervising analyst for the British Psychoanalytic Association (BPA) and British Psychotherapy Foundation (BPF). She works in private practice. A Full Member of the BPA and a Senior Member of the BPF, she is a member of the BPA's Training and Training Analysts Committees. She has taught widely on the BPA's psychoanalysis training, the BPF's psychotherapy training, and on external courses. She has a number of publications, including "Why reconstruct? Perspectives on reconstruction within the transference", published in *Transference and Countertransference: A Unifying Focus of Psychoanalysis* (Karnac, 2011), and "On authenticity: The question of truth in construction and autobiography", published in *The International Journal of Psychoanalysis*.

Michael Halton is a psychoanalyst and senior member of the British Psychoanalytic Association (BPA), the British Psychotherapy Foundation (BPF), and the Tavistock Society of Psychotherapists.

He is a member of the BPA Training Committee and teaches on its psychoanalysis training. He is a training therapist and supervisor for the BPF, and supervises and lectures at the Tavistock Clinic. He has a particular interest in technique. Among his published work are papers on Bion, the oedipal situation, and phobic states of mind (in *Transference and Countertransference: A Unifying Focus of Psychoanalysis*, Karnac, 2011). He was formerly a part-time consultant psychologist in the NHS and is now in full-time private practice.

David Morgan is a consultant psychotherapist and psychoanalyst in the NHS and private practice. He is a training analyst/therapist and supervisor for the British Psychoanalytic Association and British Psychotherapy Foundation, and a Fellow of the British Psychoanalytical Society. He provides consultation to the public and private sector, including organisations of a political and social nature, and is a regular speaker at conferences. He enjoys lecturing and teaching at home and abroad and has contributed to radio and TV programmes on whistleblowers, Van Gogh, and fundamentalism. Recently he has lectured on narcissism at the London School of Economics, and on poetry, hypnotism and also purgatory at the Freud Museum, on perversion at City University, on whistleblowing and dissent at the Institute of Psychoanalysis and the Wessex Training in Oxford. He has recently published in the *New Internationalist*. He was co-editor with Stan Ruszczynski of *Lectures on Violence, Perversion, and Delinquency* (Karnac, 2007).

Joscelyn Richards is a training and supervising analyst of the British Psychoanalytic Association (BPA). She played a major role in establishing the BPA, and is currently Chair of its Training Committee and a Member of the Board. She led the setting up of the British Psychoanalytic Council and served as its first Chair. She co-founded a psychotherapy centre in the National Health Service and was Consultant Clinical Psychologist there until her retirement. She currently works in private practice. She has taught widely, and presented and written papers on working with patients with borderline and psychotic disorders. She recently received the British Psychoanalytic Council's Lifetime Achievement Award.

Julia Sandelson is a training and supervising analyst of the British Psychoanalytic Association (BPA). She is also a training and supervising therapist of the British Psychotherapy Foundation (BPF), formerly the British Association of Psychotherapists (BAP), as well as a training and supervising therapist for a number of other training organisations. She is on the BPA Training Committee and teaches on the training in psychoanalysis. She has developed and taught theoretical and clinical seminars and workshops on a variety of subjects for the BPA, the BPF and other training organisations. She works in private practice and part-time in the National Health Service at the Maudsley and St. Thomas' hospitals.

Lesley Steyn is a psychoanalyst in private practice. She is a member of the British Psychoanalytic Association (BPA), on its Training and Scientific Committees, and teaches theoretical and clinical seminars on the BPA psychoanalysis training. She is a Senior Member of the British Psychotherapy Foundation and teaches on its training and external courses. She also supervises and is a training therapist for other training organisations. In the NHS she has worked and taught at the Portman Clinic, and is a visiting lecturer at the Tavistock Centre, supervising psychotherapy students. She has published papers in *The International Journal of Psychoanalysis* and is a member of its editorial board.

INTRODUCTION

Jean Arundale and Debbie Bandler Bellman

Interpretations in psychoanalysis come in many shapes, forms, and sizes. Foremost are interpretations of the transference, positive or negative, and of the present or past unconscious. Some analysts give priority to interpreting anxiety and unconscious phantasy, with a focus on internal objects, while others may give equal space to extra-transference interpretations, reconstructions, or enactments. All may include empathic resonances, reflections, spontaneous utterances straight from the unconscious, or long-planned interpretations delivered in stages, and so on.

Psychoanalysts themselves come in diverse shapes and forms. Historically, these variances have largely been attributed to differences between traditional schools of thought, and there have been attempts to find common ground between theoretical traditions in the face of what has been felt to be a psychoanalytic field in danger of becoming too pluralistic. In more recent years, it has been noted that within theoretical traditions there can be wide differences between the ways analysts speak to their patients, sometimes wider than between schools, in spite of ostensibly subscribing to and drawing upon a singular body of theory and its implied techniques. This has led to some concern that analysis could become too individualistic, thus leading to a culture of "anything goes".

Do we conclude that individuality reigns? Or can there be one psychoanalysis that embraces all groups and individuals, that encompasses psychoanalysis as a whole while at the same time taking into account the inevitability and importance of the analyst's unique personality and individual analytic voice?

To add a further dimension, the interaction between the two personalities and minds of the patient and analyst in the analytic space produces its own diction, vocabulary, and distinctive voice. Ogden (2014) has written that if a patient were "a speck on the wall" (p. 867) in the consulting room, he might be surprised to hear his analyst's voice speaking, during the course of an analytic day, to different patients in very different ways with very different language and idiom, yet nevertheless recognise that it is the same, his own, analyst speaking.

The acceptance of individuality in the interpretive voice can be seen as similar to the recognition of the value of countertransference. Before it was recognised as a valuable asset and important factor in the analytic process, countertransference was viewed as an obstacle in clinical work. In a similar manner, wariness of individuality in analytic practice has given way to an appreciation of the ways in which the personality and personal viewpoint of the analyst influence both the understanding of clinical material and how its meaning is communicated to the patient. By definition difficult to schematise, individuality is implicit in the literature and capable of being demonstrated.

The contributions in this book exemplify ways in which different analysts think about and treat the issue of interpretation, illustrating the distinctiveness with which an analyst expresses her own personality, creativity and understanding within the medium of psychoanalysis. Entering the realm of the philosophical concept of the particularised universal in which the general concept finds its expression not in abstraction but only in its particular manifestation, each analyst construes the theories and body of knowledge of psychoanalysis in his or her own way. Though we do not in any way feel that "anything goes", we do feel that the analytic process can embrace not only different theoretical views but also differences in how we listen to and communicate with our patients.

This book about the practice of psychoanalysis and the interaction between two personalities illustrates the individual interpretive voices of its ten authors, their analytic methods, their thinking, their understanding of their patients, and how they convey this understanding whilst remaining authentic.

Reference

Ogden, T. H. (2004). This art of psychoanalysis: Dreaming undreamt dreams and interrupted cries. *International Journal of Psychoanalysis, 85*: 857–877.

CHAPTER ONE

The voice behind the couch: whatever happened to the blank screen?

Sara Collins

Introduction

The analyst's interpretative voice, coming as it does from behind the couch, is a powerful tool, unique to psychoanalysis, which sets it apart from other forms of human interaction. Every analyst must find his own interpretive voice, and psychoanalytic theories of technique seek to articulate the nature and quality of that voice.

This chapter explores and defines a particular aspect of the analytic voice. The fact that interpretations are being heard from behind the couch has given rise to assumptions about the presence or absence of feelings on the part of the analyst. The analyst's response, based on the emotional experience with the patient, initially sidelined in the history of psychoanalysis, has taken on a more central role.

I start by looking at the origins of interpretation from the inception of psychoanalysis with Freud, his use of the couch, free association, the rule of abstinence, and the "blank screen". This leads to a focus on theoretical developments regarding the role of the analyst's emotions in forming interpretations.

I explore the complex matrix of opinions on the salient issue of the analyst's feeling-based interpretations. In contrast with the term "blank screen", I describe the analytic empathic voice as functioning like an "affective screen", thus uncoupling this term from its historical predecessor. This distinction emerges from a theoretical journey that investigates the meanings and misconceptions of the interpretive voice as a "blank screen". It also shows how contemporary influences have led to my new phrasing of an empathic analytic voice in the countertransference as an "affective screen". It is a screen, a function within the analyst, that receives and registers projections as unconscious communications from the patient. By way of interpretation, the analyst reflects the patient's unconscious split-off or repressed affect. This is done through the analyst's experience in the countertransference. I shall illustrate this with clinical vignettes.

The invention of free association

Freud began situating himself behind the couch from a need to free the patient from sensorial constraints, which visual information about the analyst might impose. Freud (1895d) wanted his patients to concentrate on recovering memories so as to get to the roots of hysterical symptoms. In order to do this, they needed to be free to travel back in time and deep into their unconscious, under Freud's guidance (and the occasional application of pressure to their foreheads), so as to recollect as vividly as possible, and with the full force of the appropriate affect, the pathogenic set of ideas that were the root cause of the symptoms. This was of crucial significance to Freud at that particular theoretical junction, since he was attempting to bypass the method of hypnosis, which he had hitherto used. They therefore needed to be free to associate.

But Freud found that despite his instructions to focus and recollect, his patients steered off course and began to talk about other things, which eventually led to his theoretical formulation of resistance. As was often the case with Freud, he ingeniously attributed psychic meaning to gaps and absences, and to what was *not* happening. He realised that while his patients were not performing the task allotted to them, they were doing something very helpful indeed: they were producing associations. He proceeded to instruct his patients to produce associations, particularly as an aid to interpreting dreams.

Freud (1900a) described this process in detail: "We ... tell him that the success of the psycho-analysis depends on his noticing and reporting whatever comes into his head and not being misled, for instance, into suppressing an idea because it strikes him as unimportant or irrelevant or because it seems to him meaningless" (p. 101).

One of the first deliberate uses of the technique was in the case of Dora, where Freud (1905e) notes that "the pure metal of valuable unconscious thoughts can be extracted from the raw material of the patient's associations" (p. 112); and it is underpinned by "a rule of psychoanalytic technique that an internal connection which is still undisclosed will announce its presence by means of a contiguity—a temporal proximity of associations" (p. 39).

In his work on the interpretation of dreams, Freud (1900a) relied on associations in order to discern meaning from the seemingly meaningless manifest content of dreams. He concluded that his method enabled his patients to free themselves from the constraints of logical rational discourse, which dreams do not follow, and to observe the flow of their association.

Freud's technique was designed to allow access to the unconscious by asking patients to deliberately let go of ego control over their thoughts and, especially, over what they actually say in the analytic session. Freed from intentional thinking, ideas would become seemingly unconnected and disjointed, but, indeed linked by a thread of unconscious meaning. In the same way, Freud (1913c) urged the analyst to adopt "free floating attention", a mode of thinking and feeling that is attuned to the unconscious of the patient as well as to that of himself.

Talking to the patient from behind the couch allowed both patient and analyst to give themselves over to the analytic task without distraction, removing the patients' capacity to check the analyst's responses through facial expressions and body language that might distort the patient's associations.

Freud states, "Since, while I am listening to the patient, I, too, give myself over to the current of my unconscious thoughts, I do not wish my expressions of face to give the patient material for interpretations or to influence him in what he tells me" (1913c, p. 134).

Here Freud spells out a reason that goes to the heart of his psychoanalytic technique—the intention to promote the patient's *internal* gaze rather than aspects of the analyst's presence or observations in the external world of the consulting room. Therefore, the rule of abstinence from looking in analytic sessions is linked to recognition of the power of the gaze in influencing and determining the patient's material. The analyst's internal gaze, too, is freed to look inward to be in touch with the countertransference feelings, which has become so important in modern psychoanalysis. Thus, freeing both patient and analyst from the restriction of the human look was to be a tool of encouraging the two participants in the analytic session to traverse the frontiers between their conscious and the unconscious, and explore depths of psychic meaning.

A clinical vignette: free association and early memory

A female patient told me about a trip she had taken to a health farm with a friend. She had planned the trip as a treat for her friend, an elderly, frail woman who had lost a great deal of weight due to serious illness. As a result the friend looked "small and shrunk". At that time in the analysis, the patient struggled with containing aggressive feelings and intense anger, often with me.

The patient described to me what happened during breakfast one morning at the health farm, when they had both ordered soft-boiled eggs. Up to that point the trip had gone well, and she had experienced no incidents of what she called "welling up of my rage". When the friend started eating her soft-boiled egg and she saw her gaze focusing on the yellow running yolk, she felt her friend had become too absorbed in her food, stopped listening to her, and consequently my patient felt ignored by her friend. She began to raise her voice and talk louder and louder in an attempt to re-engage the friend's listening, until my patient noticed she was nearly shouting in the dining room, as other guests turned their heads in her direction. The friend kept quiet, continued eating her egg, and to the patient she seemed increasingly small and shrunken. The patient was alarmed and distressed by her experience.

The analysis revealed that it was the specific sight of the runny yellow yolk on her friend's spoon that triggered my patient's rage. It reminded her of repeated incidents with her mother when she was a young child of six. The mother, a harassed, troubled woman with the responsibility of bringing up five children (the family was poor and lived in a remote part of the country) occasionally gave her soft-boiled eggs for breakfast. This was a special treat on a number of accounts. The mother had little time for preparing individual dishes for any of her children and boiling eggs was an unpredictable affair. Water would be poured on an egg placed in a cup and left for a few minutes, a process which would be repeated three times. It would be a matter of luck as to what the resultant consistency of the egg yolk would be.

The patient, an aspiring writer who had certain panache for storytelling, described the feelings of anticipation and suspense at the moment of cracking the top of the egg and inspecting its contents. She would be seated at the little kitchen table and her mother would stand over her. The egg yolk examined, the mother would pass judgement on its consistency: "too runny, too hard, just right", after which my patient would be allowed to proceed with eating the, by then much craved for, egg. But the mother would continue to hover over her daughter in the small kitchen.

My patient then recounted a sudden and painful turn of mood. The mother, having taken the trouble to prepare an egg for her daughter, would begin to talk to the seated daughter by the table in a harsh and discontented voice, talking to the child about her own childhood, described as "tragic" by my patient. But the child did not want to listen to the mother, whose stories she had heard before. Instead, she was concentrating on the warm sticky fluid of the yolk (representing mother's milk). The mother's voice grew louder and more insistent, and the girl felt an urge to get up and leave the table, but was trapped by the mother's large frame and the temptation of food in front of her. She shrunk into herself, as the mother riled at her for not listening. Her deep sadness was palpable in the room as my patient was telling this vivid story.

This vignette exemplifies the function of memory invoked through free association, which, in an analytic session, is enhanced by means of the withdrawal of the gaze. The shrunken friend in front of my patient eating an egg evoked a vital childhood landscape (both external and internal), which, within a seemingly ordinary domestic scene, captured in a nutshell essential aspects of the mother/daughter relationship: a feeding mother who is also in desperate need of her daughter's attention. Unable to contain within herself the child's need to be nourished, and retain her role as the feeding mother, no sooner did the mother provide than she became envious of her daughter's position as a nourished baby, reversed the roles, and demanded her own feed. Being with her child as a "nourished baby" became intolerable to her, since it triggered her own memories of deprivation, and she needed to project these distressing childhood memories into the child in front of her. This she did by literally "telling", transmitting horror stories to the daughter as the child was dipping into the egg yolk (representing the baby at the breast). The feeding was spoilt, and contaminated with outpourings of negativity and rage.

Moving through the passage of time and the meanderings of the unconscious to the contemporary story at the health farm, the frail female friend represented the patient as a young child: the little "her" who had wanted to shrink and disappear when her mother started shouting. She, the patient, then became the shouting mother. The friend's illness was of relevance too, as the patient had come to think of the mother of her childhood, at this later stage of the analysis, as "ill". The patient's alarm was that she too was in danger of spoiling all the magnanimous giving she had done, by what she felt was an "unpleasant episode of shouting at my friend". Indeed, the trip as a whole was an attempt at reparation and expression of gratitude on the part of the patient, while she was working through her unconscious aggression in the analysis.

This vignette is reminiscent of the Proustian iconic madeleine, a treat an ailing aunt gave the child narrator on Sundays. The little sponge cake in *Swann's Way* has become an enduring literary icon of the past remembered in the present. As an adult, the narrator eats the madelaine during a troubled period and it opens up the past. The similarity between the literary example and the clinical vignette is that both are sensual memories, each quite specific to a time and a place, and related to a damaged maternal figure. Both of these are significant, focused memories, one in a psychoanalytic way and the other in a literary sense. They evoked and encapsulated whole swathes of childhood in which the longings for love from a damaged object, and its psychic corollaries, are collapsed into one emblem. These "nutshell" episodes are triggered by a form of sensual free association. Being, most probably, "screen memories", they are linked to early pre-verbal experiences which, in themselves, are primarily sensual. But in the psychoanalytic technique of speaking to patients from behind the couch the objective of facilitating memory relies on associations, including sensual triggers on the one hand, and on physical abstinence, such as the withdrawal of the gaze and touch, on the other. Both elements of this technique have in common the underlying goal of encouraging patients to focus on their own internal world rather than on the person of the analyst, calling up the past through the present and using the analyst not so much as a real person but as a vessel that receives, contains, and metabolises their internal stories.

The function of the couch and neuroscience

There are two distinct elements incorporated in the technique of talking to patients from behind the couch. The first is the specific arrangement of being placed behind the patient. The second is the actual element of *lying* on the couch, which, itself, has implications for the differential mental functioning of patient and analyst in the consulting room.

While Freud employed the couch initially for his own practical reasons, and was not aware of any neuropsychological implications for his patients lying down rather than sitting up, a contemporary view, espoused by Grotstein (1995), lends support to Freud's research into the unconscious from an unexpected angle. Grotstein maintains that lying down combined with the withdrawal of eye contact induces a shift in the brain activity from one hemisphere to the other. The change would be in the way the person responds to data, which would shift from left to right in right-handed people, and the other way around in left-handed people. Grotstein describes research from infant observation that showed variations in very young children's attentiveness when they observed material sitting up, or, alternatively, lying down. These changes in states of alertness were also recorded in electroencephalographic as well as hemispheric shifts. The quality of the alterations was in terms of level of control and mental organisation. The lying down person moves to a looser, freer, more random, and less discriminate mode of functioning. Grotstein concludes that: "This 'right-brain' shift in the lying-down position in analysis would be demonstrated by the nature of the patient's associations. These would be 'free' i.e., optimally disconnected from 'left-brain' editing, censorship, and control and would instead be organised by the unconscious." (1995, p. 397).

The above findings illustrate, from a neuroscientific angle, how the absence of eye contact, the reliance on the analyst's voice, and the patient lying on the couch promote free association, an essential tool on which the analytic enquiry into the unconscious relies.

Understanding the analyst's empathic responsiveness

The blank screen is a metaphor describing the analyst's receptivity as an impassive and unemotional attitude. It is similar, though not identical, to the metaphor of a mirror, another common simile describing the analyst behind the couch. A blank screen lends itself to receiving impressions from another source, whereas the mirror is designed to reflect whatever is in front of it. The "detached surgeon" was the analogy recommended by Freud:

> I cannot advise my colleagues too urgently to model themselves during psycho-analytic treatment on the surgeon, who puts aside all his feelings, even his human sympathy, and concentrates his mental forces on the single aim of performing the operation as skillfully as possible. (1912e, p. 115)

This didactic statement, sounding harsh to the contemporary psychoanalyst's ear, is known to have been Freud's declared rather than actual method, as evidenced in numerous comments in his case studies, and stories about his manner with his patients. Perhaps this was a case of "do as I say rather than do as I do".

However Fliess (1942), the son of Freud's contemporary Wilhelm Fliess already allowed for mild feelings of empathy with a small measure of identification on the part of the analyst, so as to understand the patient. But any intense emotions were considered problematic, and were thought to result from insufficient resolution of the analyst's own emotional difficulties.

These metaphors of "blank screen", "mirror", and "surgeon", are often linked with analytic neutrality. However, I believe that neutrality and the "blank screen" are not the same. As a result of tying the two together, it seems that writers such as Loewald (1960), Hoffman (1983), and Stern (1991), in their attempt to put to rest the blank screen concept, have also discredited the possibility of a neutral analytic stance, which, to my mind, is a conceptual act akin to burying the household utensils together with the coffin. For, while analytic technique can be focused on analysts being emotionally responsive to their patients, the registering of such responses being a major analytic tool, they can still remain "neutral" in the sense of not being judgemental, partial, or moralising. Stern, for example, in his sharp critique of the blank screen analytic attitude equates it with neutrality by stating:

> So few analysts are willing any more to defend the blank screen metaphor of the analyst's role, at least in its stark form … that to attack it has become a gratuitous act, useful only as a kind of chest-beating. And yet every time one is ready to consign the issue to

oblivion, one reads some new article, or hears about someone's defense of *neutrality*, [my italics] and the tired old argument comes to life. (1991, p. 51)

The difficulty with abandoning the notion of neutrality alongside the blank screen is in the presumption that a re-assessment of analytic boundaries may follow, for example, in giving the analyst a sanction for self-disclosure. Another consequence of abandoning neutrality could be a plea for greater involvement of the analyst's own real personality in the analytic process, and the conception of the analytic process as interpersonal and egalitarian. This would lead to the breaking of boundaries between analyst and patient, and putting a burden on the patient who would feel encumbered by the analyst's feelings, which are unrelated to the patient.

The question of the analyst as a new object

As early as 1934, Strachey stated a position that challenged Freud's detached surgeon analogy by asserting that the patient was aware of the analyst as a real person, and not just as a transference figure. According to Strachey, the "real" analyst represented a model that showed a new and different way of dealing with conflict between (essentially sexual) impulses and the superego. Repressed impulses, upon becoming conscious with the aid of analysis, are accepted and tolerated by the analyst, thus showing the patient a more accepting, benign, and less punitive superego model. Although Strachey adhered to the classical view of the source of neurosis being a conflict between repressed impulses and the superego, he believed that the resolution of the conflict depended on the patient's recognition of a new way of dealing with this clash of opposing internal forces. This new way would be through identification with the actual personality of the analyst and through acceptance of her interventions. What is deduced from Strachey's argument is that the analyst is not just a real object, *not* a blank screen or a mirror, but that she is also a new object offering herself to the patient for new identifications and introjections. The intrinsic idea behind this is that the patient's conflicts result from a harsh superego (in Strachey's terms), or from a severe internal object (in contemporary analytic terms), which the patient needs to defend against and manoeuvre his way around, in some way. But the analyst's presence and interpretations foster the reintrojection of a new, less harsh object, modifying the old one, and making patients realise that they do not need to relate to themselves with the same habitual punitive attitudes.

Loewald (1960), in promoting the notion of the analyst as a real object, which he argues, alongside many others, goes counter to the classical idea of the analytic blank screen, states that:

> There is a tendency to consider the analyst's availability as an object merely as a device on his part to attract transferences onto himself. His availability is seen in terms of his being a screen or mirror onto which the patient projects his transferences, and which reflect them back to him in the form of interpretations. ... This is only a half truth ... Increasingly, ... the analyst becomes not only potentially but actually available as a *new object*, by eliminating step by step impediments, represented by these transferences, to a *new object-relationship* [my italics]. (1960, p. 18)

My own view of "the analyst as a real object" is that while it is certainly true that the analyst is a real object in the physical world, his psychological reality, subjectively experienced by the patient, is determined by the transference. The "analyst as a real object" is a difficult claim to uphold, since it is somewhat at odds with the main preoccupation of psychoanalysis with the internal world, dominated as it is by primary processes and fantasy. Nevertheless, this issue of the real analyst can come to the fore towards the ending of the analysis when analyst and patient know each other well. At this point, patients are better able to distinguish between the analyst as a transference object and as a "real person".

The British school with its object relations theories largely contributed to creating a distance between their own theories and other theoretical orientations, which insisted on the analyst as a "real object". Stephen Mitchell (1997) has shown, in dramatic terms how, since Klein insisted on distinguishing between real objects and fantasised internal objects, the analyst functions like "a war correspondent" (p. 107), commenting via his interpretations on raging battles between fantasised internal objects—a very different portrayal from the impassive analyst of the classical view. And Weissbourd (2004) observes how this metaphoric portrayal of the analyst "radically alters the pace and intensity of analytic treatment, replacing the *blank screen* [my italics] with a continual commentary that puts the analyst directly within the range of fire, as a frequent recipient of the patient's projective identifications" (p. 308).

We therefore see that the departure from the classical position, which held that the analytic voice was to be devoid of emotional content, grew in two quite different and opposing directions on the two sides of the Atlantic. On the US side, it was believed that the blank screen notion did not sufficiently account for the analyst as a real person, a move to democratise the analytic relationship. This group, represented by Loewald (1960) and others, is linked to developments in the field of intersubjectivity and the relational movement in the US.

In the opposing direction and led by the object relations school, it was held that analysts became involved in becoming constant recipients of projections from a tumultuous internal world when analysing the unconscious, inevitably engaging their feelings and giving the analyst's emotional responses an important place in the analytic discourse. This grew out of influential developments in our understanding of the dynamics of the countertransference, which led to further emphasis on analysts' awareness of their feelings during an analytic session and how they deal with them, that is, the degree to which they respond by containment, possibly enactment, or a mixture of both. This constant scrutiny of the analyst's emotional states and how she deals with them led to the important question of, "Whose feelings are these?", the reply to which question was that the dynamics of the emotional interchanges between analyst and patient are explained by projective processes going both ways. In the first place, patients project unwanted aspects of themselves onto the analyst, which the analyst may understand, interpret or contain, react to emotionally, or observe as an enactment that needs understanding. This entire array of responses, it is now understood, makes up what is called the "countertransference". However, it should be noted that this latter dichotomy between the classical unaffected view of the analyst, and the Kleinian "war correspondent" view, drew its own criticisms; and the two positions were mediated through further contributions to object relations theories, mainly those of Winnicott's (1949) "transitional object" and Bion's "container/ contained" (1962), as will be discussed later.

The analyst's empathic experiences: a historical progression

In correspondence with Freud, Fliess (1942) used the term "trial identifications" (in Stern, 1993, p. 53), "which were understood as mild feelings sampled by the analyst as a way to gain an empathic grasp of the patient's experience" (Stern, 1993, pp. 53–54). This opened the debate over the function of the analyst's feelings that is clearly still alive today. Referring only to gentle feelings of benevolence towards the patient, Fliess explained the importance of these feelings as being in the service of empathy. Since then we have seen a continuum of growing involvement and interest in the analyst's emotions, both in kind and intensity, in theories on analytic technique. This increase parallels the growing investigations regarding the function of the countertransference, exemplified by Winnicott's (1949) seminal paper "Hate in the countertransference". In contemporary psychoanalysis in some quarters we can see a movement towards an interpretative approach that is based almost exclusively on the analyst's countertransference, a practice questioned by many.

Through these advances in clinical theories on countertransference, analysts are poised to look at their own emotions quite differently. Far from being "blank" or "detached", they use their emotional experiences to the full in the here and now of sessions. They offer themselves as sensitive tools for receiving and experiencing, as well as enacting, aspects of their patients' internal life, which, by virtue of being unconscious, patients (and often analysts) are not aware of. We might say that both analyst and patient are working through their unconscious experiences, but the crucial difference is that analysts are the ones who are trained to detect subliminal emotional states and enactments, and attempt to distinguish between those that are their own and those that are induced by the patient, and to understand and interpret them. In this view, the analyst who is a "blank screen" is largely seen as enacting a form of withdrawal and refusal to engage, a form of countertransference that needs to be open to analytic self-scrutiny.

Sandler (1976) and Hoffman (1983) show how the notion of countertransference has developed *after* Freud, mirroring the changes to the concept of transference *during* Freud. In relation to transference, while Freud initially regarded the transference as an obstacle to the patient's recovery, and saw it as part of the resistance manoeuvres his patients unconsciously employed, he later came to see the transference as a major source of information about the patient's unconscious alongside dreams and free association. Similarly, countertransference was regarded as a hindrance to the analytic process by Freud, and indicative of insufficient analysis on part of the analyst. However, as with transference, this position regarding countertransference soon became unsustainable, and, as shown above, Fliess (1942) began to move away from it.

However, it was not until Paula Heimann's (1950) landmark paper that the experience of countertransference, originally regarded as an unwanted intrusion into the analytic process, came to be regarded as a positive and necessary vehicle for analytic practice.

Referencing Fliess, as well as the old notion of the mirror metaphor, Heimann (1950) observes: "the notion that a good analyst does not feel anything beyond a uniform and mild benevolence towards his patients, and that any ripple of emotional waves on this smooth surface represents a disturbance to be overcome. This may possibly derive from a misreading of some of Freud's statements, such as his comparison with the surgeon's state of mind during an operation, or his simile of the mirror" (p. 81).

Here Heimann qualifies the criticisms of Freud as a "misreading" (ibid.) of his intentions, or a misinterpretation of his mirror metaphor. But she pursues her decisive idea that:

> … the analyst's emotional response to his patient within the analytic situation represents one of the most important tools for his work. The analyst's counter-transference is an instrument of research into the patient's unconscious. (1950, p. 81)

In this statement she decisively adds the countertransference as an essential research tool into the unconscious, alongside Freud's original ones of free association, dreams, and transference. And so it has remained, at least within the British school.

From this conception, significant implications for clinical practice followed. To the analyst's "free floating attention" is now added *"freely roused emotional sensibility* [my italics] so as to follow the patient's emotional movements" (ibid., p. 82). This seminal contribution by Heimann does not just add another device to the analytic toolbox; it becomes an indispensible way through which patients make their unconscious voices heard, by means of projection and projective identification.

The "blank screen" today: the fate of a phoenix-like metaphor

A fuller picture of the analyst's communications as a voice from behind the couch emerges post-Heimann. The analyst is not performing a cerebral task, immunised by her training against intense feelings and influences from patients. Far from it, analysts are required to be acutely aware of their feelings and open in order to receive the full array of emotional experiences aroused in them as communications from their patients' unconscious. But the question is: what are the implications of these ideas and what function does the analyst's own analysis have in her daily analytic work?

Heimann answers this question by stating that:

> The aim of the analyst's own analysis, from this point of view, is not to turn him into a mechanical brain which can produce interpretations on the basis of a purely intellectual procedure, but to enable him, to *sustain* the feelings which are stirred in him, as opposed to discharging them (as does the patient), in order to *subordinate* them to the analytic task in which he functions as the patient's *mirror reflection* [my italics]. (ibid.)

Heimann, then, seems to reinstate the simile of the mirror in the debate over the function of the analyst's feelings in the session, but this time the mirror is of a very different nature to that referred to during the Freudian era. Here the "mirror" image is articulated in its evolved form, deepened and expanded by the use of the analyst's emotional experiences within the analytic situation. Nevertheless, little has been made of this representation of the analyst since Heimann's allusion to it as a "mirror reflection" (ibid.).

In homage to Freud, however, Heimann traces the roots of her contributions on countertransference in Freud's own original discoveries of resistance and repression. She understands Freud's experiences of his patients' resistance as his countertransference experience, the first to be reported in psychoanalytic history, even though it was not named as such at the time. Sandler (1976), in an extensive review on developments in object relations theories and on the analytic voice since the abandonment of the "blank screen" concept, also discusses the changing significance of countertransference developed *after* Freud. These changes, he maintains, parallels changes to transference that took place within Freud's own writing. His account of the need to incorporate the countertransference "is that the analyst has elements of understanding and appreciation of the processes occurring in his patient, that these elements are not immediately conscious and that they can be discovered by the analyst if he monitors his own *mental associations* (my italics) while listening to the patient" (Sandler, Dare & Holder, 1973).

This is somewhat different from monitoring actual feelings (and strong ones at that) as advocated by Heimann. It would seem that Sandler's review does not stress the representation of emotions to the extent that Heimann does. In contemporary psychoanalysis, counter-transference has continued to occupy an ever-growing place in the discourse on technique. It is now considered a major (and occasionally the only) source of information through which to consider the analytic material. Presentations of clinical material in seminars and papers often report in detail, alongside the verbal exchanges, what the analyst feels in each part of a session. The analyst then proceeds to demonstrate how these feelings inform the interpretation given to the patient. For example, if the analyst thinks that the patient's material conveys a state of despair in relation to a maternal object, then the analyst feels this to varying degrees. The presence or absence of the feeling in the analyst would be weighted with significance and submitted to analytic scrutiny and thought.

A clinical vignette: reverie in the countertransference

P is a man in his late forties who is highly articulate and bright but difficult to reach. He presented at first with marked detachment and with grandiose fantasies that he could make me take away his painful feelings. As the analysis progressed he became enraged before breaks. He expressed his anger by lateness, missing sessions and withdrawing during sessions. At the stage at which the following vignette took place he believed that the remedy for his bouts of rage with me was for me to cancel my breaks.

Anticipating a session near a break, I feel dread and find myself wondering how many more weeks there are before my holiday. In the session he reports that his mother, who had hosted a large family gathering in her home, put him in a bedroom next to a room full of noisy children at the top of the house. The noise stopped him from having a "decent night's sleep". This he reports in a rational and bland manner with no awareness of any feelings of protest or anger, though he presents it as a "misjudgement" on the part of his mother. He describes the weekend in great detail but with no affect.

I say how difficult it is for him that he is disturbed by angry feelings, which he experiences as a disturbing noise from inside himself. I suggest that perhaps the weekend and the coming break have aroused some of these dreaded feelings that he now tries to push away.

He responds with "Ahah", and becomes silent. This "Ahah" is said in a tone that implies a question mark at the end of it, as though P is partly agreeing and partly asking me to say more, though in a dismissive way.

This response makes me feel angry and distanced. I understand that my anger and dread about seeing him are *his* split-off feelings of anger and dread, communicated through projective identification, while he remains distant and aloof, in an attempt to protect himself (and me) from his rage.

I say (as though I have been asked for a clarification) that hearing about the break has disturbed him. It is like noise that stops him from keeping his feelings asleep. He feels that keeping a distance is the only "decent" way to deal with his emotions, which he dismisses as childish.

He responds again with "Ahah", in the same tone of voice, and becomes silent. I feel exasperated. I feel I am with a patient who insists on keeping me at an arm's length while demanding more. In the silence that follows my mind wanders and drifts. I find myself thinking about my cat. I conjure up thoughts of a particular habit my cat has of digging her nails into my chest in a rhythmic motion, one paw then the other; and how this feels scratchy and uncomfortable, but also warm and intimate. I remember someone explaining to me that this is an instinctual activity in cats, and that kittens do it in order to stimulate the flow of milk from their mothers.

I wonder why my mind drifts at this point and why it conjures up this particular scene. I realise that his repeated "Ahah" feels like the rhythmic scratching of my cat. I think that at the moment my patient is angry with me (the cat scratching) for bringing up the break and, in his terms "insinuating" an unconscious need to stay close to me (the cat on my chest), which he defends against by distancing me.

I say that it makes him angry when I talk to him about the break, which reminds him that he needs me and would like to stay close to me all the time, and he finds it impossible to talk to me about this need.

Discussion

This vignette is advanced in order to demonstrate a particular analytic function, which I call an "affective screen". This puts analysts in contact with patients' split-off primitive feelings, and enables containment, thinking and forming interpretations.

In the first part of this vignette, though registering my angry feelings, I could not be sure of what they meant. I waited, and in the meantime I interpreted primarily the symbolic unconscious meaning of the story. I talked to the patient about the noisy children at the weekend and the sleepless night. Later, after the his two responses of "Ahah", the affect of anger became more pronounced in the countertransference. Then, with the help of the reverie, I understood my anger in terms of the current transference. I saw that it embodied the patient's conflict between the need to be close to me (to be on my chest) and his rage against me for bringing up the break and its attendant painful feelings (the scratching).

The interpretation that followed the second response of "Ahah" was therefore a result of taking the reverie into account while containing the emotional impact of the patient's attempt at distancing and silencing me. The subsequent interpretation was a result of the emotional work on my part as analyst, in which the analyst functioned as an "affective screen". This function facilitates the capacity to experience, contain, and return to the patient with an interpretation, rather than enact the distance as a result of a powerful countertransference. Thus, the reverie reflected, as though projected on a screen, the patient's split-off affects of neediness and rage.

In subsequent sessions and over a long period, I talked to the patient about his neediness for his mother/analyst before a break and how he wanted to be very close to me in a kind of blissful way without any disturbing feelings. I also spoke to him about his rage towards his mother/analyst for leaving him and how he withdrew from contact with me in the session, attempting to leave me before I could leave him. I said to the patient that something happens to him in his state of withdrawal. He becomes too angry to listen to what I say or engage with what I am saying, and his mind goes to sleep. He feels all he can do is try to elicit comfort from me by keeping me talking. He can then listen to my voice, which soothes and comforts him, but secretly also not listen to *what* I say as punishment for leaving him, since he is too angry to engage with me and since I do not accept his demand not to have a break.

Steyn (2013) takes this point further and discusses analysts' avoidance of this critical work as defensive. She posits that the analyst's awareness of his wish to avoid the painful experiences of being projected into, and the difficult work that is required in the actual feelings involved in *being* a transference object for the patient, are an integral part of the analytic project. This is illustrated in the above vignette. As emphasised by Steyn, the analyst must possess the capacity to bear archaic affective states (elicited by the patient), thus providing a screen for the patient's primitive disturbances, a function within the analyst's countertransference.

This echoes what Bion wrote of the analyst having to experience borderline patients' emotions:

> I do not think such a patient will ever accept an interpretation, however correct, unless he feels the analyst has passed through this emotional crisis as a part of the act of giving the interpretation. (1967, p. 291)

Towards a notion of the analyst's empathic voice as an "affective screen"

A different perspective on the nature of the analytic voice is offered through a debate over symmetry or asymmetry in the consulting room, in terms of who owns the greater emotional content in the relationship. From this perhaps unexpected standpoint, the fate of the "blank screen" metaphor is revived, though with a modified meaning, as I shall show. Surprisingly perhaps, the concept of the blank screen has proven resilient. For example, Hoffman (1983) draws an analogy between that metaphor and that of Bion's (1962) "container"—the metaphorical mental space in the analyst into which patients deposit unconscious and unwanted aspects of themselves. Hoffman's view is that both portray the analyst as somewhat devoid of emotional contents of her own, functioning as a kind of empty vessel that contains and reflects the patient's unconscious affect. He puts forward a bid for greater equality in the analytic relationship in allowing more of the analyst's feelings and personality to be present, although it is not clear whether he means this to be in the interpersonal sense. Hoffman's juxtaposition of the "blank screen" and the "container" is very interesting in as much as it brings together a historical view of the analyst, long considered "dead and buried" (the blank screen), together with a contemporary and currently used clinical notion (the analyst as "container").

Hoffman's emphasis seems to be on the analyst's actual personality, rather than on recognition that the effervescence of emotions experienced by the analyst in the countertransference belongs to and is *on behalf of* the patient. Indeed, Heimann (1950), to whom Hoffman extensively refers, posits that the analyst is her patient's own "mirror reflection" (p. 82) thus:

> The analyst's counter-transference is not only part and parcel of the analytic relationship, but it is the *patient's creation* [my italics], it is part of the patient's personality. (1950, p. 83)

Therefore, the analyst is both a container of and a screen reflecting the patients' emotional states, open to receiving their creations/projections through attention to the countertransference. For this, analysts must maintain the capacity to experience the full range of feelings projected by their patients.

A clinical vignette: F

F, a twenty-six-year-old male patient, arrived at his appointment, having missed the session on the previous day, because he had taken his three-year-old daughter to a playgroup, an experience he said he did not want to miss. He had told me about it in a session beforehand, in a way that suggested it was a "reasoned" and "rational" decision:

F: Quite a lot is happening; a lot is going on. It feels quite emotional. D [the daughter] had a massive temper tantrum this morning. She wanted to carry on playing. I had to get her ready for the playgroup. She was screaming and kicking and didn't want to get into her clothes. She wanted to go back to bed. G [F's wife] came in and asked if she could help. D was so distressed and I put her back into her bed. Afterwards she became glued to me like she had just had a trauma and kept saying, "Daddy stay home. Daddy stay home." I told her she was going to meet her friends and play with them and that I had to go to work.
    Afterwards G said, "Maybe we are doing something wrong. We give her too many choices." I felt angry with my wife and we could not communicate about it. I felt as if she was criticising me for the way I handled D. I was confused.

The patient said all of the above quite quickly and breathlessly. I felt he tried to tell me that for him something terrible happened in the morning, and that he needed to convey the intensity of it.

I thought there was a great deal in the material about oedipal rage and a description of oedipal constellations of various kinds. I could not tease out the various strands as to whom might be the desperate dyad that was clinging together, and who was left out. I felt flooded by the material, by his emotional state and the sudden gush of intensity, the "temper tantrum". I wondered whether what I was experiencing were *his* primitive feelings of chaos and disruption caused by the powerful feelings, something he had, up to this point in the analysis, defended against.

I: You feel you have been traumatised by what happened this morning with your daughter, by how intense your child's feelings could be.

F: Definitely, I felt traumatised all day.
  There was silence for while.

F: [Continues] D is very obsessed by me. She has been like so for a while. I feel guilty because I think it hurts G as she doesn't get a look in with D. I felt angry because I thought G was criticising me when she came in and said, "Can I help?" and when she said, "Maybe we are doing something wrong." She probably wasn't. In the end we talked about us and not about D. (He said this with regret.)

I: It is difficult to talk about yesterday's session that you missed. As if you would be talking to someone who is jealous of your closeness to your daughter, and I would resent you for it and be critical of wanting to do things with her, rather than being in the session with me.

Discussion

In the first part of the session, the patient's main unconscious anxiety was the eruption of strong feelings through his child. The analysis had focused on the patient's tenaciously held belief that he could get rid of his feelings, thus acquiring "a quiet life". Though he had suffered trauma in his early childhood, this was the first time the patient had mentioned "trauma". On this occasion, through his child, and with the help of the analytic work that had gone on before, he could allow himself to be closer to his feelings.

The analyst's initial state of confusion and chaos was an identification with the patient's own sense of being overwhelmed by these sudden emotions (i.e., trauma), an experience he could not imagine being able to cope with. The patient feared and believed that his feelings would cause him to stop functioning.

Utilising this countertransference, the first interpretation addresses this: "*You* feel you have been traumatised ..." In this simple way the analyst offers an understanding that the patient was the one to experience trauma in this situation. The patient responds by accepting the interpretation and by being able to focus on himself. What then emerges is oedipal guilt. The material that follows focuses on an important element in the overwhelming chaos: the patient feels guilty about missing the session. He feels compelled to project his clinginess into his child, so he does not experience it himself. Denying dependency, he then feels he excludes the object on whom he depends, in favour of being with someone who is dependent on him. He believes that the object then feels left out and becomes angry and critical of him.

The choice of the initial interpretation was primarily determined by the uncomfortable experience in the countertransference, which was then mediated by analytic thought. I would suggest that this interpretation was an "affective screen" intervention. It served the dual function of reflecting to the patient his state of being in an aftermath of an internal trauma, and of containing it. But an affective screen interpretation is *not* a direct mirroring of what the patient is saying or feeling. Rather, it is a reflection of what the patient cannot feel consciously and therefore projects onto the analyst in an attempt to communicate something unknown and painful. Thinking of the analytic situation as a restaging of the mother–infant relationship, this makes it all the more salient that the analyst simulates the maternal function of receiving the infant's projections, containing them and reflecting back a metabolised version.

The patient seemed to have accepted the interpretation and felt some relief, which then enabled him to recognise the extent by which he had been affected by his child's tantrum ("I felt traumatised all day"). After absorbing this recognition during a silence, he seemed able to develop the theme and we began the work of teasing out some strands of the feelings that had overwhelmed him.

Later on, the session began to feel flat and somewhat repetitive, as though we were staying on familiar, but unfertile ground. I felt ill at ease and somewhat guilty. Was I missing something? I could not identify it.

Still talking about the previous day the patient then said:

F: I feel sad about it (meaning the missed session). I feel sad that it
      happened. I feel sad that I am wasting the session today, as if I am

not here, not present. I also felt angry at work. Somebody gave me a shoddy piece of work to look at; it was shoddy and unfinished.

The patient said this when I felt uncomfortable and uneasy about the quality of my work at this point. I felt dissatisfied with it, as though something important had been left out. I thought it could be the patient's guilt at leaving somebody out (me, yesterday) and his fear of retaliation.

I: You feel that there has been something unsatisfactory here today. Yesterday your daughter's clinginess helped you a bit with your anxiety about the break because you were the adult in relation to her and to your wife. But that is not the whole story. Something is missing.

F: I feel confused by my reactions. There are lots of strong feelings, not just one. I now feel sad that I didn't feel close to G in the immediate aftermath of the temper tantrum. I was just angry as if it was her fault. And I did feel a bit thrilled that D only wanted me. I feel bad.

I: You felt that you won over D's affections when she preferred to be with you. This gave you pleasure but it also made you feel bad as if, for a while, you didn't want your wife there. Like you wanted to feel you didn't need me yesterday, and today you worry I would feel excluded and be angry and critical of you.
There is silence for a while.

F: I now feel despairing that I missed yesterday's session. I did it for all the right reasons, but still I felt terrible and blue yesterday in the playground, when I should have been happy.
F gives out a loud sigh.

F: (Continues) I am confused. I am in a muddle. [Now the break is coming], I can't take a session off if I want to be with my daughter.

In the rest of the session and in following sessions we talked about the patient's attempt to deal with his anger about his dependency on me, and his struggle with triumphant feelings that caused him to feel guilty. We understood that missing the session was his defence against a needy wish to cling to his analyst, and that he protected himself against these needy feelings by being competitive with his wife and winning his child's affection and dependency. In this way he became the parent who his daughter clung to, rather than clinging on to his analyst to meet his own childlike needs.

When the session became flat and repetitive I felt somewhat perturbed, as though I was not looking after my patient well. This, I see as being in an empathic identification with the patient's own "bad feeling" about letting down his analyst the previous day. The patient was not conscious of his guilt. He needed to protect himself from this guilt since he was afraid of my retaliatory criticism and anger. But this important anxiety and guilt about letting down his objects (which he does through triumphant exclusion and dismissal) was experienced in the countertransference in the form of the analyst's temporary dissatisfaction with her work. Again, in this part of the session the analyst functioned as an "affective screen" on which the patient projected an unconscious feeling of guilt, which could not be experienced due to anxiety.

Summary: the essential nature of empathy

As with most psychoanalytic concepts there is a wide range of views on and definitions of empathy. These are summarised in a number of comprehensive reviews, for example, Bolognini (1977, 2001, 2009), Bolognini & Borghi (1989), and Feiner and Kiersky (1994), all of which comment on the diverse strands of thought on this notion. What stand out are simple statements, such as Ferenczi's (1928) definition of empathy as the ability to put oneself in someone else's shoes, and Deutsch's (1926) focus on empathy as being an *unconscious* affective contact between the analyst and the patient's infantile needs. Thus, empathy is entering into the patient's subjective experiences, into their internal world, and feeling what it is like to be them.

Attempts at further elucidation have led to the use of "identification" (e.g. Deutsch, 1926; Fliess, 1942). Thus, identification on part of the analyst is basic to empathy. This is true of human interaction in general, as it provides the recipient of emotion the psychic means for knowing how the other feels, by testing how one would feel oneself in the same situation. Thus, empathy in psychoanalysis is entering imaginatively into the subjective experience of patients, into their internal world, and understanding what it is like to be them. Patients, for their part, communicate their unconscious affect to their analysts through projective identification.

A more robust line of enquiry has come through developments in the research and understanding of the countertransference, a mechanism closely linked to projective processes. Klein (1955) reminds us of the normal function of projection in ordinary human affairs and flags up her premise that projective identification is the basis of empathic communication, since the baby projects distressed parts of himself into the mother. Segal (1964) sharpens the link between empathy and projective identification by stating that the latter is the *earliest* form of empathy, since it occurs naturally as the very first form of communication and emotional relatedness between mother and baby. This line of argument might be taken as far as stating a position that the *only* means available for a mother to empathically relate to her baby is by absorbing her infant's projections, that is, by allowing herself to be projectively identified with the baby.

Conclusion: from the "blank screen" to the "affective screen"

This chapter charted developments in the analytic voice. It focused on views regarding the role of feelings in analysts' responsiveness, along the route of advancing our understanding of the nature of countertransference. A variety of contributions were considered, focusing on salient junctions in this progression. Starting from the analyst as a "blank screen" behind the couch, through the analyst as a new object, the chapter then elaborated on the nature of the analyst's empathic responsiveness, and concluded with the experiencing analyst functioning as an "affective screen".

Acknowledging that each analyst must develop her unique voice, I specifically explored and hopefully illustrated how analysts can give empathic expression to emotions felt in the countertransference, thus functioning as an "affective screen" in the service of the patients' psychic movements within the session.

The analyst with an essential voice of empathy is an analyst who, in a self-aware manner, accepts the inevitability of being projectively identified with the patient in the countertransference for a while, by experiencing what the patient cannot consciously feel, and uses this experience in forming interpretations. That is, the empathic analyst is not resistant to experiencing his patient's projections at a real emotional level. Interpretations are based on the analysts listening to the voice of their own feelings, combined with their knowledge and systematic thinking. This will provide what has been termed in this chapter an "affective screen" to the patient's conflictual difficulties.

The analytic act, then, becomes a restaging of the mother–infant unconscious relationship, in which the mother affords herself to her infant's need to project toxic feelings without retaliation. This is the basis of human communication and empathy. But, the difference between the mother–infant relationship and the analytic session is in the act of interpretation, which is the privilege of psychoanalytic practice.

Perhaps analysts may need to be aware of instances when they become resistant to experiencing their patients' affects fully. How these resistances can be detected may be the subject of further exploration.

References

Bion, W. R. (1962). *Learning from Experience*. London: Tavistock.

Bion, W. R. (1967). Reverence and awe. In: *Cogitations* (pp. 284–292). London: Karnac, 1991.

Bolognini, S. (1997). Empathy and "empathism". *International Journal of Psychoanalysis, 78*: 279–293.

Bolognini, S. (2001). Empathy and the unconscious. *The Psychoanalytic Quarterly, 70*: 447–471.

Bolognini, S. (2009). The complex nature of psychoanalytic empathy: A theoretical and clinical exploration. *Fort Da, 15*: 35–56.

Bolognini, S., & Borghi, L. (1989). Empathy. *Rivista di Psicoanalisi, 35*: 1076–1098.

Deutsch, H. (1926). *Occult Processes Occurring During Psychoanalysis*. New York: International Universities Press, 1953.

Feiner, K., & Kiersky, S. (1994). Empathy: A common ground. *Psychoanalytic Dialogues, 4*: 425–440.

Ferenczi, S. (1928). The elasticity of psycho-analytic technique. In: *Final Contributions to the Problems and Methods of Psycho-Analysis* (pp. 87–101). London: Hogarth, 1955.

Fliess, R. (1942). The Metapsychology of the analyst. *Psychoanalytic Quarterly, 11*: 211–227.

Freud, S. (1895d). The psychotherapy of hysteria. In: *Studies on Hysteria. S. E., 2*: 253–305. London: Hogarth.

Freud, S. (1900a). *The Interpretation of Dreams. S. E., 4*: 1–627. London: Hogarth.

Freud, S. (1905e). Fragments of an analysis of a case of hysteria. *S. E.*, *7*: 7–122. London: Hogarth.

Freud, S. (1912e). Recommendations to physicians practising psychoanalysis. *S. E.*, *12*: 109–120. London: Hogarth.

Freud, S. (1913c). On beginning the treatment. *S. E.*, *12*: 121–144. London: Hogarth.

Grotstein, J. S. (1995). A reassessment of the couch in psychoanalysis. *Psychoanalytic Inquiry*, *15*: 396–405.

Heimann, P. (1950). On counter-transference. *International Journal of Psychoanalysis*, *31*: 81–84.

Hoffman, I. Z. (1983). The patient as interpreter of the analyst's experience. *Contemporary Psychoanalysis*, *19*: 389–422.

Klein, M. (1955). On identification. In: *Envy and Gratitude and Other Works 1946–1963* (pp. 141–175). London: Hogarth, 1980.

Loewald, H. (1960). On the therapeutic action of psychoanalysis. *International Journal of Psychoanalysis*, *41*: 16–33.

Mitchell, S. A. (1997). *Influence and Autonomy in Psychoanalysis*. Hillsdale, NJ: The Analytic Press.

Proust, M. (1913). *Swann's Way* [Revised translation by D. J. Enright]. London: Vintage, 2005.

Sandler, J. (1976). Countertransference and role-responsiveness. *International Review of Psycho-Analysis*, *3*: 43–47.

Sandler, J., Dare, C., & Holder, A. (1973). *The Patient and the Analyst: The Basis of the Psychoanalytic Process*. London: Allen & Unwin.

Segal, H. (1964). *Introduction to the Work of Melanie Klein*. London: Heinemann.

Stern, D. B. (1991). A philosophy for the embedded analyst: Gadamer's hermeneutics and the social paradigm of psychoanalysis. *Contemporary Psychoanalysis*, *27*: 51–80.

Stern, D. B. (1993). Discussion. *Contemporary Psychoanalysis*, *29*: 47–60.

Steyn, L. (2013). Tactics and empathy: Defences against projective identification. *International Journal of Psychoanalysis*, *94*: 1093–1113.

Strachey, J. (1934). The nature of the therapeutic action of psychoanalysis. *International Journal of Psychoanalysis*, *15*: 117–126.

Weissbourd, K. (2004). Kristeva's Klein: A review of Melanie Klein by Julia Kristeva. New York: Columbia University Press, 2001. *Contemporary Psychoanalysis*, *40*: 304–309.

Winnicott, D. W. (1949). Hate in the countertransference. In: *Collected Papers* (pp. 194–203). New York: Basic, 1958.

CHAPTER TWO

Do interpretations tell the truth?

Jean Arundale

"… psychoanalysis is a joint activity of analysand and analyst to
determine the truth; that being so, the two are engaged—no matter
how imperfectly—on what is in intention a scientific activity."

—*Bion*, 1992, p. 114

Dictionaries tell us that the term "interpretation" denotes the
process of explaining the meaning of something and assigning
the proper significance, rendering something clear or explicit.
The meaning of interpretation in psychoanalysis is similar to this but in
the end also quite different. When two personalities come together, the
analysand and the analyst, with the intent to explore and to understand
one of them at the deepest level, the interpretive voice carries with it,
along with *logos* and meaning, an emotional freight that opens paths
and connects, that touches and reveals hidden or undeveloped areas of
the internal world. We like to think this has to do with telling the truth.

Freud's original emphasis emerging from *Studies on Hysteria* (1895d)
and *The Interpretation of Dreams* (1900a) was on a particular type of
interpretation involving his topographical model of depth psychology:
how to make the unconscious conscious. In this classical model the aim

was to uncover latent or unconscious meanings so that they could be examined consciously, thereby achieving insight into inner conflict and disguised wishes or phantasies that disturbed the personality. In the work of uncovering the patient's truth, a reconstruction of the past was central, as well as an understanding of unconscious aspects of character; later revisions of Freudian theory also included unconscious functioning in the here-and-now, "the past and present unconscious" (Sandler & Sandler, 1984).

In the Kleinian development, which evolved out of the classical technique, a shift to a somewhat different register was made: from how to make the unconscious conscious to, how does it all work? How does this person's mind and personality function, as shaped by his emotional relationships? What are the qualities of character, ego and superego states, defensive organisations, activity and thinking patterns, belief systems? Following the Kleinians, there was a renewed rigour in understanding and interpreting the transference, the countertransference, the superego and Oedipus complex as experienced in the analyst-patient relationship.

In seeking psychoanalytic truth, the Kleinians tend to favour an intuitive approach, a direct link with the patient's emotional state, mental patterns, and instinctual processes. This is not only "gut feeling" but conditioned by experience with the patient, knowledge of the patient's history, internal world, and immediate projections. Anna Freud would probably have objected to this approach, saying this is "wild analysis", and Freudians would want to wait for supportive associations, to proceed slowly from surface to depth, respecting defences to a greater degree.

At the beginning of the psychoanalytic movement, Freud believed that his dynamic theory of how the mind works would guide every new analyst in his clinical technique, so that for some time he thought it unnecessary to outline technique formally in papers or to lay down hard and fast rules for others to copy. Freud thought it was obvious that analysts should naturally be using theory as well as empathy and intuition to find the unconscious wishes, phantasies, fears, and defences that lay behind neurotic ways of thinking and behaviour. As he often reiterated, he wanted individual analysts to develop their own styles and techniques: his only imperative was that they should understand and digest the basic principles of psychoanalysis (1911–1915 [1914], p. 87).

When Freud did begin to publish papers on technique, he outlined the basic concepts of the method: free association, dream interpretation, the analysis of resistances and defences, transference, and working through (ibid.). Freud promoted, along with "free floating attention", a particular kind of active listening that enabled the analyst to attune his unconscious "like a receptive organ towards the transmitting unconscious of the patient" (ibid., p. 115), seeming to sanction a kind of intuitive connection as a valid if not prioritised method. I consider this an interesting conjunction between Freud and Klein; both suggest that analytic truth falls into the domain of the analyst's intuition in the present immediate contact with the patient. Bion, in writing of the analyst's intuition when memory and desire have been put aside, said, there is "the coming together by a sudden precipitating intuition, of a mass of apparently unrelated incoherent phenomena which are ... given coherence and meaning not previously possessed ..." (1967, p. 127). This, Bion describes as the "selected fact", a crystallisation of the current analytic situation that has been brought to the analyst's attention by an accumulation of events in the patient's material.

Issues around what is correct technique in psychoanalysis have been continuously debated: how much clinical evidence is needed in order for the analyst to have confidence in her understanding of unconscious process? How should interpretations be framed in terms of timing, dosage, and depth? How much truth can the patient bear? How do we test which analytic methods are the most fruitful? Possibly it depends on the patient one has on the couch: one person may thrive on the direct, intuitive approach, becoming enlivened and freed, linking with what they recognise as unconscious emotions and fears, whilst another may become intimidated or defensive. For another person it may be that quiet reverie stimulates thought and helps him to be in touch with himself and the other. Some may find the slower approach stultifying, so that emotionally nothing much happens in analysis. As always, the likelihood is that it is a combination that succeeds in the end, a *both/ and* rather than an *either/or* approach to psychoanalytic truth. Consistent receptivity and spontaneous responsiveness from the analyst's unconscious need not be contradictory.

At the centre of the endeavor to grasp the truth of the patient is the aim of revealing unconscious phantasy. It would be difficult to imagine that any psychoanalyst would disagree with the proposition that to interpret unconscious phantasy, capturing it in a metaphorical form, is the simplest, clearest, and probably the most effective way to transform problematic mental contents that have been repressed, split off, or unrepresented. Sirios (2012), representing the Freudian tradition, points out that metaphor constitutes the best interpretation, drawing together emotional, cognitive and pictorial aspects in a memorable spontaneous iconic moment. However, this most desirable form of interpretation is not always possible and we need other kinds of interpretations and interventions in our armory with which to speak the truth. The examination of beliefs, emotional patterns, and enactments, along with intuition, and the "selected fact", play important roles in the analysis of the patient I will present in this paper. Further frames of reference relevant to the work with my patient are dealing with the pathological superego (O'Shaughnessy, 1999), destructive narcissism (Rosenfeld, 1971), projective identification (Klein, 1946), and developing the mind as an instrument with which to think (Bion, 1962a).

Transference interpretations, of course, are where these elements are primarily revealed. However, Melanie Klein, contrary to what is often believed, was aware of the importance of extra-transference interpretations and the way in which current objects and everyday life contain unconscious elements of the past. She wrote in "The origins of transference" (1952, p. 54) of the "total situation" that has as its components transference, current life, and past experience. To quote:

> … our field of investigation covers *all* that lies between the current situation and the earliest experiences … It is only by linking again and again later experiences with earlier ones and *vice versa*, it is only by consistently exploring their interplay, that present and past can come together in the patient's mind. This is one aspect of the process of integration which, as the analysis progresses, encompasses the whole of the patient's mental life. (*Klein's*, 1952, p. 56)

The process that Klein describes was essential to the "total situation" and the pathological organisation of the patient I will discuss.

I will now present clinical material to illustrate my attempts to tell the truth to my patient.

Clinical material: Ms T

Ms T was a woman in her twenties, who had been attending analysis four times per week for three years at the time of the sessions I will discuss.

She had a personality disorder, a high degree of psychotic anxiety, and was at times very disturbed, although she was highly intelligent and accomplished in many ways. During this period, she was in the habit of coming into sessions and dramatically pouring out her distress, often crying and wailing, about whatever was preoccupying her—difficulties with her boyfriend, her inability to talk properly to her friends, her time-table, her eating disorder, her cleaning obsessions. From previous experience, I knew she would go on to whip herself up into an emotional frenzy; that is, if I simply listened and waited, she would escalate the intensity of her emotional state and her sense of helplessness. Not knowing what to do to work on the problem and gain some resolution, she would project into me and heap all of her problems into my lap.

My countertransference was highly disturbed as I experienced her helplessness and rage. Basically, Ms T didn't know how to use her mind to think. I needed to intervene, which I did in terms of attempting to calmly talk to her about herself, reflecting back to her what her beliefs were about herself: that she wasn't loveable, that no one liked her, that she had trouble looking after herself, that she could not work or put her life in order, etc. Often I interpreted these things in the transference: suggesting to Ms T that she couldn't believe I could care for her knowing her as I did, that she expected me to tell her what to do, or that she wasn't sure of how to use her mind to think with me. However, I was also learning from experience with Ms T that whatever I said would be disagreed with or objected to, on the grounds that I hadn't quite understood exactly what she meant, or that what I said was not helpful, or that any idea that could come out of our exchange could not possibly work.

After this routine had taken place many times, I realised that we were enacting a scenario, from the past with her mother, in which everything said to her was shot down or rejected and she was left to feel hopeless about everything. During one especially intense episode, I waited and kept still, feeling useless, until I found myself reacting strongly to her, bursting out and saying something to her that sounded as if I were a cross, exasperated mother and she was a small child who needed to have everything spelled out and explained exactly, who was being provocative and irritating, and who needed to be told off. This intervention, born of an emotional reaction on my part that hit on the truth, opened the way to a flood of new material reflecting truths and insights. When I realised that we had been undergoing an enactment scenario and that it was my irritable remark that had broken us out of enactment, revealed because I no longer stifled my feelings, I was able to say to Ms T, "But you don't need me to explain this to you. You pull me into a situation in which you get me to talk to you like you are a small child who is irritating and doesn't know anything." "Yes," she said, in immediate recognition, "I do this all the time with everyone; I want others to look after me. I also say stupid things that make others think I'm not intelligent, for the same reason, but also I need to play the fool. I don't want others to think I'm a threat. When others say they are having problems, I tell them I have similar ones. Why do I feel I have to mirror them and their problems?" She went on to explore how at college she had behaved in a silly way with friends, as if she was ignorant, keeping her head below the parapet in class, and not performing visibly well, so as not to attract envious attention, as if she was not allowed to know or to have more than anyone else. This led to us forming an understanding of how envious she was and how afraid of envy she was from others.

There followed a period of more thoughtful work and reflection during which Ms T was able to see her part in her own difficulties and take responsibility for them. Her angry outrage, so often the staccato accompaniment to her free associations, was in diminuendo.

After two months of this calmer work, Ms T came into a session after a weeklong break feeling suddenly angry upon entering the consulting room: "I feel so angry and upset. I didn't know that's what I was feeling, I have been lots better. All that anger is back, I've gone backward, I feel just like I felt earlier toward G [her boyfriend, who had been away working on a project]. He has ruined my life. I give him everything and he gives me nothing back. He is so selfish." She went on to rage against G, and against me for being away for the break, indicating the extent of the separation and abandonment issues in a girl who was rarely separated from her mother.

This re-irruption of Ms T's rage coincided curiously with an event that had made her ecstatically happy. During the break she had spent a lot of time writing a long, reasoned email to G, carefully laying out her contributions to the difficulties in their relationship, showing how she was aware of her part in them: her angry attacks, accusations, and controlling behaviour. In the letter, she had outlined how she had been thinking a great deal about this and how she had changed due to analysis, and she spoke of her intentions to make their relationship work better in the future. She told him she had been getting her life together, and felt excited that they would meet later in the summer when he returned.

When she received his email in response, she was ecstatically happy; he wrote about how much he loved her in a beautifully written love letter, and she went on to have a good, sociable weekend with friends. Arriving at her session on Monday, after having been so happy, she was surprised that when she entered the consulting room the anger and rage returned, and the session was filled with ranting and crying. I spoke to her about how, upon encountering my actual presence, her anger was provoked and suddenly I had become G, the one who went away.

Then in the next session she was painfully sorry and frightened about having exploded in rage towards me, feeling an excruciating regret that she had spoiled our relationship like she spoiled all her relationships. She proceeded to mount a superego attack on herself, vicious and destructive. "Why am I so angry?" she wailed. "I'm angry with G, with my mother, with you. Then I feel guilty, and then angry that I feel so guilty. I lose all my sense of stability and feel I have *nothing*, absolutely *nothing*, no man, no family, and no job. The last weeks I felt you and I were friends, well not friends but friendly, that I'd made progress, able to work, plan my future, but it's all gone now and I'm back where I started." Seeing her self-destructive attack, I said, "I think it's anger itself that makes you feel so bad and guilty, that you deserve the punishment of not having anything good in your life." "*Of course!* Why should I be angry with G when he's done nothing to deserve it? Why should I be angry with my mother when she brought me up, did her best, but I hate her. I feel violent when I'm with my mother, just so tense and angry [and she gripped her arms across her chest, making fists, showing me how the violent rage was expressed painfully in her body]. And I shouldn't be angry with you; you are trying to help. I do this over and over again. I can't stop it. I blame everyone."

Gathering my thoughts together after this torrent of rage, I focused on the transference: "You don't believe I can bear the angry feelings you have toward me, that I will stop caring about you and won't want to continue to work with you, that you have spoiled our relationship." Ms T appeared to take this in but did not respond to my interpretation. Instead she said, "You are right in saying I want to be rescued by a man and not to finish my degree. I don't think I can do both, to have a life of my own and also a man. I still have this strong wish to give myself up and do whatever G wants and then I get angry about it when I can't be myself or have my life." She cried and wailed in hopelessness.

In the next session Ms T went on to describe how a process had been set in motion in which she had the impulse to destroy everything positive she had: her friendships, her social life, her degree, her analysis. She felt on the brink of wrecking her life and I spoke to her of how dangerous this was, that the destructive side of her, about which we knew and had spoken repeatedly, was in a murderous destructive rage that threatened to leave her with nothing. My thoughts and interpretations at this time were directed towards the negative therapeutic reaction fuelled by guilt and unbearable pain around Ms T's aggressive attacks on her objects and destructive attacks on all possibility of goodness in her life. I spoke, interpreting that she was in a monumental tantrum, wishing to destroy everything in sight, a furious, screaming baby wanting revenge on her mother and me. When she felt that she had spoiled our relationship, she felt she might as well spoil everything she had. In the grip of destructive narcissism and an ego-destructive superego, she told me she felt there was literally a person inside her gut screaming "NO", something powerful in her over which she had no control and which was endangering her with psychic catastrophe.

In a following session she told me that the previous night she had wanted really badly to email me to tell me to watch something on TV.

MS T: I didn't email; I knew it wasn't my place. But I thought that if I were a psychoanalyst like you, I would want to watch it. A comedian was in a show about a ventriloquist and his dummy. It was deeply moving, strange, funny, and sad. The dummy represented parts of people and they said to him things they wanted to say to him about himself.

ANALYST: You wanted to share with me something meaningful about yourself, that you recognise there are parts of you and other people that have something important to say to you.

MS T: I hope you watch it; it was really, really good. One of them said, "I really love you; I'm just afraid of the shouting."

ANALYST: This is about your relationships: those you love, you end up shouting at and being angry with. You love me but you shout at me rather than think, or feel, or be here with me in an ordinary way.

I thought about how Ms T made all her relationships into a situation where she was the ventriloquist and everyone else was her dummy into which she projected what she wanted them to think and feel, and became angry when they had their own thoughts that weren't identical with hers. She insisted that others should speak as she projected, so terrified was she of loss and separateness, disallowing others as separate individuals who are different, and think differently. This basic understanding of her dilemma was helpful and crucial, but the task of putting this into words, into a truthful interpretive voice, was only beginning. The ventriloquist/dummy metaphor in its many guises formed the basis for our analytic work for some time.

Towards the end of this session Ms T recounted a dream about being in her hometown, going to see her mum. She was on a runaway bus and the landscape was post-apocalyptic, devastated, with only wild animals running in the streets. Her associations were to an anarchic video she had seen about animals: violent, exciting, anti-establishment. She said, "I think the animals were not just about me being angry; it was mournful, there was nobody left but zoo animals. I thought earlier this week on the tube, there was no one else on the train and I had a phantasy about the end of the world; no one was left. Then a man got on and I imagined I finally found someone but he was awful." I said to her, "You attack and kill off all your objects and feel you are utterly alone and mournful. Then you find me but I'm a big disappointment when I don't think exactly as you do and then you destroy me as someone helpful who is here for you." She responded, saying that she was helped when I talked to her about how she projected into others and told them how to think.

In the next session Ms T began to argue with something I said. I interpreted that she felt murderous when I didn't act as her dummy and think exactly as she wanted. She wanted to control me by telling me what to think rather than hearing what I had to say, which she might actually have found useful. Further, she believed me to be just like her, that each time I said something she believed I was trying to get her to agree with me and think my way, to force my thoughts into her; she thought my words were not exploratory but definitive. This prevented us from exploring her mind. After I said these things, Ms T surprised me by agreeing that she recognised them as true, saying she was always trying to control what others thought of her, projecting good images. This was the way she tried to get everyone to like her; it had always been that way, she said.

In a session the following week, she told me about the phantasy she had had when turning into my street. She smelled smoke and imagined my house had burnt down. In her phantasy, she came to the house and some men were there, accusing her of starting the fire. She denied it but I was there and I didn't believe her. I interpreted to her that in her world of phantasy she wanted to eliminate me, to burn down my house, when she was angry with me. I talked to Ms T about how she thought that if she didn't control my mind and tell me what to think I would think the worst of her. Before arriving for her session, she imagined she had demolished my house containing the unhappy mother and child, believing she had to return to the burnt out sessions she had previously destroyed.

After this session Ms T had a kind of depressive breakdown in which the pain of recognising herself as destructive and the feelings of guilt about attacking her objects overtook her. She expressed humiliation and despair, feeling I could never like her or believe in her when I saw this side of her. This was the split-off part of her that she tried so hard to hide from others, with her projections, charm offensives, and the pleasing, compliant part of her personality.

Soon she moved away from her despair and returned to being quarrelsome, demanding that I agree with her and attacking whatever I said. It became clear to me that I had to speak some home truths in order to overtly avoid being Ms T's ventriloquist's dummy. In a Friday session, I said that when she didn't get what she wanted, she became a spoiled brat who cried and made demands. These direct words came from me somewhat forcefully and had the effect of shocking her. I continued, saying that she knew that she behaved badly but she also knew how to behave well when she wanted to. To this she did not put up an argument, but said, "I always think it is G who is the asshole but it is me; I'm the asshole. The truth is I'm an angry, mean person," and she began to cry and wail, asking how anyone could want her, what she could do if that's how she is, etc. I said, in truth, that the only thing worse than being an asshole is being one and not knowing it. Only if she knew it could she begin to do something about it. Ms T continued to wail that something took her over and she couldn't help it. But on Monday she returned in a very different mood. "It really helped on Friday to come face to face with being an asshole," she told me, but at the same time she said she could feel herself wanting to deny it. She spoke calmly for the whole session, saying she wanted me to know that she had thought about everything all through the weekend. She said she felt there were two ways she could take this: accept the truth and feel shitty about herself or try to defend herself. "I have to think about how not to be so mean and angry. I remember reading about psychoanalysis and how you try to find your true self in order to develop. But the true self is not always good; it's a self I have to change. I'm not nice, I'm a really, really angry person."

Ms T was to lose and regain these insights time and again, moving between blaming others and self-attack. I saw her pathology as an attempt to set up a narcissistic world in which only she and her wants prevailed, an attempt to take over her objects and force them to be and to give her what she wanted, feeling enraged whenever she was denied. She believed in magical thinking by which, if she could convince me and others of her goodness by projecting a good image of herself into our minds, this would make it true. She would then possess these good qualities without having to work for them in reality, to make an effort. It became apparent to me that I would have to speak the unvarnished truth to her on a regular basis, that she could become an angry spoilt brat, destroying things if she didn't get her own way. She used her mind to operate on others, not as an instrument with which to think.

Ms T's beliefs were powerfully charged with emotion when she was in touch with them, for example, her beliefs that she could never have what she wanted, that she always spoiled her relationships, that she had no friends, or that she would end up alone like her mother. She completely believed them as facts while, contrariwise, she often displayed them as untrue.

Her capacity to dream and to remember dreams was functional but she treated her highly exaggerated emotions and thoughts as absolutely true: if she felt something, she automatically believed it to be true. It was important that I helped her to become aware of how she exaggerated and therefore distorted her view of situations and the other's view of her. This hyperbole was intended to force a placating reaction from her objects, not the truth.

In attempting to conceptualise this patient's dilemma, her excess aggression, combined with terrifying childhood dreams, could be seen as uncontained within a merged relationship with a lost, lonely mother bringing up her only child without the mediating influence of a father. Mother's relationship with her daughter was placating and, as the mother and child clung together in their mutual unhappiness, the patient would pour out her misery and rage at her mother. Unable to contain or deal with the rage, mother's placation evoked more fury because it was essentially untrue; when mother placated her, trying to mollify and smooth things over, Ms T would become further enraged, reducing her mother to silent intimidation, projecting her helplessness into her mother as she often did into me. Only a large dose of the truth could be of value, along with a will to use self-understanding in a constructive way. That mother, a non-responding, non-receptive object, did not speak the truth, led my patient to seek it in analysis. However, she believed she had to force her thoughts into the analyst in order to be heard and understood.

Use of the mind and learning to think

Britton (2003, p. 98) discusses the way in which we treat our beliefs as if they were knowledge, when actually we need to test them regularly for their reality content and truth-value, and to emancipate ourselves from false beliefs. This, Britton states, is a vital function of psychoanalysis. For my part with Ms T, caught up entirely in splitting, projective identification, and the belief she could control the minds of others, I struggled to help her see how the continual projection of her ideal image, or sometimes defensively her negative image, into the minds of her objects, left her empty and impoverished, and prevented her from knowing what others actually think by enquiring or listening with curiosity. I tried to help her to listen to me, to hear what I was thinking instead of insisting that I agree exactly with what she thought, or what she wanted me to think or to be. I found myself saying things like, "I have the equipment and understanding to help you think. I know where we're going, you need to listen, take in, digest, metabolise."

Helping Ms T to think about what she wanted in her life was nearly impossible; she changed her mind over and over again in absolute split-apart ambivalence. Thus, Freud's view of the basic function of the mind as "trial action" could not come into play. She clung to what she "should" think, what she pretended to think, or what she thought G or I wanted her to think. She used her mind to demonstrate to me that everything was impossible, rather than thinking how to make what she wanted possible. Thus, she communicated by demonstration, evacuating her nihilistic despair.

Ms T's demandingness had the quality of trying to force me to think for her, with the consequence that she further eroded the skills and capacity to think for herself. Thus, the analysis became a question of how to interpret in order to develop these mental instruments or to find out what prevented a thinking process. I spoke to her about how she cried and felt helpless, wanting me or someone else to fix things, wasting time and not working or using her own mind.

My patient needed an object in order to think but when she was in an object relationship she believed that overreaction, exaggeration, and force were needed to push her thoughts into the object, originally her non-receptive mother. In order to think together, she needed genuine exchanges with an object, and if the other didn't speak the truth, she could not interact and find her own truth. In sessions with my patient, truth was hard to find in a zone so full of projective missiles aimed at the analyst whenever she did not think exactly as the patient did, demonstrating how, having little expectation of being understood, she needed absolute agreement (Britton, 2003, pp. 176–177).

Truth telling

In considering the issue of truth telling in psychoanalysis, the question arises, is the truth really therapeutic? What if the truth is intolerable? What if the person in analysis cannot acknowledge or accept difficult truths about himself? Does the truth really heal and make one free?

Inherent in the whole Freudian project is the idea that uncovering the truth about the self and the vicissitudes of instinctual life is necessary for recovery from neurosis. Based on a deep, humane acceptance of the emotional and developmental life of human beings, truth seeking epitomises the very nature of psychoanalytic treatment. Freud stated this directly in "Analysis terminable and interminable": "… we must not forget that the analytic relationship is based on a love of the truth— that is, recognition of reality—and that it precludes any kind of sham or deceit" (1937c, p. 248).

In regard to truth seeking, Brenman (2006) points out that Freud at one stage viewed himself as a conquistador attempting to discover the riddle of the sphinx. Brenman was acutely aware of how difficult it often is to experience psychic truth and that "the process of psychoanalysis aiming at the discovery of the truth about ourselves is a mixed blessing, by no means always welcome" (ibid., p. xxi). The truth, Brenman goes on to say, can be overwhelming and disruptive of psychic equilibrium but nevertheless, when it can be accepted, provides the basis for creative developments in the personality.

Bion overtly placed truth seeking at the very centre of his innovative work, famously stating, "… healthy mental growth seems to depend on truth as the living organism depends on food. If it is lacking or deficient the personality deteriorates" (1965, p. 38). In "On arrogance" (1958), he compared being able to face the truth about one's sufferings to Oedipus' relentless search for the truth, regardless of the consequences, even at the risk of catastrophic change.

Bion enshrined "learning from experience" as the primary way we learn the truth, and he went on to elaborate that what he termed "K" is "germane to learning by experience" (1962b, p. 47). The figure K Bion designated to mean the drive to know, the epistemophilic urge for truth and knowledge, which he puts on equal footing with "L" (love) and "H" (hate), altering Freud's dual instinct theory into a threefold triangular drive system, intrinsically intermingled but nonetheless distinct and distinguishable. I think my patient wanted to know the truth but complicated the search for it by firing things at the person trying to help her find it. Little by little as time went on she could hear me and value self-knowledge and use it in experience.

Conclusion

Bion insisted on putting aside presumptions and preconceptions about the patient, speaking within the truth of the moment, focusing a beam of attention onto what is unknown. Although he presented his ideas in an abstract, scientific way, in his clinical work he favoured his "beam of darkness", his intuition (Bion, 1970), and waited for the "selected fact". In the case of Ms T, the "selected fact" that organised my knowledge and experience of her was my comment to her that she behaved like a spoilt child, demanding her own way. Although envy played a part with her, and my patient's attacks could be construed as envious spoiling of the good breast, envy did not in my view drive the patient's onslaughts; it was her controlling, spoilt, omnipotent insistence that others behaved as she wanted and thought as she did, in absolute agreement, conditioned by her belief that no one could understand her.

Of further relevance to my technique with Ms T, is Bion's remark that, "the more 'real' the psychoanalyst is the more he can be at one with the reality of the patient" (1970, p. 28). He wrote:

> If the psychoanalytical situation is accurately intuited—I prefer this term to "observed" or "heard" or "seen" as it does not carry the penumbra of sensuous association—the psychoanalyst finds that ordinary conversational English is surprisingly adequate for the formulation of his interpretation. Further, the emotional situation serves to make the interpretation comprehensible to the analysand although resistances require some modification of the statement as too optimistic. (1967, p. 134)

Even when Ms T could recognise herself in my interpretations, resistances appeared and our truth did not stay with her for long. In moments of self-reflection she would say, "I don't learn," wailing in despair. Bion appeared to believe it is the truth itself that is transformative, that the move from preconception to realisation in his logico-deductive system, the mental event that he labelled the "transformation in K", had its effect in consciousness, not requiring effort on the part of the subject to apply and use it in life. To Bion's formulation I would add that along with insight there needs to be pearls of intent to implement in life.

Having said that my patient needed a stable object, she made it difficult for me to be one through her hyperbole and guided missiles. I have suggested that her hyperbole was due to a failure of introjection by her original object and an attempt to force her way in. As she began to see that I not only survived her *Sturm und Drang,* but remained robust, took in her thoughts and emotions, and was able to think about them (at least some of the time, when I wasn't pinned up against the wall), she could experience me as a new object different from her original object— her battered, intimidated, and placating mother. This work in the transference enabled Ms T to have better relations with her objects, strikingly so with her mother. Things also improved with her boyfriend and they moved in together. On the occasions when she regressed into picking a fight with me, particularly on Fridays and before breaks, she could feel some real remorse afterwards, without the automatic superego attack on herself.

The advantage of working with patients who have such exaggerated narcissistic characters marked by intense aggression is that the psychic patterns are *writ large* as if under a strong microscope. However, it would be a mistake to think these configurations are confined to a small sample of analytic patients. Indeed, it can be argued that all human beings share in these patterns to some degree, and that at deeper levels in the personality lie narcissistic structures that, however much we are socialised into a relational field, create difficulties in allowing the other to be truly separate and outside one's omnipotent control.

Acknowledgement

I would like to thank Elizabeth Spillius for her helpful consultations on my work with this patient.

References

Bion, W. R. (1958). On arrogance. *International Journal of Psychoanalysis, 39*: 144–146.

Bion, W. R. (1962a). A theory of thinking. In: *Second Thoughts*. London: William Heinemann Medical, 1967 [reprinted London: Karnac, 1984].

Bion, W. R. (1962b). *Learning from Experience*. London: William Heinemann Medical, 1967 [reprinted London: Karnac, 1984].

Bion, W. R. (1965). *Transformations*. London: William Heinemann Medical, 1967 [reprinted London: Karnac, 1984].

Bion, W. R. (1967). *Second Thoughts*. London: Heinemann Medical [reprinted London: Karnac, 1984].

Bion, W. R. (1970). *Attention and Interpretation*. London: Tavistock [reprinted London: Karnac, 1984].

Bion, W. R. (1992). *Cogitations*. London: Karnac.

Brenman, E. (2006). *Recovery of the Lost Good Object*. (Ed. G. Fornari-Spoto). London: Routledge.

Britton, R. (2003). *Sex, Death and the Superego: Experiences in Psychoanalysis*. London: Karnac.

Freud, S. (1895d). *Studies on Hysteria. S. E., 2*: 1–306. London: Hogarth.

Freud, S. (1900a). *The Interpretation of Dreams. S. E., 4–5*: 1–627. London: Hogarth.

Freud, S. (1911–1915 [1914]). Papers on technique. *S. E., 12*: 85–173. London: Hogarth.

Freud, S. (1937c). Analysis terminable and interminable. *S. E., 23*: 216–253. London: Hogarth.

Klein, M. (1946). Notes on some schizoid mechanisms. In: *Envy and Gratitude and Other Works 1946–1963*. London: Vintage, 1997.

Klein, M. (1952). The origins of transference. In: *Envy and Gratitude and Other Works 1946–1963*. London: Vintage, 1997.

O'Shaughnessy, E. (1999). Relating to the superego. *International Journal of Psychoanalysis, 80*: 861–870.

Rosenfeld, H. (1971). A clinical approach to the psychoanalytic theory of the life and death instincts: An investigation into the aggressive aspects of narcissism. *International Journal of Psychoanalysis, 52*: 169–178.

Sandler, J., & Sandler, A. M. (1984). The past unconscious, the present unconscious, and interpretation of the transference. *Psychoanalytic Inquiry, 4*: 367–399.

Sirois, F. (2012). The role and importance of interpretation in the talking cure. *International Journal of Psychoanalysis, 93*: 1377–1402.

CHAPTER THREE

Hearing, being heard, and the fear of interpretation

Debbie Bandler Bellman

L ong ago, in a science class as a child, my teacher posed the following question: If a tree falls in the woods and no one is there, does it make a sound? Although a scientific explanation was beyond me, the more "philosophical" aspects of the question stayed with me. Is it sound if no one can hear? If it were, what sort of sound would it be? Would different people hear it differently if they were there to hear? And would the tree make a different sound if it weren't alone?

In thinking about this chapter, I have played around with this question from long ago. Is an interpretation an interpretation if not heard by the patient? Certainly each patient hears interpretations in his own way, and the same patient hears differently at various times in the analysis. But am I only considering what the patient hears, or am I also talking about what the analyst hears, and how patient and analyst hear each other? And what do I actually mean by "hear"?

My focus in this paper is on speaking to the patient in a way that he can hear; there is no point to an interpretation that cannot be heard. To my mind, an interpretation is no more or less than an attempt to communicate something to the patient about himself that could be meaningful to him in the context of his experience of the analytic session, which is a setting in which the patient is not, unlike the tree of my childhood science class, alone. I would like to stress that I am not addressing the vast question of what types of interpretation are given and when; nor am I specifically addressing the issue of the timing of interpretations, though both are related topics. Rather, I am suggesting that a consideration of what can be heard can influence what is said and be incorporated into different types of interpretations. Although we are all inevitably and necessarily guided by our theoretical frame, as well as constrained by the limits of our self-awareness, a benefit of the idea of "hearing" is that it is tied neither to any particular psychoanalytic orientation nor to any specific concept.

In her paper "Transference: The total situation", Joseph (1985) writes, "… interpretations are rarely heard purely as interpretations, except when the patient is near to the depressive position. Then interpretations and the transference itself [become] … less loaded with fantasy meaning. Patients operating with more primitive defences of splitting and projective identification tend to 'hear' our interpretations … differently …" (p. 453). Joseph is speaking of the ways in which patients distort what is said. She highlights the importance of recognising the distortions and understanding their meaning so as to further understand the transference and, by implication, to interpret it. Although distortions are not only inevitable but also necessary in regard to what they reveal about the transference and therefore about the patient's internal object relationships, I believe there is also a place for thinking about and finding a way for the patient to "hear" in the sense I am using it, which is to hear something of what is meant, even while far from anything that could be thought of as the depressive position.

For the patient to be able to hear the analyst, the analyst has first to be able to hear the patient. This brings to mind the idea of "listening", so clearly and eloquently elaborated in Casement's book *On Learning from the Patient* (1985). In order to hear, first one has to listen. I think that in many ways patients guide us as to how to interpret specifically to them. For example, early on in her analysis, a young woman spoke of a child she was teaching. She said the child needed to be taught "slowly, carefully, little by little". This patient was telling me something important about her own capacity to take in, to hear. At this point I did not know why she felt she needed me to proceed slowly, carefully, and little by little, but I felt this was what she needed me to do.

Although, like Casement, I would advocate a kind of free-floating listening and hearing, I have found it can be helpful to be able to hear what I would call the patient's *fear of interpretation*. It is my contention that, much as patients may want to understand and be understood, there is inevitably, and to varying degrees, also a dread of both. If the analyst can hear the nature of the patient's fear of interpretation, I think it is more possible to speak in a way that can be heard.

Hearing the literature

In the literature, even from the early days of psychoanalysis, the idea of interpretations being heard is often implicit—at times more explicit. Given that analysis has always been an interpersonal process regardless of how it has been variously conceptualised, this is perhaps not surprising. In "The dynamics of transference", Freud (1912b) describes how his attention was drawn to the inevitable emergence of transference in the psychoanalytic situation. Although he regarded transference, particularly negative transference, as posing resistance to the analytic work of free-association, he nevertheless was compelled to hear it, to conceptualise it, and to find a way of working with it. Freud's comment that when the transference has become essentially negative "there ceases to be any possibility of influence or cure" (ibid., p. 107), contains the idea that treatment is jeopardised when the patient ceases to be able to hear as useful, meaningful, or indeed benign, anything that the analyst says. Put another way, one could say that the patient's *dread* of the interpretation, and of course of the analyst from whom it comes, has overwhelmed him.

In his classic paper "The nature of the therapeutic action of psychoanalysis", Strachey (1934) delineates and explores the components of what he terms a "mutative interpretation". Using both Freud's structural and topographical models, and stressing the centrality of transference interpretations, he maps out factors that combine to enable an interpretation to have a mutative, transformative effect upon the patient's psyche, specifically upon archaic aspects of the superego. Implicit in his detailed mapping out of the circumstances under which an interpretation can be mutative is an assessment of what the patient can hear. For example, the patient must have retained a sense of the reality of the analyst; that is, the patient is not in a psychotic transference.

Many later papers concentrate more explicitly on what the patient can hear, even if not spelled out in these terms. For example, in "Patient-centered and analyst-centered interpretations: Some implications of containment and countertransference", Steiner (1994) writes about analyst-centered interpretations as alternatives to those that are patient-centered. Borderline and psychotic patients—or patients in these states—can experience interpretations about their states of mind as persecutory and can react with increased anxiety, while interpretations centered on the experience of the analyst can be felt as more containing. The implication is that these two kinds of interpretations can be experienced very differently by the patient, regardless of the correctness of the content of each. Further, it could be said that in the examples described by Steiner, analyst-centered interpretations could be *heard* while patient-centered ones could not; patient-centered interpretations were *feared* while analyst-centered ones were not.

Since the 1990s, the increasing emphasis on psychoanalysis as an interpersonal process, as well as the conceptualisation of it as an intersubjective one, has spawned more focus on "attitudes" or "qualities" of the analyst in the analytic relationship that facilitate the engagement with the patient and the deepening of the analytic process. A number of authors have, for example, explored or alluded to the role of authenticity in analytic technique and experience (e.g., Bader, 1995; Ogden, 2004), whilst others have taken a fresh look at empathy and impediments to it (e.g., Bolognini, 2009; Steyn, 2013, republished in this volume). It could be said that this spotlight on the interaction between patient and analyst, together with the recognition of the person behind the interpretation, a recognition I feel goes beyond both classical and subsequent views of countertransference, indicates attention to those aspects of the analytic process that facilitate patient and analyst each hearing the other.

Hearing the interpretation

Hearing the interpretation has something to do with the patient's being able to take it in as having to do with himself and his experience, and to let it resonate emotionally. There is a sense of recognition that "this is me", and often an experience of feeling understood. The patient's recognition of himself in the interpretation suggests it has been heard at many levels, from the surface to depth, and I would agree with Carpy's (1989, p. 289) warning against seeing interpretations as useful that the patient does not subjectively feel but which the analyst nevertheless feels are true about the patient at a deeper level.

Parsons (2014) writes of interpretation as stemming from a kind of unity of intellect and feeling in the analyst that can enable the patient to have a corresponding experience. He says, "The key idea I am proposing is this: *interpretation puts into words the analyst's experience of bringing mind and heart together in trying to understand a patient, in the hope of bringing mind and heart together in the patient so as to facilitate a corresponding experience of self-understanding*" (p. 181). "Bringing mind and heart together in the patient" corresponds to what I mean by emotional resonance. An appreciation of what the patient might be able to hear, informed by an understanding of the patient's fear of interpretation, can influence the timing of the interpretation, the level of the interpretation, and the words that are chosen, as well as the actual vocal tone of the interpretation. If what can be heard is taken into account, then I think an interpretation has more possibility of "facilitating a corresponding experience of self-understanding" in Parsons' terms or, in Strachey's (1934), facilitating a mutative analytic experience that furthers integration. Whatever the analyst's theoretical model is, however one conceptualises the impact on psychic structure and the internal world, the aim is to enable the analytic relationship and process to proceed to greater depth.

Clinical illustration

Near the start of my clinical practice, which was as a child psychotherapist, I treated a nine-year-old boy who was failing in school. Unable to learn, he gained recognition as the class clown. For some time my interpretations seemed to fall on deaf ears. This was regardless, for example, of whether I was commenting on his play, on his defensive use of clowning, on his fear of failure, on his anxiety that I would think he wasn't smart—the list could go on. One day, when he performed an exceptionally ridiculous stunt, I said I wondered why such a clever boy could act so stupid. This comment caught his attention, and marked, I felt, the beginning of our working together, the beginning of his curiosity about himself, and the beginning of a treatment alliance. (This clinical example is cited in Bellman, 2012).

I tried to unravel why my comment, spontaneously offered, and which was really more of an observation than an interpretation, had such a profound effect on the treatment relationship. Certainly one could argue that all that had gone before had made an impact and led up to that moment, but I felt this was not the whole story. The difference between my previous comments and interpretations and the one about his stunt seemed to be that I had taken on board the extent of his damaged narcissism and embraced this awareness in my comment. His expectation that anything I said would make him feel even worse about himself than he already did had prevented him from taking in any interpretations, including putting into words his fear of me because he expected I would make him feel worse. This expectation, which I later felt constituted his main *fear of interpretation*, caused him to block out anything I said. He needed me to be able to hear his fear, to take it in, and to speak in a way that conveyed that I understood the depth of his low self-esteem and how he had needed not to hear in order to protect himself from anticipated verbal blows.

What I have described above is a conscious and retrospective understanding of what I think was an unconscious "intersubjective" process, a process Ogden (1997) describes in his paper "Reverie and metaphor: Some thoughts on how I work as a psychoanalyst", and which resulted in my spontaneous comment. He writes,

> To complicate matters still further, it has increasingly seemed to me that my experience of each analytic situation is to a very large degree a reflection of the specific type of unconscious intersubjective construction that the patient and I are in the midst of creating. The sort of unconscious engagement with the analysand to which I am referring results in the creation of a third subject, the "intersubjective analytic third" ... The experience of analyst and analysand in (and of) the analytic third represents an experiential base, a pool of unconscious experience to which analyst and analysand contribute and from which they individually draw in the process of generating their own experience of the analytic relationship. (p. 720)

By wondering why such a clever boy could act so stupid, I indicated first that I thought he was clever and then that I was aware he acted like he was not. What he could recognise was that he acted ridiculously;

that was his "this is me" experience. I do not think he recognised himself in the first part of my comment, but I suspect it resonated with at least an unconscious hope, and opened up the possibility that he was not as stupid as he felt he was and thus that he could feel differently about himself.

In the proceeding analytic work, he continued for a long time to need me to take his very low self-esteem into account in my phrasing of comments and interpretations. He felt very internally persecuted and projected this onto his objects, causing him to fear and expect attacks on his narcissism. Gradually he became able to both own and look at his inner hurts, and it became possible to analyse these aspects.

I began to be interested in factors that enabled my patients to hear interpretations and comments as well as factors that prevented this, to take these into account in the framing of interpretations, and to gradually develop the idea of fear of interpretation. Taking these into account has become an integral part of my interpretive voice, spanning the transition from analytic work with children to analytic work with adults. With adults, of course, I phrase things differently. In a similar situation I might not spell out that I thought they were clever—but I also might. Before exploring some of these factors, I would like to briefly mention what could be considered *pitfalls* to thinking in these terms.

Pitfalls

It could be argued that there are pitfalls, reasons not to think in terms of what the patient can hear. These might stem, for example, from the possibility that the analyst might be avoiding difficult aspects of the transference and countertransference, particularly the negative or erotic transference and countertransference. That is, the analyst could avoid taking up difficult and uncomfortable aspects of the analytic experience on the grounds that the patient could not bear to hear about them, while it is really the analyst who cannot bear to articulate and face them with the patient. Equally, the analyst might feel guilty at the possibility, and at times clinical advisability, of arousing increased anxiety in the patient, and conclude that the patient is not ready to hear. To put it another way, thinking in terms of what the patient can hear could open the door to countertransference anxieties masquerading as technical considerations.

I do not, however, feel these pitfalls are essentially different from those inherent in analyses where what the patient can hear is not a consideration. Indeed, I feel there are more pitfalls to not taking hearing into account. These would include the possibility of re-enacting in the analysis initial trauma to the patient's narcissism or, with a patient whose superego is harsh and primitive, increasing the patient's sense of persecution. Additionally, a patient may feel the analyst is proceeding at a pace that is too fast, and something of the background sense of working together—the treatment alliance—could be lost. Beyond this, the patient may feel that the analyst is making not necessarily incorrect but somewhat generic interpretations, ones that do not take his individuality and vulnerabilities into account.

Factors facilitating or preventing hearing

Factors facilitating or preventing hearing, particularly in regard to the fear of interpretation, could be in the analyst, in the patient, or in the interaction. Although it is in some ways artificial to differentiate, as all three of these locations are simultaneously present, for the sake of clarity I will explore each separately.

In the analyst

As mentioned, the analyst needs to be able to hear the patient. As Ogden put it: "The development of an analytic sensibility centrally involves the enhancement of the analyst's capacity to feel the alive moments of an analytic session in a visceral way, to be able to hear that a word or a phrase has been used, has been 'made anew' (Frost, 1918, p. 697) in an interesting, unexpected way ..." (Ogden, 1997, p. 720). In order to "feel the alive moments", the analyst needs to be able to hear herself. This entails being in touch with her current state of mind, with the countertransference, and with how the one influences the other. I remember the beginning of a middle-aged man's treatment some years ago. I was not long qualified and eager to prove my capacities, but also worried I wasn't ready to practise independently. My patient presented as belligerent and argumentative, which I found both unnerving and irritating. When I attempted to explore his aggression, he reacted with angry outbursts and I began to feel rather useless. When I could eventually process, digest, and consider my reactions, I thought that he had entered treatment expecting to be both dominated and found lacking. In order to protect himself from these painful experiences, he had identified with the aggressor, thus ensuring I would be the one to feel badly about myself. Once I understood this, I could hear what I had previously heard as aggression as driven instead by anxiety. Having heard the underlying anxiety, I could interpret it. My patient could in turn hear my interpretation. Subsequently, the transference shifted to one of much less belligerence.

One could say that my interpretations of my patient's aggression had not been heard because, as I hadn't sufficiently heard his anxiety, my comments were incomplete, and this would also be true. But the point I want to emphasise is how my own anxiety and fear that I would be found lacking as an analyst initially resonated with the countertransference. This influenced how I heard and understood both the countertransference and the affective, verbal material, and in turn influenced the transference. I had not been able to hear the patient's fear of interpretation, which was his expectation of being dominated and found lacking. In this instance, what I have called the analyst's "state of mind" pertained to undertaking analytic work independently. In other instances it might be less directly professionally related; I am sure we are all familiar with how tiredness or preoccupation can affect our experience of our patients.

A further factor affecting the analyst's ability to hear the patient—not illustrated in the example just given—is her capacity to hear her thoughts as they enter her mind during the session. Together with this, she needs to have trust in her own unconscious processes and the "unconscious engagement with the analysand" (Ogden, 1977, p. 720). This all takes time and experience to develop, and will develop uniquely. As Gabbard and Ogden (2009) said, "Becoming an analyst necessarily involves creating a highly personal identity that is unlike that of any other analyst" (p. 325).

Next in regard to facilitating factors would be the analyst's theoretical frame, enabling her to find a way of thinking about what is going on in the patient, and between herself and the patient. This frame is part of the analyst's "holding environment" (Winnicott, 1965a). If any of these factors are not sufficiently present in any given session, I think the analyst's hearing capacity will be, at that moment, at least marginally impaired. Given that we are all human, this is not an infrequent occurrence.

Ultimately, I feel the analyst's capacity to hear is dependent upon her receptivity, her capacity to take in, process, digest, synthesise, and understand at a deep emotional level what the patient is trying to communicate about his state of mind or, in Parsons' terms, his "mind and heart".

In the patient

As with the boy mentioned earlier, a patient with very low self-esteem, usually accompanied by a severe, primitive superego, can experience much of what the analyst says as a criticism. Equally, a patient who relies on splitting and projection as main defences can feel highly threatened by interpretations that verbalise what has been split off or projected, and can frequently distort what has been said. A patient with difficulty with introjection would have difficulty taking in and metabolising interpretations. As with factors impeding the analyst's hearing, those affecting the patient's are numerous, and will differ according to the individuality of the patient, the transference, and the stage of treatment.

At the same time, I believe that all patients have at least some fear of interpretation. Much as patients may want to understand their difficulties and excruciatingly painful as these might be, their difficulties have, by the time of entering treatment, become a way of life that is known, and thus they usually bring at least a modicum of a sense of safety. Interpretation, which concerns the unknown, threatens this. Put theoretically, interpretation threatens defences, defences felt to be necessary in order to deal with the internal and external object worlds.

Developmentally, the extent of the patient's fear is likely to be linked to the extent of early difficulties and how these have affected the establishment of basic trust. Where early difficulties are considerable, hope or expectation that the analyst will endeavour to maintain a "background of safety" (Sandler, 1960) within the analytic setting is overshadowed by the fear and indeed expectation that the analyst will not. The analyst's interpretations are thus anticipated with much foreboding, setting the stage for not hearing, mishearing, or feeling unheard. The dread of interpretation in these instances forms a kind of background, or overarching fear, which strongly influences how comments are heard.

In the interaction

The idea of hearing the patient links with getting to know one's patient as an individual, and brings to mind Winnicott's (1960) ideas on getting to know one's baby as part of providing the holding environment necessary for development. A mother may or may not need books on early child care to help her, but they are no substitute for getting to know her baby. As analysts, we need to be grounded in a theoretical framework, but equally, this is no substitute for getting to know our patients. Otherwise there is, I feel, a risk of making generic interpretations that will not resonate at any deep level in our patients. I have occasionally been accused of making a generic interpretation, and the patient has always been right. My comment, while not incorrect, will have been one where I was not fully in touch with the specificity the patient's experience in the here and now of the session.

Essentially, by getting to know one's patient, I mean getting to know something about his experience of himself, of others, of the worlds inside and around him. In the transference, this would be how I am experienced by him, and in the countertransference how I experience him. As the analytic process and the transference and countertransference deepen, one gets to know one's patient better. The patient also gets to know the analyst better, in the sense of becoming familiar with those aspects of the analyst's personality that come through verbally and non-verbally in the nature of the holding presence and interpretive style on offer.

In the early days, while patient and analyst are unknown, or relatively unknown to each other, the fear of interpretation is often greatest, and I am particularly mindful of how mine are heard. I am still cognisant of this later in the analysis, at some stages more than others, but by later I will have some idea of how interpretations are experienced by my patient and will have incorporated this knowledge into the way I speak. Such incorporation could be considered an extension of the function of the analyst as part of the "facilitating environment" (Winnicott, 1965b) or "new developmental object" (Hurry, 1998). That is, the analyst, as part of the environment for the patient, provides something that can facilitate the development of the patient through the development of the process of the analysis. What is provided is hearing in a way that can be used to frame interpretations so that they can be heard. Such framing would constitute part of the "holding" aspect of the good interpretation (Winnicott, 1960).

Winnicott (ibid.) considers empathy to be a crucial ingredient of the holding environment, "But the environmental provision is not mechanically so. It is reliable in a way that implies the mother's empathy" (p. 592). Listening for how interpretations are heard, particularly listening for the shape of the fear of interpretation, entails, I feel, what can be thought of as a kind of dual empathic identification. That is, empathic identification with the patient in regard *both* to the patient's current emotional state *and* with how the interpretation is likely to be received and heard.

In the course of getting to know one's patient, however, there may be aspects that the analyst finds it difficult to know of, and this will diminish the analyst's capacity to hear and thus influence what is said. Countertransference feelings stirred up by these features may be very challenging or painful for the analyst, or might touch on facets of the analyst's personality or anxieties that she would rather not dwell on or even know about. It could be said that, in regard to these aspects, the analyst has a *fear of both hearing and interpreting*; to do either fully would confront the analyst with what is warded off. Although this is in some ways similar to the patient's fear of interpretation, it is also different, in that it would usually—after the analyst's own training analysis—be a response to certain aspects of a patient or specific phases in treatment, as opposed to a more far-reaching underlying anxiety. Nevertheless, the importance of self-analysis, consultations with colleagues, supervision, or occasionally further analysis to try to work through "blind spots"—countertransference in its original sense—is pertinent here.

Clinical illustration

Ms E was a single woman in her early thirties whom I treated analytically some years ago. She sought treatment for a symptom that particularly disturbed her and which made sexual relationships impossible. She could not bear to be touched by men, a symptom that started in adolescence after being abused by a distant relative. She also suffered from periodic bouts of acute anxiety, and had several near-phobic symptoms. These latter did not worry her so much, as they warded off what she feared would be overwhelming anxiety. Despite these difficulties, she was well functioning in a number of ways, and had a satisfying professional career and many friends of both sexes.

In our initial meetings, Ms E described her life before the abuse as "happy". She was the middle of three children, with an older sister and younger brother, and felt her parents had been available to her despite their busy professional lives. At the same time, she had a sense that she saw her early childhood through "rose-coloured glasses". She said she wanted desperately to understand her symptom because she wanted to be able to marry and have children, and was keen to start analysis.

I was quickly struck by the discrepancy between Ms E's early presentation and what it felt like to be with her. Her demeanour and affects were cheerful, as if she didn't have a care in the world, and she described the abuse in clear and factual terms. I, however, found her story extremely disturbing, and felt confused, as well as suffused with great anxiety.

Although she attended regularly and on time, talked with apparent ease, and appeared to consider and associate to my comments, I felt kept at a distance. My interpretation that she feared being "touched" by my comments made some sense to her, but seemed not to truly resonate. I felt she couldn't bear to hear my comments at any sort of deep level, and suggested she couldn't bear to let them in because she feared to do so would feel like a repeat of the abuse. This made more sense to her. Having let herself hear a little more, in the second month of analysis Ms E grew very anxious. She spoke of feeling overwhelmed and fearing she wouldn't be able to manage her work. I commented on her fear I was making her worse, and her dilemma: she wanted me to be able to "hold" her anxieties yet feared she would find this abusive. She grew calmer in the session but her anxiety subsequently escalated.

I felt increasingly helpless in the face of what seemed a phobic process and a doomed treatment. I wondered whether she could indeed not allow herself to be contained in treatment because this became equated with the abuse and was therefore experienced as a re-enactment of it, or whether it was because I had not yet found a way of enabling her to feel held safely. To put it another way, was it that she would experience any interpretation as being touched and therefore as crashing through her defensive barrier, or was it that I had not yet been able to hear an aspect of her fear that would enable me to put something into words in a way that could be heard and experienced as containing?

Ms E spoke of her fear that I would smother her, and how she wanted to save herself by leaving analysis. She explained that recently she had needed to force herself to come to her sessions. I suggested she felt I was forcing her like her relative had forced her both to touch him and be touched. She grew confused and panicky, and urgently asked, "But is analysis supposed to help me be touched? The thing is, I don't want that!" I said that if she thought the aim—my aim—was to enable her to be touched, then I could see she would feel forced into an intolerable situation because she could not imagine ever wanting to be. She began to listen intently, and asked, "But if that isn't the aim, what is? That is what brought me here. I thought I wanted it." I said she was discovering what she both may and may not want, and that over time analysis could perhaps make it possible for her to feel she had more of a choice. Ms E's reaction to this was dramatic. She grew significantly calmer, and returned again and again throughout her ten-year treatment to this interchange.

What Ms E had needed me most to hear was her terror of being forced. Interpretations had to be fended off for several main reasons. She feared they were not only forced upon her but would also force her to act without choice. She also feared interpretations would force into awareness her own sexual desires, which she unconsciously felt had led to the abuse. For her, "hearing" equalled "being forced".

Before I could wholly hear and interpret *her* fear, I had first to process *my* responses. My countertransference experience of confusion, anxiety, and increasing helplessness was elicited in response to Ms E's projected feelings, feelings she needed me to hold, to "tolerate" as described by Carpy (1989). But I also needed to hear that my anxiety that Ms E would leave was also a fear that she would stay (Ogden, 1992). Because I thought of myself as having a good capacity to receive projections and contain anxiety, I was reluctant to know of a wish to be spared having to tolerate the very difficult countertransference. I think this reluctance, combined with a feeling of having to force myself to face the sessions, had prevented me from fully recognising this latter feeling as a countertransference response and thus from hearing the depth of her fear.

As in the instance of the boy described earlier, I had not consciously worked all of this out before the session cited above. Rather, it was in the here and now—intersubjective—experience of the session that my "mind and heart" (Parsons, 2014) came together and I could then express my understanding of Ms E's main fear.

What had been most traumatic in the abuse was not touching and being touched per se, but rather being *forced* to touch and be touched. Not surprisingly, it emerged over time that Ms E's terror of being forced had its antecedents in her early history. She had felt help-less, confused, and uncontained in the face of her mother's extreme anxieties: both intruded upon and unheard. In the transference she expected to be similarly confused, projected into, and unheard. In an ongoing way I needed to keep her central fear of being forced some-where in my mind so that I could try to speak to her in a way that she could hear.

Concluding thoughts

For purposes of illustration, the clinical example chosen above is a vivid one, as was the one from the boy's analysis. In both instances it was helpful to think in terms of what I hadn't heard, or fully heard, in regard to what can be thought of as their fear of interpretation. In the case of the boy, he dreaded interpretations because he anticipated they would confirm or deepen his view that he was a failure; in the instance of Ms E, she feared she would be forced. With both, the nature of their fear of interpretation reflected their central hurts, difficulties, and anxi-eties. Understanding and putting into words their individual fears in a way that could be heard led to a deepening of the analytic relationship and process.

At the risk of stretching a metaphor too far and using it too loosely, I will end by returning briefly to the question of the tree in the woods. Did I hear my teacher's question? I think I did in that I understood approximately what was meant; it was a scientific question about sound. Although I could not give the desired answer, the question stayed with me in a more philosophical way because that is how it resonated. Thus I would say I heard the question but took my own direction with it. In regard to thinking about how interpretations can be heard, I feel we owe it to our patients to consider how we can most meaningfully hear and speak to them, and how we can address their anxiety about inter-pretations while responding to their wish to understand and be under-stood. Which path the patient then takes will be up to him.

References

Bader, M. J. (1995). Authenticity and the psychology of choice in the analyst. *Psychoanalytic Quarterly, 64*: 282–305.

Bellman, D. B. (2012). Specifically Anna Freudian. In: N. Malberg & J. Raphael-Leff (Eds.), *The Anna Freud Tradition* (pp. 369–375). London: Karnac.

Bolognini, S. (2009). The complex nature of psychoanalytic empathy: A theoretical and clinical exploration. *Fort Da, 15*: 35–56.

Carpy, D. V. (1989). Tolerating the countertransference: A mutative process. *International Journal of Psychoanalysis, 70*: 287–294.

Casement, P. (1985). *On Learning from the Patient*. London: Tavistock.

Freud, S. (1912b). The dynamics of transference. *S. E., 12*: 97–108. London: Hogarth.

Frost, R. (1918). The unmade word. In: R. Poirier & M. Richardson (Eds.), *Robert Frost: Collected Poems, Prose and Plays* (pp. 694–697). New York: Library of America, 1995 [quoted in: Ogden, T. H. (1997). Reverie and metaphor: Some thoughts on how I work as a psychoanalyst. *International Journal of Psychoanalysis, 78*: 719–732].

Gabbard, G. O., & Ogden, T. H. (2009). On becoming a psychoanalyst. *International Journal of Psychoanalysis, 90*: 311–327.

Hurry, A. (1998). Psychoanalysis and developmental therapy. In: *Psychoanalysis and Developmental Therapy* (pp. 32–73). London: Karnac.

Joseph, B. (1985). Transference: The total situation. *International Journal of Psychoanalysis, 66*: 447–454.

Ogden, T. H. (1992). Comments on transference and countertransference in the initial analytic meeting. *Psychoanalytic Inquiry, 12*: 225–247.

Ogden, T. H. (1994). The analytic third: Working with intersubjective clinical facts. *International Journal of Psychoanalysis, 75*: 3–19.

Ogden, T. H. (1997). Reverie and metaphor: Some thoughts on how I work as a psychoanalyst. *International Journal of Psychoanalysis, 78*: 719–732.

Ogden, T. H. (2004). The analytic third: Implications for psychoanalytic theory and technique. *Psychoanalytic Quarterly, 73*: 167–195.

Parsons, M. (2014). *Living Psychoanalysis: From Theory to Experience*. London: Routledge (New Library of Psychoanalysis).

Sandler, J. (1960). The background of safety. *International Journal of Psychoanalysis, 41*: 352–356.

Steiner, J. (1994). Patient-centered and analyst-centered interpretations: Some implications of containment and countertransference. *Psychoanalytic Inquiry, 14*: 406–422.

Steyn, L. (2013). Tactics and empathy: Defences against projective identification. *International Journal of Psychoanalysis, 94*: 1093–1113 [republished in this volume, London: Karnac, 2014].

Strachey, J. (1934). The nature of the therapeutic action of psycho-analysis. *International Journal of Psychoanalysis, 15*: 127–159.

Winnicott, D. W. (1952). Anxiety associated with insecurity. In: *Collected Papers: Through Paediatrics to Psycho-Analysis* (pp. 94–203). London: Tavistock, 1958.

Winnicott, D. W. (1960). The theory of the parent–infant relationship. *International Journal of Psychoanalysis, 41*: 585–595.

Winnicott, D. W. (1965a). From dependence to independence in the development of the individual. In: *The Maturational Processes and the Facilitating Environment* (pp. 83–92). London: Hogarth, 1976 [reprinted London: Karnac, 1990].

Winnicott, D. W. (1965b). *The Maturational Processes and the Facilitating Environment*. London: Hogarth, 1976 [reprinted London: Karnac, 1990].

CHAPTER FOUR

Tactics and empathy: defences against projective identification*

Lesley Steyn

In this paper I wish to try to address some problems I have struggled
with in the approach I use, within the British tradition, that
emphasises work in the here and now with the patient's projections
and phantasy relationship with the analyst. Strachey's work (1934) was
a turning point in focusing attention on the here and now of the analytic
session: he showed that the patient's severe superego could only be
modified if "caught in the act" in the present moment when projected
into the analyst and his "mutative transference interpretation" became
a template for psychic change for future generations of all schools of
analysis (see Arundale, 2011).

Since then, work by Klein (1946), Bion (1959), Rosenfeld (1971)
and others on the theory of projective identification has developed
Strachey's vision that the analyst becomes the patient's "external phantasy object" (Caper, 1992). As the patient, in phantasy, projects parts of
himself into the analyst and then feels these parts to reside in the analyst,

---

*This paper was published in *The International Journal of Psychoanalysis*, 94: 1093–1113,
and is republished here with the kind permission of that journal. The Institute of Psychoanalysis is the copyright holder.

not himself, so, these authors show, the analyst correspondingly feels provoked to identify with the projected attributes.

My way of working is influenced by all of the above as well as by present-day analysts (Feldman, 1997; Joseph, 1981; O'Shaughnessy, 1992; Roth, 2001; Steiner, 1993) who in different ways show how the analyst working in the here and now can be drawn into impasse or collusion, re-enacting the patient's maladaptive object relations. All these authors emphasise the need for the analyst's personal honesty and countertransference introspection as the patient's defensive projective system often overwhelms the analyst's capacity to see and think. They also describe the importance, when the analyst does catch this process in the act, of interpreting at the right level to try to help the patient bear painful insight.

What these authors also show is that being projected into can be such a painful experience for the *analyst* that it can feel unbearable to suffer it—and yet this is what is required if we are to bear to know and feel what the patient cannot bear.

In his paper "The emotional experience of K" James V. Fisher writes:

> ... we should note that in "On Arrogance" (1958) Bion casts Oedipus in a role similar to that of the analyst who conveys to a patient a determination to lay bare the truth no matter what the cost and yet cannot or will not take in the emotional experiences that can be the truth of that quest. (2006, pp. 1228–1229)

What Bion describes as arrogance on his own part, in Fisher's view, is:

> ... those periods in the analytic encounter when he could not take in a patient's projections, arrogantly assuming that the projections were simply an attack on verbal communication. (p. 1228)

I have come to think that the kind of split-off "arrogance" in the analyst that Fisher understands Bion to be describing is more pervasive than we realise. I think this can express itself in ways of interpreting the patient's projective identification when the analyst has an underlying lack of belief in the reality of the psychic predicament she is describing or when she defends against it.

To my mind, and following my understanding of the authors above, what is transformative in working with a here and now approach is the analyst's capacity to take in and bear the truth of what she has become in the patient's psychic reality. What I want to show is that it therefore follows that interpretations made in clinical situations when the analyst has *not* done the emotional work of recognising and bearing what kind of object she has become for the patient will be experienced by the patient as empty tactics—even lies—rather than interpretations of integrity. At the same time, interpreting from a position of bearing this truth will be difficult and painful for the analyst and indicate a struggle inside her with great hostility not only towards the patient but towards the process of psychoanalysis itself insofar as it seeks the integration of loathed parts of the self. If the analyst cannot know about her own ambivalence towards the analytic process then she is likely to split off her hatred and project it into the patient.

The focus of my paper, therefore, is upon the real difficulties for the analyst who works with the approach I try to follow in acknowledging and dealing with her own ambivalence about being a projective-identification receiving object.

As an example I will describe a certain kind of defence that I have come to recognise in myself and think others may recognise. It involves the use of an interpretive technique that has become known as the analyst-centred interpretation advocated by Steiner (1993).

Steiner shows that when we speak to a patient we must consider the patient's capacity to bear insight into what it is that they are doing. His "analyst-centred interpretation" is a suggested technique that enables the patient to explore the content of his projections in the analyst without confronting him with patient-centred interpretations that return projections too quickly, threatening the patient with too much painful self-awareness. Like many, I find Steiner's contribution in this area invaluable and frequently find analyst-centred interpretations indispensable in relieving a stuck position when the very word "you" is anathema to the patient. However, at times I have come to find in my own work that Steiner's contribution can be misused, resulting in a situation where the analyst's tactics come to replace the painful emotional work involved in empathy.

Sophia and the misuse of analyst-centred interpretation

To illustrate, I offer a clinical vignette with a difficult to reach patient whom I struggled to work with, moving in terms of technique between trying to use "patient-centred" and "analyst-centred" interpretations as described by Steiner (1993). I think the case I am describing shows the difficulties involved when the patient does not, in the first place, see the analyst as someone who can provide understanding. What I most want to demonstrate, though, is my own great difficulty as the analyst in accepting this view of myself. (I am grateful to David Tuckett who, in consultation, showed me that I was using analyst-centred interpretation defensively in the case described.)

A thirty-year-old woman, Sophia, entered treatment following a bitter divorce. Her husband had left her for another woman and she had lost her job. She found it difficult to imagine that her husband had any rights to leave her or to any privacy from her wish to intrude into his new relationship. As a child she had experienced her parents as unhappily married and leading separate lives and felt herself to be in a special relationship with each. She had also felt bullied by an older sibling who would sometimes confide and get close to her and at other times push her aside. Her view was that anyone with sensitivity should understand how badly she had been treated and make special allowances and she felt strongly that I should share her picture. She was in debt and very ambivalent about supporting herself financially and psychically. I often felt very pressurised and provoked to act impulsively and punitively towards her, for instance, when intrusive telephone calls and demands for new session times followed missed and unpaid for sessions. At the same time I felt very constrained by her. At the time of the following vignette Sophia was attending four times a week on the couch and had been in treatment for three years. She had not attended the previous session, which would have been the first of the week, and she had left the last session of the previous week angry and shouting at me: "You just don't listen."

PATIENT: [After a long silence] Yesterday I had intended to come for my session. I set my alarm but when I woke up it had been turned off. But I intended to come. I could not believe it when I saw what had happened. And now I am here … but I can't remember where we were because since the last session I have not been thinking about it.

ANALYST: You feel very conflicted. You want to come here and try to understand yourself but you don't want to be worried about yourself—you want to turn off your alarm.

P: [Rising anger] I told you what happened. Did you not listen! It was a mistake, turning off the alarm. I don't feel it was me doing it—why don't you believe me! It has nothing to do with anything. It is a waste of time talking about that. I'm paying for this—don't waste time.

A: It seems we are not free to explore what might be in your mind that you're not aware of.

P: What do you mean, not free! I'm not stopping or silencing you. Stop talking as if I'm a tyrant. I am trying to get you to understand but it's pointless … Now I remember that I was very angry last week when I left. But that is not why I didn't come yesterday. I can't remember what we were talking about now but I do remember I was angry. What I felt was that you have power over me. You can choose to see me. That means you can say what you like to me. You are supposed to be a professional and all you do is make me feel bad about myself. You go on about how I abuse myself—it makes me feel bad.

A: I think you are afraid you cannot stand up to an abusive part of yourself that tyrannises the part of you that tries to come here and listen to your self and get help.

P: [Despair increasing] Look it is happening! Whenever I try to talk to you about what *you* do to me you silence me. You push it back onto me and start talking to me about what I do to myself. You don't want to hear what *you* do. I'm not happy. I have a right to say what I think about you without you twisting it all the time into what I do to myself. You twist everything. My problem is you!

A: Well I do see that you feel really desperately that you are trying to talk to someone who is just refusing to listen. You feel I not only don't understand, but am not even *trying* to understand, as though I'm shouting with my fingers in my ears.

P: Yes … but … I know what you are really thinking. You are thinking that it is really me—you don't really believe it is *you* doing it. I'm sick of being told by you that it is *me* trying not to understand myself. What do you think I'm here for?

A: Well, okay, I do hear that you really feel it is me not listening. But I think it is *you* now not listening to yourself because you are very afraid of your own insight.

P: You see; you are doing it again. You cannot believe it is you doing it. I knew this would happen if I came today. There is no point in this.

During this very stuck exchange I think that I viewed myself in retrospect as trapped in the kind of impasse described by Steiner (1993) where patient and analyst are at cross purposes because the analyst believes her task is to help the patient gain understanding whereas the patient wants to gain equilibrium and finds insight unbearable. My insistence on trying to help the patient see what I saw as truth about her was making her withdraw further, but I also felt that if I became too passive she would feel I had given up or was colluding with something dishonest. Therefore, I persisted in tying to make interpretations concerned with understanding—that is, that the patient could not bear to feel alarmed about the way she abused herself by not listening to herself and so on—but these did not make the patient feel contained. On the contrary, she felt that I was pushing back the projected elements that she had eliminated from herself via projective identification precisely because she could not cope with them. I was failing to register that speaking about either the content of her projection or about the projective process itself (e.g., "You are not listening to yourself" or "You are avoiding feeling such-and-such by trying to get rid of your feelings into me") is fruitless in such a situation because a patient who is splitting and projecting severely does not experience it as a split in herself but as *me*.

While it may be true that a less disturbed patient may retain some awareness of what she projects and may, therefore, be able to recognise it as *hers* when the analyst interprets it to her, a more disturbed patient uses projective identification in a more total form divesting herself entirely of the projection so that it now seems foreign. Gabbard (2000) addresses this in his distinction between "benign transference hate and malignant transference hate":

> In the former, the "as if" nature of the transference is retained so that the patient knows at some level that the analyst is not really the hated object but that she is experiencing him "as if" he were the transference object. By contrast, the borderline patients with malignant transference hate ... lose the "as if" nature of the transference and insist that the analyst really is a deserving object of hatred, that is, the original object. (p. 411)

Given the level of disturbance, my patient's immediate need, therefore, was for the painful projections to reside in the analyst and to be understood in their projected state, as Steiner explains. Indeed, by the end of the sequence I had sensed that I needed to make some switch. I thought that analyst-centred interpretations were the only way to go in order to give the patient—who could not tolerate understanding herself—a sense of being understood by me, and so I changed in the way I understood Steiner to suggest. However, when I tried to move into analyst-centred interpreting—"You feel you are talking to someone who …"—it did not work. The patient did not feel understood, she felt suspicious. Ultimately she knew that I did not really see myself as that "someone".

Why this interpretation did not "work" I found far more difficult to understand in retrospect than the failure of my patient-centred interpretations. However, gradually, with more reflection (and I am afraid more painful encounters like the above) I eventually began to realise that the patient was right that I did not really mean what I was saying when I made my apparent analyst-centred interpretation. (This was indicated by my admission at the end: "Well, okay, I do hear that you really feel it is me not listening. But I think it is *you* …") I came to recognise that, whilst I thought I was listening and trying to understand my patient's full psychic reality, in fact, underneath what I was really feeling was that I had listened all I could and was waiting for her to listen and understand my point—which was that *she* was not listening to herself. Therefore, I was not understanding the position the patient was now in, and was in a sense lying when I said I was trying to listen. Perhaps I was not unlike the mother Bion describes in his hypothetical reconstruction of catastrophic infantile experience—a projective-identification-refusing object who "dutifully responded to the infant's emotional displays" as if she were impatiently saying to herself: "I don't know what's the matter with the child" (Bion, 1959, pp. 312–313).

Therefore, my apparent use of Steiner's analyst-centred technique was more a "tactic" than a receptivity to the patient's predicament—and the patient could tell. Her comment, "There is no point in this," could have meant that she perceived an object with no receptivity for projective identification. Underneath I was waiting for her to change just as she was waiting for me to change. It was hard for me to appreciate emotionally what theoretically I thought I knew: that the patient in a state of projective identification had no choice but to see me as malignant. I was feeling underneath as though the patient somehow could, if she wanted to, *choose* to switch and see the "real" me who was not like that. Or if she could not choose, then I did not really want to *know* that she could not.

Steiner (1993) himself points to the limits of his own patient-centred/ analyst-centred distinction:

> It is clear that the distinction depends more on the analyst's atti-
> tude and state of mind than on the wording he uses. If the ana-
> lyst says: "You see me as ..." and implies that the patient's view is
> one which is in error, or hurtful or in some other way undesirable,
> then the emphasis is on what is going on in the patient and the
> interpretation is primarily patient-centred. To be analyst-centred,
> in the sense which I intend to use it, the analyst has to have an
> open mind and be willing to consider the patient's view and try to
> understand what the patient means in a spirit of enquiry. (p. 133)

This seems to fit my experience of why my interpretation failed. However, it is hard to know where to go from here. After all, it is not really a matter of choice for the analyst to have an open state of mind and genuine spirit of enquiry.

Recognising the analyst's ambivalence about bearing projections: a step towards empathy

The importance of curiosity as part of an analytic attitude is often emphasised and I have realised that in my mind it has become almost a shibboleth. What then does an analyst do if she finds she doesn't feel curious? Fisher (2006) tackles this problem:

> When the reality is that I do not feel curious, telling myself that I
> ought to feel curious is useless. (p. 1235)

Fisher then offers a suggestion: "But my noticing, my attention being focused on that observation of my own state of mind, gives me an outside chance of triggering an emotional experience of curiosity in myself" (p. 1235).

This, I find, does open up a way forward. Recognising that I cannot simply choose to be receptive—I feel what I feel—helps me think again about what is going wrong inside *me* in a non-judgemental way—why I am not wanting to know Sophia's true predicament. I can then be in a better position to be genuinely curious about myself and my lack of curiosity. The possibility opens up of a *K* attitude towards my –*K* state or, as Fisher puts it, I can "describe my attending to my own state of mind here as involving an awareness of an internal object that is curious about me and my lack of curiosity" (p. 1235).

With further reflection about what was happening to me I could begin to realise that with Sophia I was not managing being the object of intense hatred and could not cope with the hatred stirred up in myself when I was being projected into. Sometimes I was retaliating in the form of slightly sarcastic or contemptuous comments, under the guise of confrontation. Alternatively, at other times I mentally left the room in a disengaged "Ok, have it your way" state of mind. I felt guilty and ashamed about this. Often in these states of mind I would now say that I "misused" Steiner's analyst-centred interpretations in a way that made them "tactics" in lieu of real empathy. So I would say to Sophia: "I think you feel I am always trying to make you feel bad," without *really* believing that she had no choice but to see me that way. If, as Fisher writes, I can become genuinely curious about what is happening to my own state of mind, aware that *I* cannot choose it, cannot help my exasperation and irritation with this patient with whom I am supposed to be in a spirit of enquiry, I am freer to think, in a less blaming way, about Sophia, and to realise that she also cannot "choose" *not* to see me as hostile and attacking her.

I can begin to see that she *really* feels in the grip of me malevolently imposing confusion and misunderstanding. I am a liar and she has a desperate feeling that there is no integrity—she has just heard me tell a lie and I am going to tell her more. There is no "other" picture of myself as *not* a liar that she could surely also see and draw upon if she chose to switch her view.

In a sense, it could be argued that perhaps the very notion of analyst-centred interpretations is problematic because in fact we are always talking about that, that is, the patient's experience of her object. Steiner himself notes that even when analyst-centred interpretations are successful in creating a sense of containment, they do not do the full work of analysis, which ultimately must be concerned with helping the patient to gain insight, for which patient-centred interpretations will become necessary (Steiner, 1993, p. 145). However, I wonder how far this division Steiner is making between "containment" and "insight" holds, and whether Bion would agree with it. My own sense is that although there might appear to be a difference between a patient capable of feeling understood and a patient capable of understanding, in practice a capacity to feel understood/contained seems to require of the patient some insight into the analyst's emotional work with him, which involves the analyst's struggle with her own ambivalence. I shall return to this issue later.

At this point, to summarise, what I want to emphasise as crucial is:

- that the analyst, whether he frames the interpretation as patient- or analyst-centred, takes in the reality of the patient's psychic experience and does not speak as though the patient who is splitting could somehow *choose* to see the analyst differently;
- that the analyst correspondingly does not feel as though what he feels about his patient, be it K or $-K$, is his choice or fault either;
- if the analyst, due to a harsh analytic superego demanding that he listen with a spirit of enquiry, cannot accept a) his own struggle to integrate hateful, not-wanting-to understand, not-wanting-to-do-this-work parts of the self, he will not really be able to accept b) the patient's predicament.

Recognising that the patient in the grip of projection *cannot* see the analyst differently is particularly shocking and disheartening since we are trained to understand that the patient gaining a *different* view of the object is precisely what is ultimately desired for psychic change.

For example, in his landmark paper Strachey (1934) explains that a mutative interpretation occurs when the patient becomes aware that the analyst is *not* in fact like the patient's object:

> If all goes well, the patient's ego will become aware of the contrast between the aggressive character of his feelings and the real nature of the analyst, who does not behave like the patient's "good" or "bad" archaic objects. The patient, that is to say, will become aware of a distinction between his archaic phantasy object and the real external object. The interpretation has now become a mutative one, since it has produced a breach in the neurotic vicious circle. For the patient, having become aware of the lack of aggressiveness in the real external object, will be able to diminish his own aggressiveness; the new object which he introjects will be less aggressive,

and consequently the aggressiveness of his super-ego will also be diminished. (p. 143)

This certainly seems a desirable outcome, but the question is, how does the patient *see* that the analyst is not like his archaic object? Obviously, it does not happen simply through the analyst making analyst-centred interpretations, as I did above, in the hope that the patient will then immediately see the difference between the real analyst and his phantasy.

On the contrary, as Strachey points out:

> The analytic situation is all the time threatening to degenerate into a "real" situation. But this actually means the opposite of what it appears to. It means that the patient is all the time on the brink of turning the real external object (the analyst) into the archaic one; that is to say, he is on the brink of projecting his primitive intro-jected imago onto him. (p. 146)

So how does one avoid this happening? Strachey recommends that it is:

> … important, therefore, not to submit it to any unnecessary strain; and that is the fundamental reason why the analyst must avoid any real behaviour that is likely to confirm the patient's view of him as a bad or good phantasy object … If for instance, the analyst were to show that he was really shocked or frightened by one of the patient's id-impulses, the patient would immediately treat him in that respect as a dangerous object and introject him into his archaic severe super-ego. (p. 146)

This sounds quite clear. Strachey is saying that what is crucial is that the analyst should not "join in" the patient's phantasies about him, and his not joining in will enable the patient to begin to distinguish the external reality from internal reality. But is "not joining in" so straightforward? Nowadays analysts have changed their view on their own method and tend to emphasise that interpretation should be about the interaction of patient and analyst at an intrapsychic level. There is growing interest in transference-countertransference enactments, viewed as a two-person process where the analyst is really nudged or prodded into the patient's world (for example, Joseph, 1981; Sandler, 1976). Today we seem to accept, even expect that the analyst does in fact "degenerate" into becoming inevitably in some ways "like" the archaic object. The analysis *will*, therefore, "degenerate into a 'real' situation" (Strachey, 1934, p. 146) to some extent in that the analyst *will* come to enact the behaviour of the patient's archaic internal object and possibly get stuck for a while in doing so. Furthermore, there is increasing consensus that some enactment is not only inevitably part and parcel of analytic work but can be necessary in order for us to be aware of what is going on. Cassorla (2012), for example, argues that acute enactment may be needed to undo an established chronic enactment and that this does not only entail discharge but is also a movement in search of meaning.

In discussing the difference between enactments that can be useful and necessary for understanding the patient's psychic reality, and those that get stuck in impasse or descend on a slippery slope into boundary crossings and violations, most analysts, for example, Gabbard and Lester (1995), suggest much depends upon whether the enactment can be picked up, interpreted, and openly discussed, in which case it can be positively helpful to the treatment. What does this mean? Certainly it is the analyst's capacity to recognise that this "degeneration into a real situation" is *really* happening—to catch it in himself—and think about it that prevents violation. But what should the analyst *do* with such recognition? One answer could be that the recognition itself of what he has just been doing has the impact of modifying the way in which the analyst behaves with the patient without the analyst ever needing to interpret this directly to the patient. For instance, an analyst who recognises that he has been feeling hostile/seductive towards his patient will change on becoming aware of it and this change will be—consciously or unconsciously—picked up by the patient. I assume this happens often and that it is often enough.

However, at other times the analyst may actually want to say something to the patient about what has been happening between them. He may feel, for instance, that the way the two of them are interacting is an enactment of an unconscious pathological relationship and that to show this to the patient could be fruitful. In this case it might be said that it paves the way for interpreting the patient's experience of the object in an analyst-centred way that is genuinely felt. Therefore, when the analyst says to the patient: "You feel I just retaliated because what you said before made me feel bad," or, "We seem to have arrived at a situation where I am always criticising you," then perhaps sometimes the intention is not so much that the patient should see that the analyst is *not* really like that (as Strachey suggests) but that the *analyst* speaks from a place of recognising the truth that he *has* in fact (to his slight horror) been drawn to some extent into becoming that object with hostile feelings towards the patient. Furthermore, it is recognised that the analyst has done this in order to avoid psychic pain in himself.

What I am saying is that with certain patients the reality is that before the work can reach a point at which the *patient* can possibly be expected to become aware of the *difference* between the analyst and the archaic internal object, as Strachey requires, and which we certainly hope will happen eventually, a great deal of painful work first needs to be done by the *analyst*. This involves her recognising inside himself—perhaps over and over again—the extent to which he *has* become all-too-*like* the archaic one.

Acknowledging the analyst's struggle without disclosing: treading the line

If the analyst does recognise this it will be painful and far more problematic for him to interpret this to the patient in an analyst-centred way than in the situation described by Strachey (1934)—where the analyst speaks from a "clean" position (feeling inside that he is *not* like the patient's object).

The analyst is likely to feel guilty, ashamed and—perhaps rightly—to feel that he needs to do much more work in relation to himself. As a rule, the more truth the analyst worries there is in it, in terms of the analyst's real feelings, then the *less* comfortable the analyst is likely to feel in making an analyst-centred interpretation. As Gabbard (2000) writes, analysts have a tendency to "disidentify with the aggressor" (p. 417). And perhaps analysts should in fact avoid analyst-centred interpretations that they feel are "too true" of the real analyst to avoid danger or inappropriate confession. I am focusing here on hateful feelings towards the patient but a similar problem can arise with, for example, erotic feelings. After all, suppose an analyst says to a patient (who might have had a parent without boundaries): "I think you are very worried that I'm attracted to you." If the analyst says this "clean" then the interpretation may be mutative in Strachey's sense (as the patient recognises with relief in that moment both that this is indeed what she fears/wishes and that this is *not* in fact true of the real analyst). It is, however, a very different matter if the analyst realises that he in fact *does* feel aroused by the patient and tries to interpret whilst struggling with such feelings. This would make the patient highly anxious and I think most analysts would be rightly uncomfortable about doing so.

To return to the situation with my patient Sophia in the first vignette, I can now recognise that the patient was arousing hatred in me and this was what I was struggling to manage. I felt guilty and ashamed about wanting to get rid of my patient. I felt it was not a proper analytic attitude and showed a narcissism and immaturity in myself—perhaps like a not-very-grown up mother who did not want to be with her baby but felt terrible guilt about this. But what, if anything, could be said to the patient of this?

Gabbard (2000) writes:

> The more we mask our authentic countertransference hatred, anger and exasperation, the more the patient feels worse about herself. She feels no sense of efficacy. Patients need to know that they can move the analyst and that the analyst cares enough to be responsive. The analyst's exasperation may signal to the patient that he or she matters to the analyst. In the absence of such responses, the patient may feel inferior to this superhuman analyst who can transcend hatred with empathy and understanding, and she may also feel deceived if it becomes clear that the analyst is disguising his hatred. The whole analysis then becomes inauthentic, a sham. Analysts are occasionally asked if it's possible to analyse a patient that you don't like. In my writings on hateful patients, I have emphasised that one might well ask, can you analyse hateful patients if you don't hate them? (p. 412)

Gabbard writes that by disavowing her own anger/hostility and pushing them squarely into the patient, the analyst is making the patient the container of all the hate and sadism existing in the analytic dyad—cramming the anger back down the patient's throat. Therefore, Gabbbard continues:

> I would certainly not say, "I hate you." However, if a patient would say to me, "You seem to be angry with me," I might acknowledge that I was irritated or that I felt exasperated. The task is to confirm the patient's perception and let him or her know that you are not indifferent, without causing a devastating narcissistic injury. (p. 414)

Carpy (1989) argues strongly that the patient needs to see the analyst affected by what is projected, struggling to tolerate it and managing sufficiently to maintain his stance without gross enactment. It is through this process that the patient is able gradually to re-introject the previously intolerable aspects of himself that are involved. He also is able to introject the capacity to tolerate them which he has observed in the analyst.

Returning to the paradigmatic situation described by Bion (1959), where the screaming baby projects his panic into the mother, Carpy emphasises that it is *not* that the baby is unaware of the mother or feels the mother is *not* panicked but that the baby will have an experience of being fed by a mother in whom he *can* sense panic, but who is nevertheless able to give him milk. This, he says, is what makes the panic tolerable.

Following Carpy, I therefore suggest that we can think that what can be containing is that the patient or baby perceives that the analyst/mother goes on trying to help him despite the hatred and aggression she has at times towards the patient/baby and despite the fact that the cries make her feel criticised—after all if the mother/analyst were ideal there would be no crying. Often there is a technical dilemma in that we know that obstruction of projective identification increases it and yet if the analyst *can* bear to receive and contain painful projections and copes well then the patient may envy the analyst's capacity to bear what he, the patient, cannot, as Rosenfeld (1987) and Joseph (1981) point out. What I am suggesting is that it may be precisely in these "no win" situations that the patient needs to be allowed to perceive that the (not perfect) analyst does in fact *struggle* to contain the projections and is never entirely successful. This will involve the patient seeing that the analyst has some private struggle with herself with the projection.

Here is an example from my work with Sophia where I feel I allowed her to make use of her observations of my feelings. One day, during a conversation when I was raising the issue of her low fee and she was protesting, she said to me:

P: If you are trying to get rid of me then that is not ethical and you have no right. You shouldn't have taken me on if you can't cope with me.

A: You are afraid that I have become so angry with you that it is provoking me to want to raise the fee to punish you or push you out. [I must emphasise that this analyst-centred interpretation was said, on my part, *not* "clean" in the Strachey sense that I could feel comfortable that I was certainly not that object behaving in that way. Though I had thought a great deal about the situation, trying to separate what was "objectively right" from what I felt like doing to manage my own irritation, was difficult.]

P: You *do* get angry.

A: You see that and you are wondering if my anger is out of control.

P: If you need the money then that is different. [She paused for a while and then added] Maybe it's a mix.

Then she began to talk about how she knew her parents could no longer stand her living back with them since her divorce. It hurt and enraged her because she felt parents should always want their children living with them—love should be "unconditional". Sophia believed her parents should feel guilty if they did not feel this way and wanted their own space. But she also felt they both cared about her and perhaps thought it was best for her to be more independent, though she did not agree. She did not understand her parents at all—why they found it so hard to be parents—but she saw that they struggled. She also saw that as a child she had often been over indulged because of their fear of saying no to her. Often she felt that they gave in to her and then felt very resentful afterwards and treated her with hostility.

This could be read in different ways. In one way it could be said that the patient was discussing and analysing her parents/analyst in an omnipotent, patronising way, as though reversing the need and the generations, defending herself against feeling small and dependent as a child/patient. However, what I felt more strongly was the empathy she conveyed for my struggle (like her parents') with my hatred and feelings of not wanting to be with her doing this work and my attempts to behave well towards her despite this. This seemed to pave the way for Sophia to gradually feel more empathic with her own hatred towards her objects, to grapple with it and feel safer with it—including deepening the sense that she could feel more in control of her own impulses. There could be a space between feeling hatred and doing harm. She could start to acknowledge that she "felt" like hitting or murdering someone without the terror that this was the same as doing it. I noticed that she stopped saying about everything she did, "I could not stop myself."

It is noticeable that Sophia did not, in this instance, feel the need to penetrate further into the nature of my feelings about her by questioning me directly to gain further admissions in a way that could have descended into mutual analysis. Rather, she seemed relieved and able to use my acceptance of her perception—"You see that and it makes you wonder ..."—as a base to feel permitted to explore aloud (via her parents) what she felt to be my struggle with her. Neither did I feel any need to confirm or deny the different explanations she offered for my possible motives in wanting to raise the fee; instead I listened in a way that conveyed that I was wondering about myself ("Is this because I'm angry?") and accepting of her need to wonder about me. Since, as I said, I was not clear about my motives in the transference, this listening and wondering about myself was genuine and painful though not, as I say, shared in the sense of offering verbal confirmations or denials with her. I think offering myself as an object willing to explore my ambivalence to myself paved the way for Sophia to begin to be able to think about herself a bit less defensively, and even to contemplate why people might sometimes not want to be with her, without feeling that everything about her was bad.

Gradually, with us both less paranoid about being projected into, I feel that a genuine shift has occurred with Sophia, such that she "no longer fears the analyst's malign influence so much as the experience of being analysed" (Halton, 2011, p. 154). Less phobic about me, she is more consciously able to be worried about her own mind and self-destructiveness: both she and I are increasingly depicted in her inner world as people struggling with conflicts, not all good, not all bad. Her relationships with friends, colleagues, and parents have improved.

What I am advocating is not the analyst confessing to the patient—which means telling somebody something you already know. It is about the analyst conveying that she realises she too has an unconscious and so she may have been doing something without realising it. It shows the analyst is able to examine herself empathically and involves a real attitude of enquiry about a relationship dynamic—"What's happening to me? What am I getting drawn into?"—rather than a situation where the analyst conveys that she thinks she already knows.

Technically, I am saying that it is essential, as Gabbard (2000) argues above, that the analyst does not disavow in herself the fact that emotional intercourse and struggle is going on inside her. Otherwise, the analyst, under the guise of retaining a firm analytic stance, becomes impenetrable, defending against allowing her patient to perceive the truth of her struggle to contain what is projected. This then pushes the whole problem of not being able to contain feelings back into the patient rather than acknowledging that the task is very difficult.

However, at the same time, I am emphasising strongly that it is also important that the patient be excluded from the analyst's intercourse with herself—and sees that she is excluded—in order to avoid dissolving the gap between generations into confession and mutual analysis. Treading this difficult line, the analyst has to manage a stance that conveys nonverbally to the patient something like, "I know this is a struggle inside me that you perceive I am having with my feelings about you and I'm not denying it or stopping you thinking about it, but I'm not going to discuss it with *you*. Instead I am going to think about it more myself or with a colleague/partner." This is the equivalent of a mother conveying to a child, "I know I need some help with how I am with you—but from your father, not you." The patient needs to feel that the analyst—from inside herself—recognises that the feelings the patient finds it impossible to bear really are very difficult, even for an analyst, though she manages better than the patient.

From what I have said it seems that a capacity to feel contained requires from the patient a capacity to have some insight into the reality of the analyst as a separate object more capable of thinking emotionally than the patient herself. This is why I question the emotional reality of Steiner's division between patients who can feel understood/contained and those who can understand (see above). As Britton (1989) describes in his paper, "The missing link", some patients cannot bear to feel excluded from the analyst's communing with himself; but I would then suggest (as I think Britton does) that such patients have as much difficulty feeling understood/contained as they do understanding. (In fact, Britton—see below—does address the issue of patients who cannot bear to be contained, which Steiner does not.)

I would like to make a further point about the difficulty in being excluded. Analysts emphasise the significance for patients' psychic health of the capacity to be excluded, yet I find that as an analyst, feeling excluded myself can feel hard too. (Steiner [2008] also addresses this issue.) Sometimes, with my here and now approach, I find I can become like a parent firmly closing the bedroom door on my teenagers, only to keep entering their rooms without knocking.

For instance, during one recent session Sophia was telling me that, having just incurred a family trauma, she needed treatment and wanted to seek help from Victim Support because they were specialists who could understand what victims of trauma went through and would not keep questioning her.

I immediately felt irritated by this idea of myself as intrusive. I interpreted that Sophia felt desperate because she needed one kind of help but was sure I was going to insist upon giving her another kind that did not feel like what she needed. She responded that maybe she just felt too traumatised to go into it at that time.

I said even now she was feeling that I was probing. We seemed to have got into a situation where I was repeatedly pursuing or pushing her and perhaps this added to her trauma. She said, wearily: "Yes, but you are still talking about *you*."

It seems that I could not bear the experience of being projected into as unhelpful and intrusive without "coming back" in effect to try to show how well I was really understanding my own intrusiveness. Paradoxically, if the analyst's task is to take in and bear the truth of what she has become in the patient's psychic reality, then the analyst's need to interpret and show the patient that she is understanding may become a sign that she cannot in fact bear it.

Therefore, a problem I find when I try to trace very carefully in the here and now the impact on the patient of my last interpretation by interpreting continually in the transference is that sometimes it can be stifling: it can convey to the patient that I cannot bear separateness and exclusion, cannot allow the patient to have private responses, an intercourse with herself about me that I do not immediately see as well or see beyond. Above all, it can convey the analyst's anxiety (mirroring the patient's predicament) that if she remains projected into for too long, without putting it back, she will not be able to extricate herself and will lose his mind. As Rosenfeld (1987) writes:

> In some situations one can interpret too quickly what one has recognised, with the result that the patient experiences what is said as a rejection of him. What has happened in these situations is that through projective identification the analyst has been experienced concretely as expelling the projected feelings and so expelling the patient as well. (pp. 15–16)

With Sophia, although I continue to listen to her material as an expression of waves of emotion present in the sessions and the current relationship with the analyst, I do not always interpret in terms of you and me. Rather, as Ferro (2009) describes, I listen to what she says, say, after receiving an interpretation, as a response that might signal to me to modulate my interpretations in a way that facilitates her to do her own psychological work. If the interpretation is too "saturated" with transference meaning it can shut this process down. However, this stance still involves me sitting with and bearing what kind of figure I think I am currently in her psychic reality (for example, in the case described above, intrusive). Tuckett (2011) warns that some problems facing psychoanalysis have been introduced by the very success of the here and now technique:

> The kind of emotional pressure many patients exert can mean that analysis becomes talk about you and me with too little space for formal regression, current expressions of infantile sexual conflicts and other deeper elements of the Freudian unconscious, and even the loss of the original Freudian and Kleinian meaning of transference—all making psychoanalysis a denuded interpersonal psychotherapy. (pp. 1387–1388)

Dana Birksted-Breen (2012) is also concerned with the pitfalls of a here-and-now technique that can lead to concrete thinking and impasse if not grounded in an approach that includes the essential notion of an unfocused state of mind—free floating attention or reverie.

Strachey (1934) himself wrote:

> A cake cannot be made of nothing but currants; and, though it is true that extra-transference interpretations are not for the most part mutative ... they are none the less essential. If I may take an analogy from trench warfare, the acceptance of a transference interpretation corresponds to the capture of a key position, while the extra-transference interpretations correspond to the general advance and to the consolidation of a fresh line which are made possible by the capture of the key position. (p. 158)

Towards integration: the necessary sense of a shared struggle

Sophia's capacity to think (via the description of her parents' situation) about the object's struggle to look after her as well as my own attitude of enquiry into what was happening to me with her (in identification with the patient's object) involve an empathy for people caught up in something difficult together, rather than empathy for either one side or the other. To borrow Strachey's warfare terminology, there is a shared battle and the enemy to be "caught in the act" is a malignant object relationship, not the patient or analyst. Psychoanalyst and feminist theorist Bracha Ettinger (2010) makes an interesting distinction between what she calls "empathy-within-compassion" and "empathy-without-compassion". Empathy-within-compassion means the analyst's empathy (to the patient) within compassion (also toward the patient's significant primary figures); she contrasts this with empathy-without-compassion—an empathy to the patient only. In Ettinger's view, empathy (to the patient) without compassion (also to the patient's archaic and actual significant primary objects) creates internal splitting and leads to a fixation in a "basic fault" positioning.

Ettinger posits the notion that, " The infant meets the maternal subject via its own primary affective compassion" (2010, p. 1). She argues:

> The failure in primary compassion and awe leaves the subject—the infant to begin with—at the mercy of paranoid-schizoid mechanisms. The psychoanalytical phantasy to find the ultimate cause of human suffering by empathy toward the subject without compassion (toward its early environment) leads to increasing failures in the subject's primary compassion and awe—a failure which is a royal road, in my view, to splitting (Klein, 1946) and to the fall into the "basic fault". (Balint, 1968, p. 3 quoted in Ettinger, 2010, p. 1)

Whilst I would dispute the idea that analysts tend to lack compassion for the patient's primary objects, some do seem to work in a way that seems to have, as Ettinger puts it, an "over identification with the narcissistic self of the infant-I within the adult-I, which limits the I's respect and compassion toward its own non-I(s)" (p. 4).

Caper (1992) makes a similar point when he complains that Kohut in 1979 ("*The two analyses of Mr Z*") "… took at face value the patient's assertions that his psychopathology must have stemmed entirely from his mother's destructive frustration of his healthy attempts to develop" (p. 284). This technical stance, Caper says, encouraged splitting in the patient, preventing both analyst and patient from exploring the patient's own contributions to his difficulties, either with his mother or his first analysis.

What I find particularly thought-provoking, in Ettinger's work, however, is that she views the infant's primary tendency to paranoid-schizoid splitting as balanced by this "primary compassion" from the very start of life. She emphasises that this really is *primary* rather than a reaction. In other words there is a primitive tendency to split but there is also a primitive tendency to seek to transform this, that is, to integrate. Quoting Marguerite Duras—"Our mothers always remain the strangest, craziest people we've ever met"—Ettinger (2010) writes that we all have primal phantasies of a "ready-made mother-monster" who gives us not enough, abandons and devours, and that these phantasies are primal because they correspond to the basic enigmas of human existence. At the same time she emphasises that the infant in each of us hopes that another adult—father, analyst—will *not* confirm this intimate infant conviction but, on the contrary, will help us transform it. The analyst's way of interpreting can then help or hinder this integrative process via primary compassion. Ettinger writes:

> Therapeutic interpretations that pathologise this experience shape the ways in which our mothers remain the craziest people we've ever met. Interpretations … that are empathic with "the ready-made mother-monster" (without compassion to the maternal figure) and which locate a "cause" of our sufferings (the "unconsciously poisonous mother", the "intoxicating mother", the "never good-enough mother", the always "over-controlling" mother, the always "constantly abandoning" mother) turn this important, painful and vital conscious and unconscious real-phantasmatic experience into a symbolic "truth-cause" and turns the intimate mother to whom we are transconnected (whether we like it or not) into the craziest of all figures. (2010, p. 4)

Following Ettinger I think that the analyst's capacity to empathise with herself in struggling with the patient (perhaps in imaginary identification with the original archaic object) whilst at the *same* time empathising with the patient's perspective on himself as hateful, is vital in helping the patient to lessen splitting. On the other hand, if the analyst empathises with the patient alone, ultimately splitting is deepened. This seems to me to be closely linked with Fisher's (2006) point (see above) that an analyst lacking empathy with her own position with the patient cannot really empathise.

However, to achieve what Ettinger hopes for is very difficult and Ettinger does not engage in her paper with the analyst's struggle to achieve this aim. Britton (1998), however, does engage in the analyst's difficult struggle to empathise both with the patient's subjective experience and one's own objective experience at the same time, which he conceptualises in oedipal terms.

Britton describes the situation where the patient fears that the analyst's psychic reality, if it emerged, would destroy her own whilst the analyst's countertransference is that if he adopts her psychic reality his own would be annihilated. This is closely linked to Steiner's (1993) recognition that a psychic retreat is partly in response to a world lacking in objects able to distinguish between one's own and their own reality. This was certainly my experience of the situation with Sophia described in the opening vignette, where I think it felt as though we were both literally fighting for our minds. Britton says that if he compels the patient to accept his reality the situation is explosive, and if he submits to his patient's a collusive situation results and the analyst may become involved in some sort of mutual analysis. He describes how the analyst can find himself feeling that empathising is incompatible with "being analytic". This struggle to have two "realities" in mind happens, he says, when the patient has:

> a defensively organised Oedipal situation with the phantasy of a totally empathic, passively understanding maternal object and an aggressive paternal figure who is objectively personified as seeking to impose meaning. (Britton, 1998, pp. 49–50)

In other words, there is an antipathy to any point of view different to one's own. This antipathy feels to the patient as though a hateful father is interrupting the contact with the perfectly loving and understanding mother, destroying understanding and eliminating meaning. The failure of the analyst to understand the patient is then experienced not simply as a deficiency of the analyst but as a malignant attack by the father on the patient's psychic integrity.

In contrast, then, to Ettinger's idea of "primary compassion" whereby the infant is actually *predisposed* to seek a helpful father/analyst to enable her to lessen her hatred and splits in relation to the "ready-made monster-mother", Britton (1998) thus posits an opposite more pessimistic picture. He suggests an innate factor in the infant—a "psychic atopia"—or allergy to the products of other minds which increases the risk of a failure of maternal containment.

Despite the different ways of conceptualising the innate situation, both Ettinger and Britton are concerned with ways in which the analyst can help the patient to lessen splitting and point to the analyst's tendency to be pulled into interpreting in ways that actually deepen it. In this, both accord with Caper (1992) who says that the function of psychoanalysis is to assist the patient to integrate repressed or split-off parts of his personality.

What I am adding is that this is only possible if the analyst can acknowledge the ambivalent feelings in herself—her own real difficulty in being a projective-identification receiving object. This will be difficult if the analyst idealises her own capacity to bear and contain projection. If the analyst cannot tolerate guilt about not wanting to be with the patient who projects into her, which is what the process of analysis often requires, then this guilt may then become a powerful superego that demands that we listen with a "spirit of enquiry" and this does not induce an enquiring state of mind.

Caper (1992) reminds us that Freud considered the analyst's need to cure, which forces him to abandon his realistic analytic modesty, to be a defence against his own sadistic impulses. Caper argues that an analyst who has not come to terms with his own sadism and destructive impulses will have little belief in the adequacy with which such conflicts may be addressed and encompassed. This will mean the analyst will not be able to restrict himself to bringing the two sides of the conflict between constructive and destructive impulses closer together in the patient's mind, leaving the outcome of the analysis hostage to the patient's ability to resolve this conflict. Instead he will be likely to try to suppress or split off the patient's destructiveness. Caper continues:

> ... but if the analyst can recognise the sources of his need to relieve the patient's suffering in his own unconscious conflict between loving and destructive impulses, and in his doubts about the adequacy of the former in the face of the latter, he will ... be free of his need to heal the patient. This will allow him to make an interpretation that simply brings together the disparate parts of the patient. (1992, p. 286)

I fully agree with Caper but want to emphasise in this chapter that bringing together disparate parts is never "simple" because of the strength with which both analyst and patient long to keep them apart.

Trust in the analytic process does not mean we believe that a genuine spirit of enquiry *will* always prove stronger than hate, destructiveness, and narcissistic wishes to compete, eliminate different views, make ourselves the centre, or prove ourselves right. Instead, we can try to enable ourselves and our patients to bear living constantly with these conflicts never being sure which will triumph. Therefore, when we make interpretations I believe the analyst's empathy for the patient's struggle can only be genuine if the analyst also feels empathy with her own struggle to integrate parts of herself. Being projected into is sometimes a horrible experience—even abusive—but it is a required part of the job. The analyst is always hoping to find that her love for the process of psychoanalysis is good enough to survive her own hatred for the process and the outcome is never certain.

Acknowledgement

I am grateful to Debbie Bandler Bellman and Jean Arundale for galvanising me into putting down these thoughts by inviting me to write a chapter for this book.

References

Arundale, J. (2011). Here and now interpretations. In: J. Arundale & D. B. Bellman (Eds.), *Transference and Countertransference: A Unifying Focus of Psychoanalysis* (pp. 27–43). London: Karnac.

Balint, M. (1968). *The Basic Fault: Therapeutic Aspects of Regression*. London: Tavistock.

Bion, W. R. (1959). Attacks on linking. *International Journal of Psychoanalysis, 40*: 308–315 [reprinted in: *Second Thoughts* (pp. 93–109), London: Heinemann, 1967; London: Karnac, 1984].

Birksted-Breen, D. (2012). Taking time: The tempo of psychoanalysis. *International Journal of Psychoanalysis, 93*: 819–835.

Britton, R. (1989). The missing link: Parental sexuality in the Oedipus complex. In: J. Steiner (Ed.), *The Oedipus Complex Today: Clinical Implications* (pp. 83–101). London: Karnac.

Britton, R. (1998). *Belief and Imagination*. London: Routledge.

Caper, R. (1992). Does psychoanalysis heal? A contribution to the theory of psychoanalytic technique. *International Journal of Psychoanalysis, 73*: 283–292.

Carpy, D. V. (1989). Tolerating the countertransference: A mutative process. *International Journal of Psychoanalysis, 70*: 287–294.

Cassorla, R. M. S. (2012). What happens before and after acute enactments? An exercise in clinical validation and the broadening of hypotheses. *International Journal of Psychoanalysis, 93*: 53–80.

Ettinger, B. L. (2010). (M)Other re-spect: Maternal subjectivity, the ready-made mother-monster and the ethics of respecting. *Studies in the Maternal* 2 (1). Available from: www.mamsie.bbk.ac.uk/back_issues/issue_three/index.html [accessed July 2014].

Feldman, M. (1997). Projective identification: The analyst's involvement. *International Journal of Psychoanalysis, 78*: 227–241.

Ferro, A. (2009). Transformations in dreaming and characters in the psychoanalytic field. *International Journal of Psychoanalysis, 90*: 209–230.

Fisher, J. V. (2006). The emotional experience of K. *International Journal of Psychoanalysis, 87*: 1221–1235.

Gabbard, G. O. (2000). Hatred and its rewards: A discussion. *Psychoanalytic Inquiry, 20*: 409–420.

Gabbard, G., & Lester, E. (1995). *Boundaries and Boundary Violations in Psychoanalysis*. New York: Basic.

Halton, M. (2011). Phobic attachments: Internal impediments to change. In: J. Arundale & D. B. Bellman (Eds.), *Transference and Countertransference: A Unifying Focus of Psychoanalysis* (pp. 129–155). London: Karnac.

Joseph, B. (1981). Towards the experiencing of psychic pain. In: M. Feldman & E. Bott Spillius (Eds.), *Psychic Equilibrium and Psychic Change: Selected Papers of Betty Joseph* (pp. 87–99). London: New Library of Psychoanalysis, 1989, 1999.

Klein, M. (1946). Notes on some schizoid mechanisms. *International Journal of Psychoanalysis, 27*: 99–110.

Kohut, H. (1979). The two analyses of Mr Z. *International Journal of Psychoanalysis, 60*: 3–27.

O'Shaughnessy, E. (1992). Enclaves and excursions. *International Journal of Psychoanalysis, 73*: 603–611.

Rosenfeld, H. (1971). Contribution to the psychopathology of psychotic states: The importance of projective identification to the ego structure and object relations of the psychotic patient. In: E. Bott Spillius (Ed.), *Melanie Klein Today, Volume 1* (pp. 117–137). London: New Library of Psychoanalysis.

Rosenfeld, H. (1987). Impasse and interpretation: Therapeutic and anti-therapeutic factors in the psychoanalytic treatment of psychotic, borderline and neurotic patients. In: *New Library of Psychoanalysis, Volume 1* (pp. 1–318). London: Tavistock.

Roth, P. (2001). Mapping the landscape: Levels of transference interpretation. *International Journal of Psychoanalysis, 82*: 533–543.

Sandler, J. (1976). Countertransference and role-responsiveness. *International Review of Psycho-Analysis, 57*: 43–48.

Steiner, J. (1993). Problems of psychoanalytic technique: Patient-centred and analyst-centred interpretations. In: E. Bott Spillius (Ed.), *Psychic Retreats Pathological Organisations in Psychotic, Neurotic and Borderline Patients* (New Library of Psychoanalysis 19) (pp. 131–146). London: Routledge.

Steiner, J. (2008). Transference to the analyst as an excluded observer. *International Journal of Psychoanalysis, 89*: 39–54.

Strachey, J. (1934). The nature of the therapeutic action of psycho-analysis. *International Journal of Psychoanalysis, 15*: 127–159 [reprinted *International Journal of Psychoanlaysis, 50*: 275–292].

Tuckett, D. (2011). Inside and outside the window: Some fundamental elements in the theory of psychoanalytic technique. *International Journal of Psychoanalysis, 92*: 1367–1390.

CHAPTER FIVE

Double-sided interpretations and the severe superego

Julia Sandelson

Introduction

Since Freud's day there has been widespread and often controversial debate about the most therapeutic and effective technical interventions for patients with borderline and narcissistic pathology, which has gained in relevance in contemporary times. The aim of this chapter is to contribute to the ongoing debate about the technical issues involved in making contact with disturbed patients who suffer the damaging effects of an ego-destructive superego, and whose emotional functioning and development are severely impaired by "therapeutic inaccessibility" (Freud, 1923a, p. 249). Whilst supervising and teaching, it repeatedly came to my attention that some analysts and candidates often struggle with finding ways to make contact with these patients. My wish in this chapter is to help foster an understanding of how and why making a particular kind of interpretation, one that I have termed a "double-sided interpretation", can be effective. I propose to describe this interpretation and illustrate how this particular formulation can be applied in practice. I do not intend to promote the idea that such an interpretation be used invariably, but I present it here as one way of making an intervention that can enable the disturbed patient to make or recover contact

with himself and with his analyst. I will outline the theoretical aspects
that place in context and form the foundations to the background of the
double-sided interpretation, followed by the relevance of their use in
analytic work with patients, and then present and discuss some clinical
material from the analysis of a borderline/narcissistic patient who was
three years into his analysis at the time in question.

Theoretical background

Freud's structural model of the mind is built on conflict between the
life and the death instincts with their libidinal and destructive aspects.
Freud's notion of the superego evolved over his lifetime, moving
increasingly towards a structure that can be viewed as both potentially
ego-constructive as well as ego-destructive. Of the ego-destructive
superego, Freud (1923b) wrote that in melancholia it is "a pure culture
of the death instinct" (p. 53), having attracted sadism and destructiveness to it. In order to explain this self-destructiveness, Freud suggested
that the erotic component of the life drive was no longer strong enough
to "bind" within the ego the whole of the destructiveness, so that this
became "free", and was expressed as an inclination towards aggressiveness and destructiveness in a defusion of the libidinal and destructive
instincts.

In Freud's further consideration in "Analysis terminable and interminable" (1937c) of what he had earlier portrayed as the "repetition
compulsion", he described patients who hold onto their illness and
give the impression they will never change, because of "a force that is
defending itself by every possible means against recovery and which
is absolutely resolved to hold on to illness and suffering" (p. 242). This
force he attributed to the death instinct, made more deadly when combined with the compulsion to repeat.

Klein (1958) too had distinguished between an ordinary severe
pre-oedipal superego that in the process of development becomes
less severe and more realistic, and another version of the structure: an
archaic destructive and cruelly perverse superego formed in a defusion
of the instincts and linked to the death instinct, that remained unaltered
by the normal processes of growth.

Bion's model of the mind was a further development of Klein's expansion of Freud's metapsychology and as such occupies a place of central
importance in the evolution of theory and practice. Within Bion's model

of the container-contained relationship, painful emotional experience is either evaded or modified. If these painful feelings can be modified by a "sojourn in the good breast ... the object that is reintrojected [can] become tolerable to the infant's psyche" (1962b, p. 90). This introjected object is capable of knowing and thinking, and promotes mental growth. However, in the case of the internalisation of an "obstructive force" (1958, p. 90)—Bion's "wilfully misunderstanding object" (1962c, p. 309)—he regards this a "primitive catastrophe" (1958, p. 88), making normal development impossible, because such a superego not only attacks ego functions but also prevents the development of curiosity, the epistemophilic impulse (Freud, 1909d, p. 245). In *Transformations* Bion (1965) specifically associates curiosity with K, in contradistinction to the other "impulses, emotions and instincts" (p. 67) which, when combined, form L (love/loving) and H (hate/hating). The K link enables the internalisation of a containing object on which all emotional learning depends (Bion, 1962b, pp. 42–43). Bion's work is rooted in Freud's (1911b) work on the pleasure and reality principles, but in giving the K link equal status to the emotional linkages of the L link and the H link he turns Freud's dualistic theory of the instincts into a triadic theory. Indeed, Britton (1998, p. 11) views the drive for knowledge an innate ego instinct.

Although some theorists consider it innate, the wish for emotional knowledge, the K link, grows and develops within the nexus of the container-contained relationship. A K state of mind involves an urge, a wanting to know about one's internal objects, the relations between them, and the objects in the external world. Patients with no K link cannot experience and think about themselves. Bion first introduced his notion of a "severe and ego-destructive superego" in his paper "Attacks on linking" (1959, p. 107). He posits that without the installation of a K state of mind, an ego-destructive superego develops in which one part of the infant/patient is opposed to himself. This is not K but its opposite, "anti-knowing", termed by Bion –K, an attack on a K state of mind. Indeed, Fisher (2011) argues that –K, is not an absence of K but a perversion of the urge to know (p. 60).

Bion (1962b) elaborates and expands on his notion of this destructive internal object in *Learning from Experience*:

> It is a super-ego that does not have any of the characteristics of the super-ego as understood in psycho-analysis: it is "super"-ego. It is

an envious assertion of moral superiority without any morals. In short it is the resultant of an envious stripping or denudation of all good and is itself destined to continue the process of stripping ... till [there is] ... hardly more than an empty superiority-inferiority that in turn degenerates to nullity ... The emergence ... . of any tendency to search for the truth, to establish contact with reality and in short to be scientific in no matter how rudimentary a fashion is met by destructive attacks on the tendency and the reassertion of the "moral" superiority. (p. 97)

Many contemporaries of Klein and Bion, and those analysts up to the present day, link a pathological narcissistic organisation of the personality to a primitive, punitive superego—the introjection of a dangerous, powerful, and hostile object—referring to such a superego's cruelty and righteousness (e.g., Brenman, 1982). O'Shaughnessy (1999) also, with reference to Bion's description above, emphasises the difficulty of any emotional development for such patients: "This pathological 'super'-ego watches the ego from a 'higher' place and is fundamentally against the pain that comes from thinking and understanding" (p. 868).

Britton argues that narcissism is rooted in the need to escape an ego-destructive superego, that a narcissistic organisation is evolved using narcissistic object-relationships—internal, external, or both—to evade the hostile superego (2003, p. 164). Bion's contemporaries, Segal, Rosenfeld, and others, working closely together, regarded narcissism as a defence against perceiving the object as separate and different. Whether because of childhood neglect or innate aggression, the narcissistic patient has a hatred of neediness and preserves a belief in omnipotent self-sufficiency; he cannot bear to know that a separate, independent mind can see his neediness and dependence. Klein's view of projective identification, which she developed in 1957 to include envy, is that "split-off parts of the self are projected into the object [which] leads to a strong confusion between the self and the object ... [and] bound up with this is a weakening of the ego and a grave disturbance in object relations" (p. 192). Segal's view chimes with Bion's image of the mind as containing a "rival" (1962b, p. 98), an obstructive object that is at war with the patient's ego. Similarly, O'Shaughnessy (1999) describes the consequences for the patient of a murderous pathological superego that "usurps the status and authority of a normal superego and entices the ego to turn away from life, to dissociate itself from its objects and ultimately to destroy life itself" (p. 861).

Like Bion, these theorists ascribe a crucial role to envy in narcissistic organisations of the personality. Rosenfeld made profoundly important contributions to the possibility of analysing the narcissistic transference. He introduced a distinction between libidinal narcissism (1964) and destructive narcissism (1971). Both aim at the destruction of ego functions and of any object-relatedness. In libidinal narcissism, defences against any recognition of separateness between self and object play a predominant part. In destructive narcissism the destructive aspects predominate and form a Mafia gang (Rosenfeld, 1971, p. 174), a tightly woven web of highly organised, stable, fixed, and rigid defences that is skilled at deploying intimidation and/or seduction as weapons to keep the patient's libidinal self under its control. Envy appears as a wish to destroy any progress made in the analysis and to attack the analyst, as representing the object who is the true source of life and goodness. The technical question for the analyst working with the patient who functions predominantly in a –K state of mind becomes one of how to enable movement into a K state of mind in which awareness of internal psychic and external reality becomes possible, with all of the possible richness of emotional experience and capacity for thinking. How can we help the emotionally unreachable patient tolerate and "suffer" psychic pain (Bion, 1970) and maintain rather than destroy the emotional links between internal objects, and between analyst and patient, enabling contact with truth and reality? This involves the broader question of how the individual emerges from narcissism and becomes able to love.

Double-sided interpretations

Analysts are currently working in an era in which borderline patients and all those functioning at the more psychotic end of the continuum are populating our consulting rooms in increasing numbers. The endeavour of the analytic encounter with many of these patients is a challenging but satisfying undertaking. They make changes and sustain them. However, working with patients with powerful ego-destructive superegos can frequently feel like a repetitive, unrewarding, and fruitless enterprise.

Why, therefore, work with patients who consciously want help to change but who unconsciously have superegos committed to un-linking and therefore an incapacity to learn and develop? With borderline patients and those functioning at a primitive level of development the analyst's overriding task needs to be guided by finding a way to repeatedly make and/or to recover contact with the patient. The technical problems of working with such patients have been widely discussed (see, for example, Feldman, 2000, 2007; Roth, 2001; Steiner, 1982, 1994, 2006). Joseph's (1989) work in particular emphasises the importance of making emotional contact with the patient; her work illustrates the importance of "avoiding knowledge about" in favour of "experience in" (p. 7). How does the analyst help the patient recover contact with his libidinal self and make contact with the analyst when he is in an emotionally unreachable state, when an ego-destructive superego destroys ordinary ego functions: perception, attention, memory, thinking, understanding?

During a recent assessment of such a patient, who like many such patients has good intellectual functioning, she referred to her emotional life as being like "The Walking Dead" characters in a TV series: "I'm like one of those zombies who looks alive, who walks around, but is actually dead." I felt myself inwardly smiling with agreement since the title of the series seemed so pertinent and to provide such an accurate description of the patient! Her bored and boring way of speaking, her listless countenance, and apparent disinterest in why she had come for analysis gave me the impression of an empty shell, a person functioning mechanically. But this also alerted me to a powerful destructive element at work inside her. After all, the patient's libidinal desire for something better, apparently so absent in the assessment itself, had requested analytic help and had managed to bring her to the assessment.

The power and force of a severely narcissistic or borderline patient's affects can take over the mind and make it difficult for the analyst to think. The analyst needs to rely on being acutely tuned into his countertransference in order to feel and notice what the patient has split and projected. My countertransference with the above patient was initially one of puzzlement, then mounting irritation at her failure to engage in any emotionally meaningful way with me. An ego-destructive superego militates against linking; it aims to dissociate the patient from his libidinal self and to attack the link with the object at every juncture. It is my view that double-sided interpretations can help repair these links and enable shifts toward greater contact. An example of this in relation to the patient's assessment above might be phrased as: "You're telling me and yourself that you wanted to come to your session today and you also didn't want to come, perhaps because you're anxious and annoyed about needing my help." Repeated use of double-sided interpretations, in combination with an understanding and interpretation of the underlying anxiety, gradually enables the patient to become aware of his attacks on linking, and to develop a wish to preserve the link and a capacity to think within an analytic couple. This paves the way towards self-observation in a triangular relationship, the third position, and mental space (Britton, 1989, pp. 83–101), fostering the capacity to experience feelings and to think.

The function of double-sided interpretations

It is of paramount importance that the analyst finds a way to make or to recover emotional contact with the patient if the patient is in the grip of severe paranoid anxieties. How does the analyst phrase interpretations that will not be heard as persecutory? If the patient blocks contact with the analyst, the destructive self dominates and triumphs over the analyst, over his own libidinal self and the analytic work. This results in stultifying the analysis, reaching impasse or psychic stasis.

The therapeutic importance of interpreting both sides of an internal conflict cannot be underestimated. I am using the expression "double-sided interpretation" to indicate a type of interpretation that is composed of both the positive transference and the negative transference at *the same time*, that is, an interpretation that addresses both the patient's dependent, libidinal self and his omnipotent, destructive self, and which functions to reduce persecutory anxieties. Through discouraging pathological splitting and projective identification, which are attempts to rid the psyche of conflict, the double-sided interpretation has the potential to act as a transformative element in the patient's development.

For the disturbed patient struggling with an ego-destructive superego, the double-sided interpretation both binds the death drive thus relieving a high level of anxiety, and helps the patient not to become so totally overwhelmed with paranoid anxieties that he responds by regressing to the anxiety-free borderline zone of a psychic retreat (Steiner, 1993). When the analyst employs a double-sided interpretation in order to make contact with the patient's libidinal self, it lessens the inevitable splitting and defusion of the instincts, and encourages a healthier fusion of the life and death drives in which the more loving aspects are mobilised and mitigate the patient's hatred, envy, and aggression.

As just one of many types of interpretations available to the analyst within her repertoire, the double-sided interpretation is specifically aimed at gaining enough of the patient's attention to highlight and emphasise the patient's internal conflict, his loving and his hating feelings, thus encouraging him to think about and to tolerate his ambivalence, shifting towards more contact with the analyst, and to move towards greater integration. I make this sound like a process that flows smoothly along; it is not. Often the patient cannot tolerate the anxiety or sense of loss this brings, and fails to develop the capacity to understand, to integrate the conflict, and to make a shift, however brief, towards increased object relatedness and separateness.

Interpretations that encapsulate exclusively the negative transference or exclusively the positive transference tend to bring with them increased difficulties for these patients. When analysts are bombarded with a powerful negative transference they need to make an effort not to be drawn into either over-interpreting or interpreting the destructive side alone, which ultimately results in "malignant containment" (Britton, 1998, p. 28). Interpretations that are constituted purely of the negative transference only can easily be experienced as invasive and intrusive, and in such a way that the analyst is perceived as forcing dependence on the patient, who is then more likely to disappear rapidly into a psychic retreat. Likewise, such interpretations can be heard in critical and sadistic ways, or as "moral injunctions" (Bell, 2011, p. 100) because of the patient's projections of a punitive superego into the analyst. These interpretations will then increase persecutory guilt and push the patient deeper into a narcissistic position. The analyst can also become unwittingly drawn into a collusion with the omnipotent destructive internal object, the ego-destructive superego, and/or into a sadomasochistic enactment resulting in interpreting the destructiveness in isolation. On the other hand, resorting to using interpretations exclusively of the positive transference tends to fuel idealisation, and, if used frequently, are likely to arise more out of the analyst's own anxiety or guilt, or worry about losing the patient, than from the patient's reality. If both the libidinal and destructive selves are interpreted *within the same interpretation* in the double-sided interpretation, such pitfalls are more likely to be avoided.

A detailed and repeated exposure of the dynamics of the here-and-now of the transference, and a closely honed and sensitive counter-transference used to frame double-sided interpretations, will gradually orient the patient to becoming more consciously aware of a destructive self operating within him in opposition to a libidinal self, together with awareness that he loses contact with a good and helpful analyst. Double-sided interpretations communicate to the patient that the analyst both wants to understand him, and that the patient has a need to be understood. By bringing in the good and loving aspects of the patient, he is more able to tolerate interpretations of his hating and envious aspects.

As a striking example of this, one of my patients who often experienced and expressed her L and H aspects in terms of endless battles, communicated, some years into her analysis, that she had grasped that she was at war with herself, essentially with her ego-destructive superego: "I never used to know whether you were my ally or my enemy so I couldn't risk trusting what you said, but now it doesn't feel like that anymore, like I've suddenly realised it's about a war between me and me and I need you as an ally so that the good in me won't let the bad take over …".

Double-sided interpretations are also more likely to result in exposure of the more collusive alliances, the sadomasochistic relationship between the destructive and dependent parts of the personality (Rosenfeld, 1971; Steiner, 1993). When the libidinal, dependent, and non-psychotic self is strengthened or rescued from its trapped position by a double-sided interpretation, the patient can more easily resist feeling seduced or intimidated by the destructive narcissistic self. In a strengthened and more reality-oriented position, the libidinal self will feel moved to link with the analyst. The increased experience of containment, coupled with experiences of a K state of mind involving awareness of internal conflicting emotions, enable the patient to tolerate frustration more, to tolerate the experience of a "No Breast" (Bion, 1962a, p. 112). Inevitably, this is made more difficult for a patient who actively *wants* to feel despairing and self-destructive as part of masochistic pathology. Such a patient's libidinal self unconsciously willingly chooses "the submission to tyranny" (Meltzer, 1968, p. 400), and both Joseph (1982) and Segal (1993) stress the conflict between L and H over the lure of the voluptuous despair offered by the destructive self.

The double-sided interpretation can reduce confusion, and enable differentiation between the illusion of the "good" feelings of destructive omnipotence and the goodness of a helpful analyst in a more reality-oriented perception. It is important to help the patient realise that her idealisation of destructiveness is an illusion, that the conviction she holds of her "good feeling" is based on destructive omnipotence rather than on reality-based perception of a K link with a helpful superego.

Rather than functioning in a –K state of mind, repeated experiences of containment of both L and H can enable not only tolerance of ambivalence but, significantly, the development of curiosity. Since double-sided interpretations encourage the patient's awareness of internal conflict, she is more likely to start becoming genuinely curious and interested in herself, as well as in others, and to question why it is that she is so self-defeating and self-destructive. This is a function that Bion explicitly makes reference to: it is the analyst who has the task of showing the patient functioning in a –K state of mind that she does not properly question herself (Bion, 1959, p. 108).

Borderline and narcissistic patients carry a profound belief in their omnipotent self-sufficiency and superiority, which serve as defences against envy and separateness (e.g., Rosenfeld, 1964, 1971). They ostensibly and consciously want analysis to help them change, but are continuously threatened by and in the grip of attacks from an ego-destructive superego that persistently aims to dissociate the patient from herself and to attack the link with the object. In this way the patients remain unreachable and preserve their psychic equilibrium. The unconscious commitment they hold to this pattern means that deep interpretations of their emotional states can seriously destabilise them. Repeated experiences of countertransference feeling in the moment and finding a way of speaking to the patient of this within the double-sided interpretation, taking up both the positive and negative, have a better chance of reaching the patient, making contact, and affording a moment of integration. Whilst it is important to hear and interpret the underlying anxieties and unconscious meaning of the patient's material, this will be ineffective if the patient's capacity to take in and to understand has been obliterated by her ego-destructive superego. In order to make contact and thus to link with the patient's imprisoned libidinal self, it is more effective to interpret first and foremost the *process* of the session. By this I mean a close tracking of the interplay between patient and analyst (e.g., Joseph, 1989). In this way it becomes possible to understand how the patient has received and perceived the interpretation by noticing and commenting on the patient's emotional responses, both verbal and non-verbal, in combination with the use of, where appropriate, the double-sided interpretation.

Clinical example: Mr A

I wish to show the benefit of the use of double-sided interpretations through providing some illustration of the dynamic processes in the clinical work with Mr A, a patient with a narcissistic and perverse defensive organisation of a predominantly destructive and masochistic nature, in whom an ego-destructive superego and sadomasochistic enactments dominated the transference and countertransference relationship in the early years of his analysis. He is similar to those patients described by Joseph whose "malignant type of destructiveness" is in the nature of "an addiction to near-death" (1982, p. 127). Segal (1993) too describes "the sadistic pleasure of triumph over the defeated analyst but also the masochistic pleasure of triumph over that part of the self that wishes to live and grow" (p. 59).

Mr A repeatedly exploited his anxieties for masochistic purposes, provoking ways to make himself redundant from jobs and from relationships. He split off envy and hatred, projected it into others who he then, from a superior height, perceived as attacking and criticising him for what he considered his "better characteristics", such as his pride in his independence, his "one-man-band". He had good intellectual capacity but related robotically to me. It soon became apparent that he had learned through imitation and by rote all his life.

At first Mr A experienced immense difficulties in sharing the same physical space with me as well as with others, because he complained that he did not know what to say or "how to be". He said that he had no sense of himself, could not comprehend the reason for not being able to sustain more than one-night stands with women, and was almost permanently overwhelmed with unbearable anxiety. Mr A, in his early forties, had been brought up by emotionally absent parents. His mother was depressed and unable to cope with three boys, of whom Mr A was the youngest. Mr A grew up feeling terrified of his authoritarian, verbally and physically aggressive father who died unexpectedly when Mr A was still a young boy. He felt neither relief nor sadness about this loss. Despite his father's "violence", resulting in all the family members behaving in submissive ways, Mr A nurtured and cherished a great admiration for his father's aggression. Consequently he idealised destructiveness and confused omnipotence with ordinary potency.

Initially, Mr A would respond to much of what I said with the refrain: "I'm indifferent to my indifference". The dismissive way he reacted to my interpretations was associated with a kind of indifference in which he remained calm whilst I struggled to make contact. It felt as if I was meant to make all the effort to care for the analysis while he remained passively disinterested or contemptuous of my attempts to reach him and help him understand himself. His libidinal self seemed to be lost inside his superior "one-man-band" state of mind. At these times I felt obliged to tolerate and to accept the provocative way he dismissed me but I could feel that it was making me angry and sometimes provoked me into criticising him. Mr A seemed to exist in a permanent state of disconnection, only occasionally coming alive with me as an object whom he could draw into repeated enactments of a sadomasochistic nature, after which he felt superior and triumphant.

Eventually, there came a phase in the analysis when the patient began to have memories that shed light on a source of his disconnectedness. He remembered his father violently ripping the plug out of the wall socket that broke the connection to the patient's favourite TV programme, a violent attack on linking that was repeated in the disconnection with me and in attacks on his own mind, for example, in his forgetting what he was going to say mid-sentence, the appearance of a sudden fog that blurred his mind so that he could not think, sudden stammering that came over him—attacks on himself that paralysed his thinking and castrated his speech.

There were memories when Mr A recalled that his parents slept in separate beds; he remembered there was no affection between them, no linking, and no creative intercourse, which repeated in relation to himself and in the transference. Indeed, fear pervaded his home; there was an impregnable iciness in the household atmosphere, no idea of something being connected in an ordinary ambivalent or potent manner.

A further dimension of Mr A's psychic makeup was his identification with an impotent, depressed mother. In a particular week he presented as deadened and silent. He refused to give in, to speak to me, wanting me to watch him suffer in angry silence, hating me and paralysing me. In an illustration of what I have described as the double-sided interpretation, I said: "I think you'd like to find a way out of your closed-up place to talk to me but it's difficult because at the same time you're enjoying wallowing in that place where you stay silent and disconnected from me as though that makes you feel superior even though you're suffering." Mr A agreed with me, but in the process of trying to elaborate, he suddenly sounded disconcerted and disorientated, saying he didn't know what had happened but he had lost what he was going to say, even though it had just been there in his mind.

Alternating with silent periods there were sessions in which he usurped the space and took over control with a flood of speech and phantasies. He would use my words, imitating me, and would quickly build phantasies around my thoughts, incorporating me and identifying with an idealised analyst, making interpretations he thought I might have made, preventing separateness. Near the end of a session during the course of which Mr A had been unreachable, parroting my words with relish, excitedly twisting and lifting them out of context, my interpretation touched on his fear of knowing about his neediness and humiliation. I said: "I think that today you're finding ways to twist what I'm saying in order to mock me, maybe because you're afraid to let yourself get in touch with what you might really want or need from me in case it leaves you feeling humiliated." He stopped talking for the first time, seemed to be trying to think, and then pronounced triumphantly: "I've had a fantasy of my holding your hand then it turned into my holding your brain in my hands."

I felt that this fantasy in response to my interpretation showed a shift to his libidinal side, which was then quickly corrupted. It encapsulated the difficulties Mr A faced whenever he attempted to make any psychic shift towards making contact with me. The moment he and I were linked, "holding hands", he experienced such intense envy and hatred that he attacked the link between us and cut himself off from the brief moment of separateness in which he felt genuinely connected to me as a good object. Later, instead of experiencing a phantasy of possessing my mind, he managed to become aware of and to verbalise how he envied and wanted my peace of mind.

Mr A was convinced of the goodness of his destructive omnipotence, yet was aware of some confusion. He would talk about his confusion as a "lie" and "not knowing when I'm doing a dirty deal behind my own back". As soon as Mr A made contact with me as a helpful object he felt an instant need to push me away and control the distance between us. Sometimes, the moment he recognised that he had managed to "connect" and link with me, and had understood something meaningful, or felt an awareness that he had made progress, he felt immediately threatened, and the good would be instantaneously turned to bad. His destructive self would often creep in insidiously and unobtrusively, but equally frequently would erupt violently, cutting all contact.

Mr A would introduce doubt whenever he linked with his libidinal self and with me, and he would quickly convince himself that his destructive self was the truth of his whole self to the point that he had no memory of ever having felt linked in a warm and loving way with me moments earlier. Over time he began to distinguish between reality and a confusion in his internal world, which he began to challenge as a possible "lie". When he recovered his understanding—sometimes moments later, sometimes sessions later—that he had lost a sense of himself as composed of both "healthy and malicious" elements in a more ambivalent manner, he would become desperately insistent, and for me poignantly so, that I maintain a "picture of both sides of the coin" of his whole self as he knew he would lose it. He could then feel more secure that I would be able to "get under the radar" of his destructive self and make contact with him again. We both had to endure many long years together before Mr A was able to begin to consistently recognise his destructive hatred and envy of his libidinal self and of me, for connecting with me or making progress, and to manage to question and challenge this "dictator part". As such, I believe that this enabled a proper judgement of reality—an ego function, as opposed to a superego passing moral judgement (Britton, 2003).

The problem with the patient's omnipotent destructiveness was that, in his words: "I do know that there are two sides to me, but even as I'm talking to you now and telling you that I'm aware that there are two sides, the other part is telling me that what you're saying is rubbish, not to listen to you, and that I know best, so I'm drifting off and it's hard to stay connected with you." If I managed to identify and experience the very moment in which the patient would switch from functioning in a K state of mind, to his L link with me being attacked and hijacked by his ego-destructive superego, then a double-sided interpretation, together with resisting the pull to enact his projective identification of submission and helplessness, would prove particularly helpful in preventing the switch. At these times such an interpretation would release his mind just enough from the captivity of his destructive self to offer him the mental space to remember and to refocus on the existence of his libidinal self by eliciting his wish for something he longed for and that had meaning.

Repeated production of phantasy as a defence

My patient went through a period of evasion of painful emotions or thoughts by a particular defence, staying in control of me and the analysis through the proliferation of phantasies, mostly violent or sexual. He would use phantasies to dissociate and to live in, rather than allowing contact with me. Each time I would start to say something, speaking to the him that wanted to find a way to hold my hand again, he would dissociate and produce another phantasy that attacked and broke off contact with me. It was intolerable to him to experience me as separate and as having a mind of my own.

In the following clinical material I will try to give something of the flavour of this.

PATIENT: [Starts talking the second he lies down] I'm feeling much better today. I wanted to get here early but I'm amazed I ended up leaving rather late even though I didn't mean to. On the way here I was trying really hard to think about things and not just give in to them and feel like life's a waste of time, that I may as well be better off dead, and it does seem to have made a difference because I do feel better … [brief pause] But even so … I found myself having a few fantasies on the way here which weren't at all pleasant. The first one was about my cycling along and a little boy is running ahead of his mother and she's running behind him and he suddenly runs into the road and I run into him, and then the mother and I are having a big fight, she's saying it's my fault and I'm indignant and thinking it's not my fault and she's just attacking me.

Mr A continued to describe how he was having these fantasies every day (in such as way as to make me feel it's my fault in a mildly blaming way).

ANALYST: [First interpretation] It strikes me that you had a struggle this morning. You were eager to get here for your session because you felt helped yesterday, but as soon as you allow yourself to know that, you make yourself late and you turn your wish to get here into a fantasy, wanting to provoke a fight with me, feeling like a little boy who is both hurt and powerful, perhaps because you feel that I have things to say that might help you rather than you knowing them all yourself.

PATIENT: I can feel myself half trying to block you out because I don't want to hear that and it's not what I thought of by myself. I had no trouble getting up early because I wanted to get here but then I went back to bed so I ended up being amazed I got here on time. I must have cycled extra quickly. [Begrudgingly but less speedily] I suppose you're right, though even as you're saying it my mind wants to attack you and say you're not right and I am.

Then Mr A immediately went on to tell me another fantasy about causing an accident at a junction in a road between him and a car full of men who are furious, whilst he is righteous and pleased that their car is all smashed up. He added:

P: And, it reminds me of a fantasy I had a week or two ago when I was using a bomb to blow you up in the session. I feel better today, as I'm not convincing myself this is all useless and a waste of time. I don't like how hard I'm having to struggle at the moment but I suppose it's a bit better than being in complete despair.

A: [Second interpretation] Perhaps you didn't quite know how to take my words. You tried to take them in so you could feel better, but instead blocked me out and prevented yourself from getting my help by a car crash or blowing me up, when perhaps you'd like to use the session today in a different way.

Mr A talked a bit more straightforwardly about the fact that he knew he was an angry little boy so much of the time and hated it.

P: [Sounding genuine] Now exposure's on my mind. I feel deflated; I feel shame. I don't exactly want to wear my heart on my sleeve and anyway I can't ... [Suddenly, in a more inflated tone] What's just popped into my head is your break soon. I'm thinking that means I'm a bit worried about it.

A: [Third interpretation] I think you felt I deflated you, just for a second, but feeling vulnerable and exposed like a little boy frightened you so much you switched again to feeling inflated. It sounds as if you want me to think you're interested in understanding yourself and that you are feeling worried about the break, when it isn't so clear you are.

[Mr A maintained a rigid and angrily sullen silence for several minutes.]

In examining this session more closely, Mr A starts by telling me that he feels better, although at the same time he ensures that I remember, and perhaps is also warning me, about how close to the precipice edge he is standing between a wish for something life-giving and a wish for something death-giving—a child in a dangerous position in the road who could be hurt by his own aggression. Mr A shows me that he feels like a powerful, self-harming little boy who wants to provoke a fight with me. He uses a helpful superego to enable his wish to come to his session but instantly attacks and destroys this wish, his link to positive feelings for the object, and moves into getting a masochistic kick out of allying himself with his destructiveness in which he can omnipotently make his parents fight. In doing so he feels excitedly gratified by the punishment of being run over.

To enable linking, the first interpretation I give Mr A emphasises and highlights his internal conflict—his L link towards me, his wanting to come to his session, together with his hating H link that attempts to sabotage his getting to the session on time the moment he acknowledges to himself his libidinal wish. This double-sided interpretation appears to have a beneficial effect. He admits my interpretation begrudgingly, slows down and struggles to become more thoughtful. But he then quickly identifies with a hating, omnipotent destructive part of himself that bombs me and causes car crashes, and which successfully entices him away from me with the promise of excitement, albeit the masochistic excitement involved in being punished by angry parents.

It is apparent that Mr A's narcissistic self-sufficiency and his dependency are in conflict with each other. Even though Mr A manages to squeeze out through gritted teeth that he does agree with me, clearly he does not like feeling dependent and knowing I have something to offer that he cannot give himself. In order to defend himself he attacks his ordinary life-affirming wish to come to see me. At an unconscious level he experiences this wish in itself as an attack on his narcissism. His hatred of neediness and dependency threatens him with unbearable humiliation if he were to acknowledge and prioritise his needy libidinal self, so he transforms his ordinary good and loving feelings into phantasies that cut the contact between us. He is seduced back into a compulsion to repeat, this time with a more directly violent phantasy concerned with blowing up my mind. The shift he makes from using "I" to "my mind" in his sentence, "I suppose you're right, though even as you're saying it my mind wants to attack you and say you're not right and I am," reveals the moment at which he is again lured into an identification with his destructive self, cutting contact with himself and with me. This dissociative way of talking ("my mind") has a disconcerting effect on me, hearing Mr A talk as though there is a patient, an analyst, and someone else in the room, as though he and I are talking about and analysing another person, not him.

Through having to bear the proliferation of Mr A's phantasies I am feeling increasing provoked. But I try to remind myself that his continual use of phantasy (consciously thought and unconsciously produced) to attack himself and the object is a compulsive defence against unbearable pain. The temporary relief from anxiety gained from being beaten into submission by seduction and intimidation by such a powerful and terrifying superego only serves to magnify his anxiety by feeding into escalating cycles of cruelty and punishment.

I feel in danger of being drawn into competing and therefore enacting my part in this disturbing sadomasochistic game playing, and pushing Mr A back to a restoration of the status quo of an emotionally disconnected psychic equilibrium. As Britton (2003) states: "Enactment within analysis is prompted by a desire to retain a defensive organisation and probably to recruit the analyst into its personnel" (p. 77).

Therefore, I cautiously formulate my second double-sided interpretation, aware that whatever I say could potentially enable or disable Mr A emotionally. Listening carefully, and experiencing my countertransference to his responses, alerts and focuses my attention on my emotional experience and to the process of the dynamics taking place between us rather than listening only to the content of his material. Whilst the content is important, and Mr A needs to know that I have heard and understood the substance of what he is saying because it is this that partly contains him, it is, however, not this that primarily brings emotional contact by linking us. What will enable contact is my using my countertransference feelings, elicited by his projective identification, as the basis of an interpretation that helps Mr A recognise that he has both loving and hating feelings towards me.

It seems that my second interpretation, one that again hinges on linking both his libidinal and destructive selves, does this time have the effect of painfully deflating Mr A. His genuine quiet tone and his communication that he feels angry, hurt, humiliated and needy for me, his little-boy-smallness ("heart-on-the-sleeve") are, I think, a moment of Mr A feeling in touch with his psychic reality. He is unable to sustain it for long. Mr A continues by mentioning my forthcoming break. This could be viewed as his remaining in contact with me but I feel this to be a deceptive manoeuvre. Instead I am alerted to his suddenly inflated, slightly superior tone of voice, which mark an internal shift in him towards omnipotence. This, together with his use of "I'm thinking that means I'm a bit worried about it ..." as though he is making the "interpretation" that he thinks I might have said, brings on a familiar feeling in me: that Mr A has seized back control and become his own analyst. At this point I sigh to myself, feeling defeated.

My third interpretation speaks to Mr A of his deflation and his little boy vulnerability. However, I believe that he hears the second sentence—"It sounds as if you want me to think you're interested in understanding yourself and that you are feeling worried about the break, when it isn't so clear you are,"—as a barbed attack pushing him away, so that in that moment he feels wounded. I think he had perceived me as a primary object who was critical, impermeable and impenetrable, and who was as such unable to take in, modify and make tolerable his projections of painful feelings, Bion's (1962a) "projective-identification-rejecting-object" (p. 117).

It is inevitable for such a patient in the relatively early phases of analysis to be repeatedly pulled back and caught up in the excitement of triumphing over himself and me in the to-ing and fro-ing of linking and unlinking. It is essential in double-sided interpretations to ensure that the libidinal self is given as much weight as the destructive self. Due to the patient's sensitivity to exposure of his disturbance, if inadequate emphasis is placed on the emotions connected with the patient's libidinal self, he is more likely to narcissistically withdraw or to mount a defensive offensive on the analyst. Mr A's response to my third interpretation was to withdraw into an angry silence. Perhaps I could have mitigated more the degree of pain and anxiety that my third interpretation had aroused in Mr A by placing much greater emphasis on my having understood his ordinary libidinal hurt and ashamed heart-on-the-sleeve little boy.

Despite having found the brief moments of Mr A's deflation relieving and moving because of the separateness achieved, my countertransference was countered by Mr A's projective identification, which induced in me strong feelings of defeat, hopelessness, and a sense of being a useless analyst. This was hard to bear without losing all hope, which brought me to a point of feeling sorry for myself. As I experienced this, it then occurred to me that maybe this is exactly what Mr A needed from me, a sense of my compassion for him, for his needy, libidinal self which had been knocked over again and again by his triumphant superiority. With this understanding of my countertransference, as the session continued I felt in a better position to link with Mr A and to help him link with me.

The snake dream and the glimmer of separateness

Mr A started the session the following day by saying tentatively that he'd forgotten my cheque, though he'd written it and couldn't understand why he hadn't brought it. He'd left it out especially so that he wouldn't forget it.

There was a long silence during which he seemed anxious and uncomfortable, shifting on the couch. I felt he was waiting for me to comment on his withholding the cheque, perhaps to provoke me into criticising him. Or, I wondered, maybe he saw this as a power struggle or competition, perhaps because he felt it was something he gives me that allows him to feel that I need him and to feel superior about it, possibly more so because of his superego's envy of his libidinal self for having made contact and linked with me in the previous day's session.

He then told me about work where he felt under scrutiny from his boss. He was sure he was going to fail to make the grade when he gave a presentation that day and he was worried about it. He'd felt obliged to tell his boss the previous day that he was going home to work on the script last night. I said: "You tried hard to make sure that you brought my cheque today but you forgot it, as though you were trying to sabotage things here as a way to make me punish you, to tell you off for having failed to make the grade and make you feel small."

Mr A carried on talking, saying there must be something about him that "foists" feelings about himself onto other people, like his boss, because he always feels they're going to criticise him and he then finds himself feeling he has to appease them.

He then said that he had just remembered the previous night's dream:

> He was in an office photocopying but the photocopier was just spewing out mangled bits of paper and he couldn't get it to work properly. Then there were lots of small wriggling poisonous black snakes. Just one seemed to be trying to bite him and he grabbed it behind its head to prevent it striking.

He drifted into total silence, again an anxious one. It occurred to me that his anxious silence was connected with his possibly feeling criticised by my first interpretation, as though he had done something wrong, and that my not having yet responded to his dream had left him feeling more anxious. It was a double-sided interpretation but did not have the effect that I had intended of helping him link. He appeared to be looking for ways to feel criticised so I thought it likely that he had only perceived me as punishing him by hearing words in isolation from the meaning of the whole interpretation, such as "… trying to sabo-tage …" and "… failed …". In the countertransference, because of the self-satisfied tone in which he had announced the dream, I wondered whether perhaps he was trying to appease me by giving me something for having "forgotten" to bring my cheque. Then that seemed to be the end of that. I waited for him to say more. He said nothing. After a while I began to feel tense and without knowing where he was, except rigid on the couch, I commented that he had said nothing further about his dream.

Quick as a flash he retorted, saying that a snake was phallic. (He sounded pleased and smug with his cleverness, leading me to think that he *was* giving me what he thought I wanted.) His next association was a thought of the species of female spider that bites off the male's head while mating.

I felt in touch with his desires to give good things to me, counterbal-anced by his withholding, and complicated by his anxiety about what

I was really thinking about his not bringing my cheque, perhaps that I would bite off his head.

A: I think you felt that what I just said was me criticising you for not bringing my cheque so that you feel undermined and impotent, and perhaps you want to please me by giving me your dream instead, but you hesitate to go on to explore it as though you feel you've satisfied me with the gift.

P: [Nastily and contemptuously] Oh, you know how indifferent I always feel about these things. It's just a dream; they're all meaningless really. I just go along with it.

A: [Feeling acutely his attack on our work, I was able with effort to contain my irritation. I was aware of the need to address his anxiety at the same time as L and H.]

I think you're still feeling anxious about my poisoning you with criticisms for forgetting my cheque and biting your head off so that, although you would like to do well at work and to work at understanding yourself here with me, you're feeling compelled to throw out my words and reject my attempt to connect with you.

This double-sided interpretation had an effect. I felt he could take it in. His mood changed, he stopped shifting on the couch and seemed to relax, helped by my interpretation, which presumably relieved him of his own superego's persecutory anxiety about the cheque. It confirmed that previously he had felt I was attacking him with criticisms; any possibility of a creative intercourse with me had been turning into a murderous 'mating'. He responded by talking about having used the photocopier a great deal the previous day to make copies of his script given to him by his boss. Then he was silent and reflected for a while, and said nothing else was in his mind.

After a short while, Mr A said he wanted to make his boss proud of him. This reminded him of standing at his father's grave and getting upset thinking about whether his father had been proud of him. Next, he made the association of his father with the poisonous snake from the dream, and remembered having always to appease his father, connecting these for himself in a developing capacity to think. Here he could understand that it was something poisonous in him—not me—that was criticising him. The double-sided interpretation had enabled sufficient separateness between us to allow Mr A to understand and think for himself. This process involved finding a good object in me after having managed to pressure me into enacting a superego stance in a way consistent to a degree with his internal world, then reintrojecting his own projections of the poisonous black snake feelings and realising that these represented his own poisonous father. It was clear that he had initially thought I was the one mangling the meaning of and spewing out his words, biting him, and poisoning him, so that he wanted to photocopy himself into the safety of being an identical copy of his image of an analyst-me.

Mr A carried on thinking about his father for several minutes: cold, violent, unaffectionate, tyrannical, hardly ever there; how he never wanted to be in the same room as his father, feeling a never-ending sense of anxiety, only wanting to run to his bedroom, in contact with a realistic picture of himself as a boy.

In the next session, Mr A brought a dream confirming that in the previous day's session some depressive position functioning and contact with reality were achieved and worked through a little during the night. His dream, one in which he was "shocked and disappointed", conveyed to me in a dismayed and depressed tone that he had seen his father as a damaged figure, far from the powerful, terrifying person he knew from his childhood:

> It was just that my father was there—old, weak, broken-down, blind, quite decrepit—and I felt shocked and disappointed.

The dream revealed Mr A's anxiety about the existence within him of a damaged internal object, and that he was aware of a weakened, broken-down superego that he recognised as "blind" to reality. Mr A was so profoundly affected by his dream that he let me know that he found himself thinking about various aspects connected with it between his sessions. This was the first time he told me that he had thought about anything connected with his analysis between sessions, having always previously told me, with a smirk, that he dismissed each session from his mind as "unimportant" the minute he left the room.

Over the next two sessions Mr A spoke, at times with trembling voice and quiet tears, of how he was shocked at his own "blindness", horrified, and filled with guilt about the problems he could now see he had caused for himself and others, "always looking for trouble". In touch with intense sadness, guilt, and regret he spoke of his father's death when he was only a young boy, and that he thought he was crying for his father now as he never had done as a child; he wondered about the sort of "good adult-to-adult relationship with [his] dad" that might have been. He thought about the covert vitriolic and contemptuous attacks he had always made on his mother, and on all women, and commented that he knew he made them on me too. In a hesitant way he said he was sorry. He had never apologised before. I let him know that I understood that it was painful to feel so guilty, and that he was showing me that he wanted to sustain a relationship with himself and with me in ways that were satisfying and meaningful rather than destructive, just as he had managed to do over these two sessions. He agreed and thought that the reason he had always attacked women might be the way his father had treated his mother, or was it that his father was fed up with his complaining mother? This period of depressive position functioning was rather more prolonged than his previous short-lived moments and represented quite considerable progress. Inevitably, it could not be sustained as he transformed his wish to understand himself and face reality into a wish not to understand, which, in time, he would have to mourn. It did, however, herald his potential to attain increased separateness and a capacity to love.

Concluding comments

The analysis of disturbed, resistant, borderline and narcissistic patients, even when the analyst succeeds in making contact with the patient for brief moments, is inevitably repetitive, long, and at times seemingly intractable. There seems little doubt that what remains unknown is the extent to which the degree of excessive destructiveness in each individual patient is primary or defensive, and therefore, in part, whether an ego-destructive superego may or may not develop. With perpetual splitting and projective identification an omnipotent ego-destructive superego thrives and strengthens rather than weakens. The analyst needs to experience and tolerate the frustration and helplessness inherent in the patient's oscillations between minute progressions and destructive regressions, both within and between sessions. As with any other type of interpretation, the analyst has to follow the destiny of the double-sided interpretation to work out how successful it can be. Mr A's vicious superego thwarted us both to the point of despair time and again. Eventually it was made tolerable by those brief (but increasingly sustained) moments of depressive position functioning, those moments when he was aware of and acknowledged freely that he felt sad or guilty for having damaged his objects and his own capacity to engage in meaningful relationships, for not having fulfilled his career potential, and for having spoilt his capacity to enjoy life in an ordinary way.

As Britton (2003) so succinctly summarises, with severely disturbed patients it is the analyst's work to enable the emancipation of the ego from the destructive power of the superego (p. 104). It is my view that double-sided interpretations are one such vehicle that helps in moving towards that aim. By highlighting and emphasising the internal conflict between L and H, the struggle for domination and supremacy between Eros and Thanatos taking place in the internal world of the patient, the cumulative effect of using double-sided interpretations plays one part in helping release the captive libidinal self from the clutches of a destructive superego. The analyst's recognition of the small indications or green shoots of positive transference will help his embattled ego to gain strength and to resist the intimidatory power of his captor. Acknowledgement of L by the analyst, together with a growing awareness of the destructive power of his aggression, hatred, and envy, encourages reintegration with his libidinal constructive and reparative sides. Such interpretations of L and H within the same interpretation often require attention to the underlying anxiety, and need to be made appropriately within the context of the dynamic processes of the transference/countertransference relationship, the patient's material, and with an eye and ear to sensitive timing.

Bion's theory of the container-contained as the nexus of emotional development is now generally viewed as an expansion of, and as adding a further dimension to, Klein's theoretical framework, in which emotional development takes place in the movements between the paranoid-schizoid and depressive positions. Despite her expansion of Freud's theory of psychosexual development into a new theoretical metapsychology, Klein (1963) herself continued to place a good deal of emphasis on the role of the later, modified superego, which she believed "strengthens the loving impulses and furthers the tendency towards reparation" (p. 279) and the recovery of the good object.

Acknowledgment

I am grateful to Jean Arundale and Debbie Bandler Bellman for their encouragement in writing this chapter.

References

Bell, D. (2011). Bion: The phenomenologist of loss. In: C. Mawson (Ed.), *Bion Today* (pp. 81–101). Hove: Routledge.

Bion, W. R. (1958). On arrogance. *International Journal of Psychoanalysis, 39*: 144–146 [reprinted in: *Second Thoughts: Selected Papers on Psychoanalysis*, London: Heinemann Medical, 1967; reprinted London: Karnac, 1984].

Bion, W. R. (1959). Attacks on linking. *International Journal of Psychoanalysis, 40*: 308–315 [reprinted in: *Second Thoughts: Selected Papers on Psychoanalysis*, London: Heinemann Medical, 1967; reprinted London: Karnac, 1984].

Bion, W. R. (1962a). A theory of thinking. *International Journal of Psychoanalysis, 43*: 306–310 [reprinted in: *Second Thoughts: Selected Papers on Psychoanalysis*, London: Heinemann Medical, 1967; reprinted London: Karnac, 1984].

Bion, W. R. (1962b). *Learning from Experience*. London: Heinemann Medical [reprinted London: Karnac, 1984].

Bion, W. R. (1962c). The psycho-analytic study of thinking. *International Journal of Psychoanalysis, 43*: 306–310 [reprinted in: *Second Thoughts: Selected Papers on Psychoanalysis*, London: Heinemann Medical, 1967; reprinted London: Karnac, 1984].

Bion, W. R. (1965). *Transformations*. London: Maresfield Reprints [reprinted London: Karnac, 1984].

Bion, W. R. (1970). *Attention and Interpretation: A Scientific Approach to Insight in Psychoanalysis and Groups*. London: Karnac.

Brenman, E. (1982). Separation: A clinical problem. *International Journal of Psychoanalysis, 63*: 303–310.

Britton, R. (1989). The missing link: Parental sexuality in the Oedipus complex. In: R. Britton, M. Feldman & E. O'Shaughnessy (Eds.), *The Oedipus Complex Today* (pp. 83–101). London: Karnac.

Britton, R. (1998). *Belief and Imagination*. London: Routledge.

Britton, R. (2003). *Sex, Death, and the Superego: Experiences in Psychoanalysis*. London: Karnac.

Feldman, M. (2000). Some views on the manifestation of the death instinct in clinical work. *International Journal of Psychoanalysis, 81*: 53–65.

Feldman, M. (2007). Addressing parts of the self. *International Journal of Psychoanalysis, 88*: 371–386.

Fisher, J. (2011). The emotional experience of K. (Ch.3, pp. 43–63). In: C. Mawson (Ed.), *Bion Today*. Hove: Routledge.

Freud, S. (1909d). Notes upon a case of obsessional neurosis. *S. E., 10*: 151–318. London: Hogarth.

Freud, S. (1911b). Formulations on the two principles of mental functioning. *S. E., 12*: 213–226. London: Hogarth.

Freud, S. (1923a). Two encyclopaedia articles. *S. E.*, *18*: 233–260. London: Hogarth.

Freud, S. (1923b). *The Ego and the Id*. *S. E.*, *19*: 1–66. London: Hogarth.

Freud, S. (1937c). Analysis terminable and interminable. *S. E.*, *23*: 209–254. London: Hogarth.

Joseph, B. (1982). Addiction to near-death. *International Journal of Psychoanalysis*, *63*: 449–456 [reprinted in: J. M. Feldman & E. Bott Spillius (Eds.), *Psychic Equilibrium and Psychic Change: Selected Papers of Betty Joseph*. London: Routledge, 1989].

Joseph, B. (1989). General introduction (pp. 1–9). In: J. M. Feldman & E. Bott Spillius (Eds.), *Psychic Equilibrium and Psychic Change: Selected Papers of Betty Joseph*. London: Routledge.

Klein, M. (1957). Envy and gratitude. In: *The Writings of Melanie Klein, Volume 3: Envy and Gratitude and Other Works*. London: Hogarth, 1975.

Klein, M. (1958). On the Development of Mental Functioning. *International Journal of Psychoanalysis*, *39*: 84–90.

Klein, M. (1963). Some reflections on "The Oresteia". In: *The Writings of Melanie Klein, Volume 3: Envy and Gratitude and Other Works*. London: Hogarth, 1975.

Meltzer, D. (1968). Terror, persecution, dread: A dissection of paranoid anxieties. *International Journal of Psychoanalysis*, *49*: 396–400.

O'Shaughnessy, E. (1999). Relating to the superego. *International Journal of Psychoanalysis*, *80*: 861–870.

Rosenfeld, H. (1964). On the psychopathology of narcissism: A clinical approach. *International Journal of Psychoanalysis*, *45*: 332–337.

Rosenfeld, H. (1971). A clinical approach to the psychoanalytic theory of the life and death instincts: An investigation into the aggressive aspects of narcissism. *International Journal of Psychoanalysis*, *52*: 169–178 [reprinted in E. Bott Spillius (Ed.), *Melanie Klein Today, Volume 1*. London: Routledge, 1988].

Roth, P. (2001). Mapping the landscape: Levels of transference interpretation. *International Journal of Psychoanalysis*, *82*: 533–543.

Segal, H. (1993). On the clinical usefulness of the concept of the death instinct. *International Journal of Psychoanalysis*, *74*: 55–61.

Steiner, J. (1982). Perverse relationships between parts of the self: A clinical illustration. *International Journal of Psychoanalysis*, *63*: 241–242.

Steiner, J. (1993). *Psychic Retreats: Pathological Organisations of the Personality in Psychotic, Neurotic and Borderline Patients*. London: Routledge.

Steiner, J. (1994). Patient-centered and analyst-centered interpretations: Some implications of containment and countertransference. *Psychoanalytic Inquiry*, *14*: 406–422.

Steiner, J. (2006). Interpretative enactments and the analytic setting. *International Journal of Psychoanalysis*, *87*: 315–320.

CHAPTER SIX

The painful relinquishment of baseless hope: interpreting small steps towards reality

Michael Halton

Introduction

A patient, who I shall call Mrs A, sought a second analysis five times a week, a situation that lasted for many years. Her first attempt had left her untouched and dissatisfied, and in her second analysis with me she also rarely reported improvement. She claimed not to have learned anything further about herself or if she did, it was not helpful. She did not change in ways she wanted: to be a calmer, nicer, person, more at ease with herself; yet towards the end of our work there was some evidence of emotional movement, one notable feature being that she had to live with more sadness. From time to time she reported that friends and family commented on changes. For example, they observed she was a bit more open but they were surprised by the emergence of her unrelenting anxiety, her difficulties with the simple tasks of daily life, and occasionally they had glimpses of her hitherto unseen and inexplicable despair.

Before her second analysis Mrs A had a reputation as someone with a certain grace, a selfless eager-to-please manner, and a tendency to be self-deprecating. The dominating feature of her personality was to accommodate to others. We coined a term for this and called it the "obliging patient". As time passed I discovered more about the "obliging wife", "the obliging mother", the "obliging friend", etc.

After some years this accommodation gave way to reveal a very demanding patient and an analysis with rather special difficulties. We then had to find terms for this demandingness, which had transmogrified from subtle hints to overt tyranny. Her stated wish was to be "cured" and it was imperative that I did not fail in this. The story of King Canute came to mind, where the king commands his court to set his throne upon the beach. Surrounded by his followers he issues a regal proclamation to stop the tides' ebb and flow, whereupon everyone gets wet feet! An alternative version suggests Canute wanted to demonstrate that even kings lack divine powers and are subject to the laws of reality. However, this second version was a lesson both the patient and I were slow to learn.

A situation came to pass where almost no mutuality seemed possible. Any joint understanding between our two minds was beyond our reach no matter how desperately and sincerely we both tried; and neither of us spared any effort! It took some time to grasp what was at the heart of our difficulties and for me to find a way of speaking to the patient that felt helpful and had any purpose. I was greatly relieved when I realised that the person on my couch had problems using her mind to be *curious*. In *Learning from Experience* Bion states:

> A small number of patients with whom I have had to deal have presented prominently symptoms of disordered capacity for thought. In the course of their treatment opportunities for orthodox transference interpretations occurred and were taken, but the patient often learned nothing from them. (Bion, 1962a, p. 20)

I will try to show in this chapter that there are patients like Mrs A who have distinctive difficulties that need a particular understanding and technical approach in analysis. They are what Britton (2013) has called *"psycho phobic"*, that is, they are phobic of their own minds and inner lives and fear their unconscious will overwhelm and traumatise their ego.

My central argument will be that technically:

> Interpretations need to be focused not on trying to give understanding related to *what things mean*, but in describing to the

patient *at length and in detail* the difficulty they have in *noticing and attending* to their own and other people's mental states. Interpretations that intend to further curiosity or make sense of unconscious content make no (n) sense to a patient for whom enquiry is an utterly foreign state of mind.

Pari passu, such patients also have a deep belief, often unconscious, that the analyst is similarly compromised and therefore they have no expectation of being really listened too and have little or no comprehension of anyone attending to them properly with the desire to understand them.

Content and process

For many patients who we meet in analysis, it is the *contents* of the emotional problems evident in the transference that become the focus of our attention. We search for meaning in dreams, free associations, non-verbal behaviour, and subtle and not so subtle enactments in the transference/countertransference; and we craft our interpretations to convey this understanding. We try to do this with sensitivity as and when we judge it to be clinically appropriate. The emotional atmosphere, tone of voice, and timing, etc., all play an important part in this process of communication, and obviously it is not just the words spoken or their symbolic meaning that require our attention.

The *process of finding meaning*, whether it is related to elucidating the transference/countertransference dynamic, uncovering unconscious phantasy, or analysing drive derivatives, is rarely an easy and simple matter, yet most of the time, to some degree or other it can be taken for granted. The two vital aspects of meaningful communication in personal relationships that make this possible are emotional connectiveness and cognitive comprehension, and they usually go hand in hand, one linked with the other—what Melanie Klein (1952) often referred to simply enough as "love and understanding". We mostly take them as given because they operate below the level of consciousness. This is generally the case with less disturbed patients but can even be true with individuals who are borderline or psychotic.

All patients present challenges to analytic work, however they do not *necessarily* pose significant problems for the analyst in finding and conveying something that is *meaningful*. The analyst may be confused or divided over which aspect to pick up and at what level, and technical matters of framing interpretations that reach the patient emotionally may often be the most salient challenge. But if these difficulties occur between the analyst and patient, they often do so in a way that can be worked through.

The relative ease, with which the analyst is able to follow the patient's material and the patient's reciprocal capacity to attend and follow the analyst's interpretations, indicates that the patient has internalised an early object relationship that heuristically speaking is "good enough". They have a mental apparatus that can be used at least some of the time to attend and reflect on their own inner state and the inner states of others.

I wish to stress that under propitious circumstances, emotional experiences in early infantile life are linked and accompanied or followed by an unforced and natural meaningfulness that is married to a curiosity about the nature of internal and external events. Some essential component of conscious attentiveness has been established.

In "Attacks on linking" (Bion, 1959), which contains many brilliant ideas, Bion proposed that the prototypic symbolic links in the mind that connect feeling and thinking are the primitive breast and penis. Britton (1989) developed these ideas and took a major conceptual leap forward with his theory of triangular space and the third position of observation. Birksted-Breen (1996) added something further that was implicit in Britton's conceptualisation, which enriches the concept of maternal containment. Tucked away in a footnote she states:

> Containment, in my view, involves this bisexual aspect. I think that it is not a purely maternal function as has been suggested by Bion and others but *already* combines both the maternal function of *being with* and the paternal function of *observing and linking* [emphasis added]. In order to contain her infant, a mother (and an analyst) has to receive projections empathically (the maternal function) and also take a perspective on this (paternal function). (1996, p. 651)

I take Birksted-Breen to mean that a mother capable of true containment has negotiated the primal scene and integrated the primal couple, and therefore the capacity for both the maternal functions of feeling and the paternal functions of observing and thinking, separate but linked, as described by Britton.

Sadly, there are a number of patients who for whatever reason experienced insufficient love and understanding in infancy. When we meet them as adults in analysis, mutuality and shared meaning in the analytic encounter is painfully rare and the function of mindfulness cannot be assumed. One of the most striking features is the difficulty they have in attending to their inner world and obtaining understanding from their analysis which can foster curiosity and progress.

Meaningfulness

The hidden workings and underpinning of meaningfulness depends on unconscious and pre-conscious connections between different aspects of experience. Thoughts accompanied by feelings, past memories linked with present experiences, the senses operating in concert to enrich one another, etc. These underlying networks are usually taken for granted, much like we take breathing, walking, or riding a bicycle for granted. We instinctively do it, or we learn to do it instinctively. These programmed connections laid down in early infantile life are unconscious; they enable communications to have depth and resonance, and enable us to feel things are convincing and make sense.

At around six months the infant discovers that there are other minds as well as his own and this organises an intersubjective perspective where mental states become the focus of meaningful relating (Stern, 1985). The infant seems to sense that he has an interior subjective life of his own and so do others. He becomes relatively less interested in external acts and more interested in the mental states that accompany them. He tries to effect the mother's direction of attention so that he can get her to share his own experience of excitement and pleasure. Trevarthen (2001) concludes from numerous studies of infant development that primary intersubjectivity, that is, the attention of mother and baby to each other, precedes secondary intersubjectivity where joint attention is given to a third object.

The absence or impairment of this underlying network that makes things meaningful presents a severe stress for the adult ego in someone who lacks this substrate, and creates huge difficulties in the transference and countertransference for both patient and analyst. The analytic difficulties in part repeat and reflect the difficulties that were posed for the fledgling infantile ego in its original faulty development.

Ego deficiencies

In a paradigm-changing series of papers (1957, 1959, 1962b) culminating in *Learning from Experience* (1962a), Bion studied adult individuals who lacked certain ego functions and this capacity for reciprocity. They could not tolerate anxiety or frustration and took measures to *evade* rather than modify unpleasant experience. Intolerable experiences together with *functions of the ego* were evacuated defensively, leaving parts of the mind unable to develop capacities for rudimentary thought, and with fundamental deficits in cognitive functioning and mental representation. More recently other authors such as Britton (1989, 2011); Botella & Botella (2005); Levine, Reed and Scarfone (2013) have taken up Bion's work and focused on the nature of psychic states that are largely unrepresented.

The early structuring of the infantile mind and how meaning is established is an extremely complex area and beyond the scope of this chapter. However, for the purposes of exploring Mrs A's difficulties, I want to focus on Freud's central paper that was a starting point for Bion's theory of thinking. In "Formulations on the two principles of mental functioning" Freud (1911b) points out that in normal infantile development the pleasure/unpleasure principle that strives towards gaining satisfaction draws back from and *evades* any event that might arouse unpleasure or frustration. He states;

> It was only the non-occurrence of the expected satisfaction; the disappointment experienced that led to the abandonment of this attempt at satisfaction by means of hallucination. Instead of it, the psychical apparatus had decided to form a conception of the real circumstances in the external world and to endeavour to make a real alteration in them. A new principle of mental functioning was thus introduced; what was presented in the mind was no longer what was agreeable but what was real, even if it happened to be disagreeable. This setting up of the reality principle proved to be a momentous step. (1911b, p. 219)

Crucially for my purposes he goes on to say:

> The increased significance of external reality heightened the importance, too, of the sense-organs that are directed towards that external world, and of the consciousness attached to them.

Consciousness now learned to comprehend sensory qualities in addition to the qualities of pleasure and unpleasure which hitherto had alone been of interest to it. A special function was instituted which had periodically to search the external world, in order that its data might be familiar already if an urgent internal need should arise—the function of attention. Its activity meets the sense-impressions half way, instead of awaiting their appearance. (1911b, p. 220)

In neurosis and psychosis one finds a mental turning away from reality because in part or in whole it is found to be unbearable. In Mrs A the function of attention that meets the sense-impressions halfway was crucially deficient. She appeared to lack curiosity and her external world lacked significance. Her experience appeared to be shallow because she removed herself from contact with her internal world in order to protect herself from overwhelming confusion.

Bion found Freud's ideas about the pleasure principle and the discharge of psychic tension indispensable to his model for the development of thought. Unlike Freud, he found that both the pleasure principle and the reality principle were present from birth rather than following developmentally, one from the other, and took this further in his idea of a psychotic part of the personality under the sway of the pleasure principle and a neurotic part of the personality influenced by the reality principle (Bion, 1957). The psychotic part of the personality hates both psychic and external reality, and opposes any move to the establishment of thinking that links them. Pre-proto-mental tension or what Freud called excessive accretions of stimuli are dealt with by evacuative action and evasion. The infant can achieve this by crying or through the use of muscular and expressive movement. In the case of Mrs A, as we shall see later, her incessant talking achieved the same end. It conveyed little meaning other than indicating the presence of raw unprocessed distress. What was evacuated through speech and breathing was either this unthinkable and hated psychic reality, or she used her speech as a verbal form of action to evade her inner reality; consequently, her personality was deprived of material for thought.

There are different groups of patients who have little expectation of being understood and have varying aetiologies (Britton, 1998). Some consciously seek intimacy (Halton, 2011) whilst others avoid deep contact at all cost and rarely seek psychological help. Others are in a lifelong search for cure and move from one idealised remedy to another. I think Mrs A belongs to this latter group, and I believe Klein was referring to these people when she observed that serious deprivations of good experiences in early infancy can lead to the illusory belief in the existence of a supremely good and idealised object (Klein, 1955, 1957).

It is not surprising then that patients with fundamental difficulties of this nature have enormous problems connecting to interpretations offered by the analyst to further the expansion of self-awareness. To be helpful, interpretations have to be accessible to the conscious experience of the patient and the patient must perceive the analyst as separate and motivated by benign intentions. But even if they are able to see the analyst as helpful there is an additional problem if the patient is phobic of her own inner workings and the chaos lurking within.

In thinking about the phenomenology of psycho-phobic patients, Britton (2013) has made a helpful distinction between Klein's notion of the death instinct as, (a) an inborn fear of annihilation arising from within, and, (b) an innate hostility to the outside word. Britton sees these as clinically separate entities: the former is a potential source of endogenous trauma; the latter is an aversion to otherness. Together or separately these may be exacerbated by actual exogenous trauma. Both are related to Freud's description of unpleasure caused by excessive accretions of stimuli. At one moment the patient feels the terrors threatening from within and at another it is clear the phobic reaction is to the external threat posed by the analyst.

These patients are chronically troubled and find basic issues like listening to interpretations directed to their inner workings, or being interested in what the analyst *has to say* hugely difficult. They appear to lack the appropriate reciprocity with their speaking partners that Stern (1985) observed in normal development. No matter how sensitively the analyst offers understanding, the patient instinctively fears insight because repressed or split-off memories also carry primitive states of terror.

If interpretations intended to give understanding are instinctively taken to be dangerous then it is clear they have to be ignored or neutered. Analysis is a danger zone for the patient, which has to be navigated with great care. Splitting and projective mechanisms designed to protect the ego from the return of painful experiences that have found some representation, (Bion's "alpha elements" and Freud's "return of the repressed"), are less rigidly structured compared to defensive mechanisms that operate to protect the ego from the emergence or imposition of confusion from unrepresented "beta elements" (Bion, 1962a). The former protect against unwanted pain but do not threaten the ego's very existence. The latter defences are needed to prevent onto-logical disaster to the ego from unknowable forces and annihilation. One might characterise the difference as between fear of envy, depres-sion, and loss, versus fear of crushing otherness, disintegration, and annihilation; the stakes are not comparable.

Chaos and annihilation were fundamental fears in Mrs A and fuelled an urgent campaign of false hope to find salvation through a mad omniscient form of knowing. "Knowing" in this sense was not a desir-able and pleasurable aspect of learning about life or an attempt to get at the truth but a desperate matter of life and death itself. Knowing was "a must have", a "possession", "a thing", not something that could be loved or cherished for itself; it was felt to be vital to her survival irre-spective of the cost of acquiring it!

The transference/countertransference phenomenon at times partly resembled patients who have been described as possessing Asperger-like qualities (Polmear, 2008). There was a disharmony between affect and intellect to the detriment of both. It took great effort to focus on what I was saying and to bring this together imaginatively with what was going on in her thoughts. However, her deficits in attention seemed closer to those seen in children with ADHD as interpretations were responded to more with a lack of recognition and/or active avoid-ance than the entrenched indifference one usually sees in Asperger and autistic states.

Clinical case: Mrs A

By the time of her second analysis Mrs A was 53 and living alone with her husband. Two of their children were married and the third study-ing abroad. She had a settled home life and was fond of her family but uncertain about her maternal abilities and constantly anxious that her lack of confidence would lead to some unspecified calamity. She was desperate to be seen as a good mother yet she derived limited pleasure from her children and was relieved they had left home. Similar worries plagued her about her work as a teacher and she was keen to take early retirement. Her husband seemed to be caring towards his family, but most of Mrs A's efforts seemed designed to anticipate his desires at the expense of relating to him or doing things together.

She appeared to be trapped in a state of mind that was anxious but incurious. She had imprecise, non-specific emotions and much that impinged on her awareness left an undifferentiated non-specific trace. In the early part of analysis she did not feel deep emotions, neither anger nor love. She moulded herself into whatever shape circumstance required and seemed to set aside her own opinions to allow others to have theirs. This was not running with the hares and hunting with the hounds, because she did not lie about what she thought; she simply had a way of calmly eliminating anything contrary in herself, hence her superficial graciousness.

Mrs A occasionally hinted at complaints if her husband pursued an interest such as bridge but she made no effort to join him. She often felt needy for something but anxious her suggestions would disappoint them both. One of the few activities she partly enjoyed with him was attending concerts; however, it seemed to me she was attending "his concerts" and her experience was sullied by drifting off. She rarely remembered the composers or the music and knowledge seemed to be acquired tangentially without going into things properly.

Reading was also difficult and she could reread the same passage many times over, becoming easily tired and losing interest. Like traumatised children, she could not pay close attention to detail, had difficulty maintaining attention and appeared not to listen easily. At times she showed impaired organisation of thought and seemed to strongly dislike any sustained mental effort. However, she was clearly bright and at other moments had no intellectual impairment. She was conscientious and guilt-ridden and worked hard to hide her difficulties, but her close family noticed her timidity and day-dreamy sluggishness, and saw how easily she could be discouraged and withdraw. She seemed to have some of the characteristics of the passive inattentive type of ADHD predominantly seen in girls (Myttas, 2009).

Background

Mrs A had a tragic beginning, which most likely had a significant impact on her impaired functioning. Her father was an intelligence officer in the US military during the Korean War. Her mother died in a car accident during a long journey trying to reach him whilst escaping from an advancing unit of the North Korean army. Barely twelve months old, she and her four-year-old sister survived the accident uninjured. She and her sister were nursed in a military hospital and then by nannies until father remarried a few years later and the family moved back to the USA. She accommodated her new stepmother but never really took to her like her older sister. She was "daddy's girl" but felt burdened by having to be her dead mother's representative, as she shared her dark complexion whilst her older sister was fair. She felt obliged to propitiate her father's melancholic and narcissistic needs and experienced him in some vague way as insatiable but felt it was vital to satisfy his wishes.

Her omnipotent view of herself as the idealised mother/provider reversed and reflected the traumatic early loss of her mother and the projection of her own infantile clamouring for survival. After marrying she felt anxious and mildly depressed and saw an analyst for several years before coming to settle in the UK with her husband and three children. Her analysis with me lasted thirteen years. She had no idea why her first analysis was unsuccessful; neither was she helped by various body-based therapies that she tried in order to experience emotions.

Analysis: first period: complacent accommodation

At our first meeting Mrs A told me, "I have difficulties in holding on to things and I find it's difficult to remember and reflect. I easily feel lost and flooded and go blank or empty. I think I've felt this way all my life."

Early on she found the analysis with me alive and challenging, and explicitly valued what she called my "lively approach". She compared this to the measured quality of her first analyst, who from her description rarely worked in the transference. However, beyond this she showed little interest in her first analysis. Her appreciation for my "lively approach" on the surface gave the appearance of a positive transference, if a little idealised. I thought it may have been linked with a lost mother who once provided some interesting and rewarding possibilities. Though I realised her problems were deeply rooted, I was also encouraged by her search for vitality.

However, as time went on, her analysis became a difficult undertaking. In spite of her strong desire to be understood, nothing I said really got through. I remember thinking that if we did an audit, the interpretations that gained her attention, let alone achieved a purchase on her emotions, would be in the region of less than 0.1 per cent! She never seemed to listen properly to me or herself and her thoughts were interchangeable like disposable refills.

In *Brazilian Lectures 1*, Bion notes

> Some patients cannot … listen to what they themselves say. They have no respect for what they already know so that their experience and knowledge are of no use to them. The question is not simply one of the relationship of the patient to the analyst but with the patient with himself which may be so bad that he cannot even make use of what he already knows. Nothing can be done about his unconscious knowledge because he can make no use of his conscious knowledge. (1973, p. 80).

Having tragically lost her mother at such an early age I thought Mrs A was desperate to be meaningful to someone, as she felt she had failed at some primary level and was now projecting this experience. Together we were enacting a number of irreconcilable paradoxes. She was coping with not feeling alive by making me carry the aliveness; I must not be a dying object but someone who satisfied all her needs; this was the converse of her attempts to be the idealised maternal object that could satisfy everybody else's needs. However, if I was the person who gave her something vital and useful, how could I also be the repository of her useless self, which she felt I clearly was? The solution seemed to be that I had to be her inadequate failing self that produced a miracle!

Analysis: middle period: "We must try harder!"

As the analysis proceeded my perceived liveliness waned and Mrs A was disappointed. I felt increasingly helpless, failing, and frustrated; I was tormented by not being able to pursue any enquiry or investigation. She felt my efforts to understand never provided "answers" or brought the relief that she fervently believed should be forthcoming. All I did was forever open up crippling uncertainty.

She blamed me, but mostly herself, for not conveying her thoughts well enough. As far as she was concerned we must both be more vigilant, to keep on, keeping on and try harder. She sought to be understood but could not understand. She needed me to keep trying but was not interested in the understanding I produced. I had to listen with rapt attention to an endless stream of ideas that she believed were essential to our endeavour. She seemed to greedily pursue something out of reach with an implacable determination. For my part her thoughts struck me as repetitious, and so generalised and superficial that the most striking feature was their patchwork surface. There was almost nothing "free" in her associations, only a highly organised and packaged kind of thinking. Yet I knew I must try to contain my helplessness and despair and wait for some clarity. It was some time before I realised that through her endless talk she was giving me indigestible *distress in a verbal form*, which was intended to unburden her psyche of accretions of stimuli as Freud described.

During this period however, I still thought the problem was how to get through to her and I constantly felt I was not grasping things properly. I made renewed efforts to understand her better or find pithier, more direct ways of framing interpretations. Once or twice I unwittingly got caught up in trying to find some bunker-busting interpretation that would penetrate her reinforced concrete of impermeability. Only after many failed attempts at a variety of more sensitive approaches did I come to realise the problem lay with not really understanding her inability to use her mind. There was a frustrated enquirer and an uncomprehending witness and at any given moment one of us could be in either role. As her thoughts had no resonance and lacked overtones or undertones of meaning they had little capacity to evoke a train of thought in me except compliance. I did not yet grasp that we were enacting a fundamental psychic problem. Mrs A's inflexible psychic structure required that I fit in with her and when reversed through projective identification it left her feeling she had to slavishly accommodate to me.

As interpretations necessarily went beyond what Mrs A had consciously thought and said, she felt I used interpretations to impose my thinking, believing them to be proof positive that I had not listened to her properly. Imprisoned, I slowly learned firsthand through my countertransference how Mrs A was imprisoned by her own handicaps. She had an urgent need to regulate herself and therefore was not open to learning from the outside world. She felt bombarded with sensation and exhausted by it, and had to withdraw, even when alone quietly reading. However, she was convinced that I must supply endless albeit meaningless interpretations to aid in this regulation; if I was quiet in a session it meant I withheld my ideas for good or bad strategic reasons.

At this stage the idea that I simply might not have something to say, or there were things to which there were no answers, was not just unacceptable but totally unbelievable! Analysis had to be the repository of manic hope because she could not feel anything with real conviction.

Being ignored by Mrs A was the counterpoint to having one's existence recognised. My countertransference experience was often either deadness or exasperation. The trouble was that Mrs A had exactly the same experience when I made an interpretation that made sense to me; she then felt ignored, deadened, or exasperated. She regaled me, saying, "You must say something that's useful otherwise there is no hope and how can we continue without hope? I know you understand more than you say!" When she felt a session was a failure there was always tomorrow. Endless talking created the illusion of endless presence, like the background noise of a radio playing. The reality of my *actual* presence had no real relevance and I wondered, would I be noticed if I fell asleep or left the room? Her pleasure-seeking ego was drawn to the sun on her body with its mind-bleaching effects and her favourite radio programme was *Smooth Classics*. Sex too was a means to enter a dreamy, seamless, autoerotic state.

Whether she talked in a frantic or soporific way, I could never find someone in the room to speak with. If she talked rapidly I trailed behind, muddled, and as I puzzled over something, she had moved on. The picture of a baby came to mind frantically trying to relate to an indiscernible presence. When she spoke in a slow breathy way her speech had a sing song quality that seemed self-soothing and reminded me of the pre-speech, musical noises of a neonate (Marwick & Murray, 2010). Unfortunately, as little of what I said held her interest she insisted, "I need to tell you everything in my mind then you will get it!"

I would like to illustrate how talking metaphorically to Mrs A was nearly always a technical mistake, as she took elements concretely and became confused at the incompatibility or the juxtaposition of our respective ideas. For example, one Monday she reported that alarming noises had been coming from her car. After some time I said, "I think you have had a number of alarming worries going round inside you over the weekend." She instantly replied, "But I am not mechanical;, I don't think like a car engine!"

We later clarified that it was not the perceived insult of being compared to a machine that had really disturbed her but my move from her concrete concern about her car to her internal mental state which had caused the confusion and panic. My curiosity about whether there was an untoward noise that was also felt as something coming alive and attacking her from inside could not be allowed to have meaning. In a calmer moment I tried another approach and asked if she was worried she wouldn't get to her session or return safely home. Was she anxious her mind or the mind of her analyst had malfunctioned? Or were the noises signalling that the weekend separation had been a car crash and she wondered where her lost mother/analyst was? But it was impossible to establish a shared focus of attention to consider any of these thoughts.

On another occasion Mrs A brought a dream where she was preoccupied with a yellow dress. I linked this to another element in the dream to do with bananas. From previous material I knew her associations to bananas were linked with a phallic father and a memory of childhood luxury, the dress to a time of secret rebellion and sexual awakening as a young woman. The colour yellow also featured in her conscious thoughts and was the colour of my consulting room walls. I said, "It seems in the dream that the colour yellow is linked in your mind to something like forbidden fruit." I intended my comment to be tentative and preliminary to opening up the dream. She replied sincerely, "What you say doesn't make sense; the forbidden fruit in the bible was an apple, and anyway, apples are mostly green and red!"

The effort to seek meaning is normally a powerful integrating drive but instead Mrs A had a powerful need to force ideas together or keep them apart. Integration seemed beyond her and she could only make muddled amalgams. Her predicament reminded me of a small toddler failing to place three-dimensional shapes, triangles, squares, etc., into a box with corresponding holes. Mrs A resorted to force, gave up in frustration, or had a chance success. Our problem was that the failing toddler/patient did not seem to learn from trial and error, and the toddler/analyst was slow to grasp that interpretations directed at understanding the metaphorical meanings of things was futile.

Waiting and bearing something in the countertransference before speaking, or waiting tuntil Mrs A seemed more receptive, was not a way forward, as her mental states moved so quickly that we had no experience I could point too. I often felt that by the time I had reached the end of an interpretation, even a simple sentence, what I was addressing had disappeared and my words hung in the air. Keeping things simple and addressing limited aspects of the patient who was present was no easy matter as a cast change could be accomplished in a nanosecond.

We existed under a constant tyranny of superego "shoulds": she should try harder and be a better patient; I should be a better analyst; everything should be resolvable. This was linked with a deep sense of shame as she believed things went wrong because she was inadequate and possessed some hidden flaw. Helplessness was a moral imperfection and could be fixed by more effort. Her self-esteem required the absence of anxiety, and she was constantly guilty and ashamed. Many times she protested, "But isn't analysis meant to change me?" Inevitably, we were on a collision course!

Tortuous cohabitation

There was an important change when Mrs A moved from accommodating to feeling more openly persecuted. I came to see that my so called vitality was conferred on me to ensure I colluded with her illusions of hope. The traumatic horror that lay behind her "hope" and "need to know" was conveyed very movingly by one of her dreams:

> A baby dressed in pink is in a large hospital ward/church with beds all around with motionless people in them. A floaty female figure in white, possibly a nurse, comes towards the baby with a bottle—or is it a syringe? As this figure approaches the baby's mouth the baby turns her head away and seems frightened—will she be poisoned? Some priests or monks enter dressed in black performing some menacing ritual but then their bodies dematerialise leaving only their clothes to take on their human shape. The baby is frantically moving its head from side to side and has a bloated tummy and its eyes are rolling in a mad way.

Increasingly, the sessions were full of panic. I began to grasp that although her dream was meaningful, most of her deepest experiences were not representable in words and when verbal means failed, action then followed by means of evacuative speech. However, talking was also starting to fail her and daily sessions became indispensable to deal with the increasingly severe trials of life. Every session began with some worry or other. A shop had a closing down sign—had the business gone bust? What would become of the owners? A broken child's play watch, in the street—should she leave it on a wall or ask the neighbours if they recognised it? She prepared a meal and made herself ill eating every last morsel. Feeling she did not get anything substantial from analysis led to an intrusive greedy attempt to acquire something by other means. She wanted to borrow magazines from my waiting room and was very upset when I tried to explore what this might mean rather than just agree. What was the problem if she returned the magazine the next day?! After most sessions she ate to quell the feeling of emptiness.

Just before a summer break Mrs A spoke about not being able to throw a dry crust of bread away, but my interpretation that she had lost her mother and her world had collapsed so early in infancy that nothing could be allowed to be lost again—not analysis over the break, nor a crust of bread—brought little acknowledgement. Sometimes she could feel a faint recognition if I used the word haunted rather than missing. I wondered, did her mother die before she could ever truly love anyone or know what missing felt like, and now could she only register the haunting presence of an absence?

At this period she was driven by having to know, as she felt knowing was the means to terminate the awfulness of not knowing. If she could know, she could fix things, and repudiate the menacing thought that some things were irreparable. It was as if she was defiantly determined to stay alive at all cost; survival was what mattered, not to what end or by what means. It was as if we were dealing with a biological drive beyond thought.

The fate of interpretations

It is worth broadly describing the various fates of my interpretations, Mrs A's responses and the defensive structures they revealed.

There were instances when the moment I spoke, the evidence (i.e., the presence of some palpable emotion) on which I based my observations vanished in a flash. I came to understand this as a psychic flight, a phobic response to perceived danger of being invaded and poisoned, as in the dream, and the immediate confusion as to whether I was benign or malevolent.

At other times interpretations were instantly smothered with her own excited thoughts that barely related to what I had said. It was as if *attending* to something that came from me was unbearable. This kind of reaction had both a defensive and competitive component, the verbal equivalent of the familiar children's game where two or more people cover each other's hand with their own and this is repeated until the hand at the bottom of the pile moves to the top again. My interpretations seemed to threaten to obliterate her thinking and vice versa; it seemed vital therefore that she stay on top and have the last word.

The immediacy of what I said went unnoticed and all she heard were repetitions of previous comments so nothing was new. She half listened to words she recognised or took the opening words without waiting to find out what I was saying. It was as if her thoughts were the essential lifeline. She frequently repeated words or fragments of interpretations from previous sessions but the original sense was lost or the remembered ideas were meaningless and inappropriate to the new context in which she forcibly placed them. Her focus was on disjointed details rather than meaningful wholes.

Specific words could haunt her; what had I meant when I said: "You are worried"? Why had I said "worried" when I had previously said she was "anxious"? Mrs A asked me not to confuse her and pleaded that I speak in a less obscure manner. In moments of desperation she looked up the meaning of words like "sadness" and "anger" in the dictionary.

The repetitive talking also acted like a drug that had a terrible hold on her. Like the baby in the dream she repeatedly turned her head away and kept her mind in constant movement; otherwise I thought she would be overwhelmed by the endogenous trauma of her bloated mad state. When insight did occasionally break through it agitated her and left her feeling out of control. It came unbidden in a momentary flash that was not coherent and could not be firmly grasped. Insights were like bits and pieces of alarm that were lost as soon as they appeared. She could not fathom that understanding was a process.

Endogenous threat verses exogenous threat

There were times when it was clear she felt the menace did not come from me but from within herself and her frantic talk was an effort to keep something emerging from the depths. She trembled with panic, and her experience seemed on the border between a psychic and somatic event. These brief glimpses of a terrifying inner presence helped me understand why she had such a lack of desire to think something through. She was in the grip of a basic fear that Winnicott (1945) has aptly called "not going on being". Inside was an unspeakable chaos that seemed to be a –K internal world without a stable body ego or differentiated environment. It was as if these basic differentiations were never properly established before her mother's death.

In response to the increasing loss of equilibrium, the next phase to follow was rather bullish. Argument took over as the preferred method to evade internal chaos. Her previous hypersensivity hid reserves of stubborn determination to defend herself. If I began an interpretation with "I wonder if ..." this signalled the poison to come and she broke in with some comment. Unable to reconstruct what I had just said, we both got lost in a labyrinth of words. When I managed to slow things down and reconstruct what had just taken place between us, she felt I was just demonstrating that I could think clearly. What use was this to her as she could not understand what I said so she was still left in a muddle? An alternative reaction might be: "I know that," or, "OK, you're right," followed by, "but how does that help me?" The transference/counter-transference dynamic seemed to me insoluble; she couldn't listen to me and she felt I never listened to her! I tried to catch myself before being ironic as I am sure it was an expression of my impotence and impatience but more importantly because she had difficulty in reading my intentions and took me literally.

She was desperate to be understood but what was I to understand by her desire for understanding? Her version of listening seemed no more than one person hearing the other out before waiting to speak again.

Again I found Bion helpful as a guide. He writes:

> ... the patient must be shown that he has no interest in why he feels the way he does. Elucidation of the limited scope of his curiosity issues in the development of a wider range and incipient preoccupation with causes. (1959, p. 108)

Last period: bearing no hope and tolerating not knowing: the technique of description

The last period was more fruitful in establishing some semblance of a joint understanding but this too was painful and hard-won. Mrs A's failures in symbolisation and her lack of curiosity about emotional relatedness seemed linked to an inability to mourn, but how could she mourn an object that was poorly or incompletely represented. As I have noted, interpretations of content or past-to-present links rarely achieved any useful purpose. Links between different themes or ideas, or between similar experiences at different moments in the same session were also for a long time rarely successful. She had difficulty seeing emotional situations from perspectives other than her own and lacked what Britton (1998) has called the "third position", or the capacity to observe herself whilst being herself. There was certainly no gain in trying to talk about different parts of her as she was only conscious of her immediate state and this approach would have confused matters further.

As my understanding of her trauma increased, I realised the manner and focus of my interpretation needed to change. Helpful interpretative work had to be based on simple descriptions of immediate experience to have a chance of being heard and taken in. This meant avoiding the pitfall of becoming an authority on her unconscious while having no partner to share my discoveries with. It was only the emotional atmosphere that existed in any contact between us that would make the difference, along with the consistency daily sessions provided.

Repeatedly describing the predicament we were in, where we were unable to find a way to listen or understand each other, brought some recognition of concern and did manage to catch her attention from time to time. For example, after one difficult, prickly interaction I said, "How painful it is that you feel you can't reach me and you feel I can't reach you, in spite of us both trying so hard!" This led to a fleeting change in the atmosphere from persecution to sadness and regret.

Earlier in analysis Mrs A's belief was that by telling me everything in her mind I would assemble it into sense but what I needed to interpret was her dread of senselessness, of the random unknowable non-sense of the child's lost watch or the shops closing down, the terrible loss of something that could barely be remembered or the mutual incomprehension that so often took hold between us. It might please me to find symbolic meaning in these events but even if there was real meaning it could scarcely reach and comfort Mrs A when what she really needed to know was that I could bear not knowing.

Comfort of sorts came when I addressed the restrictions in her mental functioning so she could slowly observe these problems in herself. By sustaining interest in the barrenness of her world and not trying to go beyond it, she slowly came to believe I had a genuine interest in getting to know her. She was relieved to be unburdened by the needs of others: father had needed her to replace his dead wife; stepmother had needed acceptance as a replacement mother; her husband needed a companionable wife; her children needed a contented mother; and her analyst had needed a patient who could develop.

The more I found ways to sympathetically analyse her limitations the more small steps we made. For example, one Monday session she came into the consulting room and noticed the wastepaper basket by my desk was full of tissues. She lay down on the couch and after a pause said with considerable alarm, "The basket is full of tissues!" After another pause, her mood calmed and she continued more intellectually, "Maybe something happened to the cleaning lady and she didn't come." I had in my mind that during the preceding Friday session she had been worried her difficulties in listening wore me down. I also knew she was worried about her stepmother's illness and felt guilty at not being kinder. She was worried she would be left burdened with her elderly father if her stepmother died. However, I mentioned none of this and instead said: "I think you were frightened because when you saw the wastepaper basket full it came as a shock. You didn't expect it and you didn't know why. It didn't make sense and it scared you." She replied: "Yes but do you have a cold?" I remained silent. "I don't know if you're ill, but the cleaning lady must have come because the waiting room looks tidy." I then said: "What really frightened you was being confronted with something that didn't have a clear answer and it threw you into confusion and panic." She said she felt tearful but did not know why because I had a kind tone in my voice. She went on: "I have never been able to really let go of my feelings, really cry, I don't think I ever will, no matter how much I trust you!"

We were both moved by this moment. She could not conceive of letting go because it was not just linked with being ridiculed for losing control of her feelings but of losing control of her mind, her urine her faeces, and complete psychosomatic disintegration.

Complete trust is what Mrs A really wanted, but she was looking for a wholly benign figure that could never exist. Once the reality principle is accepted, things are what they are, but never completely, never 100 per cent.

The wastepaper bin incident, in which my interpretations focused on her mood and the atmosphere between us, helped her recognise her own experience and feel I was alongside her. If I had made interpretations about the meaning of her phantasy, even though there were unconscious phantasies to this effect, of making me ill on the Friday, or if I had taken up with her that I was the burdensome ill father in the transference who had no cleaning lady/wife and needed her to look after me, I think it might have been correct but it would have been heard as intellectual ideas and not reached her emotionally because of her psycho-phobic state.

As we gained understanding about the fears of her inner life, interpretations that were primarily *exploratory* rather than *explanatory* could be tolerated a bit more. However they had to be concise, patient-centred interpretations (Steiner, 1993) about her immediate subjective perceptions because at a deep level everything I said was to some extent a disturbance. Irrespective of her conscious mood, there was a jumpiness in her that was almost never absent. It was often necessary to follow an interpretation with another about how she had experienced the first interpretation and how she viewed the effect on her of what she thought I was doing. These technical adjustments helped but it would be misleading to suggest they resolved much; progress was pitifully slow and hard-won. As her functioning was pretty patchy it was very important to observe and catch the brief moments when she was able to use her mind.

Conclusion

It took some time to realise that my approach to analysing Mrs A as if she was object related did not take into account her profound developmental difficulties. What she was primarily *doing* in the sessions was to sustain a failing sense of self using talk as a form of projective identification. Talking was:

> ... an employment of the *musculature* to disencumber the personality of thoughts. (Bion, 1962a, p. 83)

Her profound resistance defended against a recapitulation of an equally profound traumatic past. Her turning away from understanding like the baby in the dream was her way of protecting herself from the exogenous and endogenous traumas of feeling overwhelmed by primitive dreads and terrors. Mrs A's psycho-phobia left her unable to develop a meaningful sense of self with which she could feel her own desires properly and recognise her personal wishes. Hence she could rarely recognise a sense of missing someone or something or experience the emotional impact from a concert she attended. She was convinced from the start she was a disappointment and this narcissistic disaster was defended against by shunning contact and potential trauma.

Tragically, Mrs A had little recognition of a mother's voice in her beginnings and she was disinterested for a long time about what her inner world had to say. This extended to her lack of curiosity about the external world in general, such as who authored a book, who composed a piece of music, or what her analyst had to say.

If I spoke and expected her to listen, I either stole her self-experience or she was subject to a poisonous injection. Moreover, if feelings of shame were uppermost she could not accept any interpretation because however true she felt it might be, my interpretive voice was felt to crush her own ideas and I was experienced as demanding a humiliating submission. Because Mrs A used her mind largely to evacuate distress and evade understanding she was prone to instinctively believe everyone else did the same. If I made an interpretation it was to retaliate, that is, to rid myself of what she had projected. This was such a deep conviction that she was not envious of my good qualities but what appeared to be my privileged position as the analyst to interpret and project with impunity.

Her form of speech revealed the very early, projective processes described by Freud, and when this failed a paranoid system developed to defend deeper chaotic id forces that had no representational content or were at best poorly represented. However, describing this situation sometimes led to momentary productive exchanges. The real hope was for me to experience and contain the full calamity of her fundamental psychic reality, and I think this was what enabled real development. Painfully, we were able to move from "we can understand" to "we must understand" to "we can only understand the best we can". Near the end of her analysis she brought a very moving dream:

> I was swimming with a little girl and holding her hand tightly. Then the water changed into sewage with shit and debris everywhere. I sank down, clutching the girl, and we went under but both managed to surface again, shaken, feeling sick but alive.

Her association was to a very long car trip: she had felt sick most of the time but managed to finish the journey because in case of an emergency there was a sick-bag. She said she could not have done it without knowing the sick-bag was available otherwise she would have panicked.

I think the very long analytic trip we did together helped her recognise her sickness and the need for support from an external container. The analytic car journey could be survived, unlike the original one where her mother had died.

The death of hope was linked with the acceptance of a tragedy that had no remedy. At first this could not be faced or mourned because it was felt to spell the death of the self and the known world. I suspect the trauma of her mother's actual death was confused with traumas or ruptures occurring earlier in infancy when there was no proper differentiation of self and object and these experiences were unrepresented in the psyche. In the place of knowledge acquired through experience Mrs A had "manic hope". However, her "hope" was an empty substitute for real belief or trust. Her traumas occurred before the capacity to symbolise adequately had been established and she therefore had an impaired capacity to daydream or fantasise. Her early life experiences were too overwhelming to be processed and *in extremis* she retreated into a psychic world furnished with ideas that had a strange literalness and inflexibility. She was full of good intentions but her hope was meant to fill a gap of nothingness or worse.

Mrs A was chronically anxious all her life and through her analysis she discovered this. Analysis did not fully remedy her anxieties but it did provide some helpful continuity, there was a coming to terms of sorts, and a sadness and appreciation of what remained. Before her second analysis hardly anything could be relinquished. Manic hope and determination seem to be the twin pillars upon which daily life was ordered. By the end we were both able to accept the second version of the King Canute story that gave recognition to reality. We faced our respective limits as analyst and patient, the limits of psychoanalysis and the limits imposed by the reality principle. Understanding brought disappointment, not the transformation she wanted, but it did bring some relief and it did afford limited solace.

Convincing movement occurred when Mrs A began to understand her own involvement in situations and how she could not stop defending herself or hearing everything as of no value, as life itself must have felt after her mother's death. The crucial step was not that she managed to prevent this happening but that she could observe herself being unable to do so. This is what I refer to in my chapter subtitle as "small steps towards reality", perhaps I should really have said "giant steps towards reality" because for Mrs A that is what they really were. She had begun to understand her own involvement in our relationship and to accept its limitations.

Freud wrote:

> The patient must find the courage to direct his attention to the phenomena of his own illness. His illness itself must no longer seem to him contemptible but must become an enemy worthy of his mettle, a piece of his personality which has solid ground for its existence. (Freud, 1914g, p. 152)

I'm not sure Mrs A no longer saw herself as contemptible, but she did develop a concern for herself that could spare her from the most extreme aspects of her critical superego. I think she did better than to see her illness as the enemy and came to accept it as a sad misfortune.

I would like to thank Ron Britton for his helpful comments on this case.

References

Bion, W. R. (1957). Differentiation of the psychotic from the non-psychotic personalities. In: *Second Thoughts*. London: Maresfield, Reprinted Karnac.

Bion, W. R. (1959). Attacks on linking. In: *Second Thoughts*. London: Maresfield, reprinted Karnac.

Bion, W. R. (1962a). *Learning from Experience*. London: Maresfield, reprinted Karnac.

Bion, W. R. (1962b). A theory of thinking. In: *Second Thoughts* (p. 80). London: Maresfield, reprinted Karnac.

Bion, W. R. (1974). *Brazilian lectures: Volume 1: Sao Paulo* (Ed., J. Salomao). Rio de Janeiro: Imago Editora Ltda.

Birksted-Breen, D. (1996). Phallus, penis, and mental space. *International Journal of Psychoanalysis, 84*: 1501–1515.

Botella, C., & Botella, S. (2005). *The Work of Figurability: Mental States Without Representation*. London: Routledge.

Britton, R. (1989). The missing link: Parental sexuality in the Oedipus complex. In: *The Oedipus Complex Today* (pp. 83–101). London: Karnac.

Britton, R. (1998). Subjectivity, objectivity and triangular space. In: *Belief and Imagination* (pp. 41–58). London: Routledge.

Britton, R. (2011). The pleasure principle, the reality principle and the uncertainty principle. In: C. Mawson (Ed.), *Bion Today* (pp. 64–80). London: Routledge.

Britton, R. (2013). External danger and internal threat. In: E. McGinley & A. Varchevker (Eds.), *Enduring Trauma through the Life Cycle* (pp. 85–101). London: Karnac.

Freud, S. (1911b). Formulations on the two principles of mental functioning. *S. E., 12*: 213–216. London: Hogarth.

Freud, S. (1914g). Remembering, repeating and working through. *S. E., 12*: 145–156. London: Hogarth.

Halton, M. (2011). Phobic attachments: Internal impediments to change. In: J. Arundale & D. B. Bellman (Eds.), *Transference and Countertransference: A Unifying Focus of Psychoanalysis* (pp. 129–156). London: Karnac.

Klein, M. (1952). Some theoretical conclusions regarding the emotional life of the infant. In: *The Writings of Melanie Klein, Volume 3*. London: Hogarth, 1975.

Klein, M. (1955). On identification. In: *The Writings of Melanie Klein, Volume 3*. London: Hogarth, 1975.

Klein, M. (1957). Envy and gratitude, In: *The Writings of Melanie Klein, Volume III*. London: Hogarth 1975.

Levine, H. B., Reed, G. S., & Scarfone, D. (2013). *Unrepresented States and the Construction of Meaning: Clinical and Theoretical Contributions*. London: Karnac.

Marwick, H. M., & Murray, L. (2010). The effects of maternal depression on the "musicality" of infant-directed speech and conversational engagement. In: S. Mallock & C. Trevarthen (Eds.), *Communicative Musicality: Exploring the Basis of Human Companionship* (pp. 281–300). Oxford: Oxford University Press.

Myttas, N. (2009). Gender disparities: Adolescent girls with ADHD. *ADHD in Practice, l*: 8–11.

Polmear, C. (2008). Finding the bridge: Psychoanalysis with two adults with autistic features. In: K. Barrows (Ed.), *Autism in Childhood and Autistic Features in Adults* (pp. 279–301). London: Karnac.

Steiner, J. (1993). *Psychic Retreats*. London: Routledge.

Stern, D. (1985). *The Interpersonal World of the Infant: A View from Psychoanalysis and Developmental Psychology*. New York: Basic.

Trevarthen, C. (2001). Intrinsic motives for companionship in understanding: Their origin, development, and significance for infant mental health. *Infant Mental Health Journal, 22*: 95–131.

Winnicott, D. W. (1945). Primitive emotional development. *International Journal of Psychoanalysis, 36*: 137–143.

CHAPTER SEVEN

Shades of doubt: scepticism, cynicism, and fundamentalism

Simon Archer

"The fundamental cause of the trouble is that ... the stupid are cocksure while the intelligent are full of doubt."

—*Bertrand Russell*, 1931, p. 28
(Kind permission for printing this quote granted by
the Publishers Taylor & Francis. The copyright is held
by the Bertrand Russell Peace Foundation Ltd.)

My analytic work has led me to an interest in the way that conscious and unconscious doubt may be played out and interpreted within the transference and countertransference. I have treated a number of very anxious patients who have been wracked with doubt. They were either full of self-doubt or besieged by doubt of their objects. A question arose: Was their self-doubt actually doubt of the object? Which came first, self-doubt or object-doubt? Freud's "Mourning and melancholia" (1917e) would suggest that self-doubt is actually object-doubt where the doubted object is "taken in" and becomes part of the self. I began to separate out in my mind two sorts of patient. One group presented with manifest conscious doubt. Extremely anxious, they were able to describe their helplessness in the face of acute or chronic doubt, for example, in situations of job or partner choice, or in other situations where procrastination dominated. The other group seemed to be wracked with shameful doubt at an unconscious level but defended against this by various means such as denial or omnipotence. This severely restricted their lives or damaged their relationships.

I have come to think of a spectrum of doubt from ordinary, constructive scepticism through to total, destructive doubt. Doubt, in the form of scepticism is the essence of scientific and artistic intellectual enquiry. We instinctively lick and taste strange food before we eat it. In infancy this proto-scepticism helps survival. To be human is to doubt. Doubt of one's own absolute certainty is central to democracy. To be inhuman is to abolish doubt. At the destructive end of the spectrum there is cynicism. In this state of mind there is envious mistrust and doubt of everything and everyone, constantly voiced in the form of denigration. This is associated with fragile "know-all" omnipotence. The degree of denigration betrays the amount of repressed but nagging self-doubt. Also located at this extreme is the total abolition of doubt. This is what underlies a fundamentalist state of mind dominated by the need to abolish a potentially traumatic sense of doubt. Doubt is a dire threat to fundamentalist systems. Denial, splitting, and paranoid projection are used to force any hint of shameful, doubt-inducing failure into others. This is obvious in fascist political systems, in which any open expression of doubt may lead to imprisonment, torture, or execution.

In his landmark study of obsessionality, Freud's "Rat Man" is besieged by doubt:

> The *doubt* corresponds to the patient's internal perception of his own indecision, which, in consequence of the inhibition of his love by his hatred, takes possession of him in the face of every intended action. The doubt is in reality a doubt of his own love—which ought to be the most certain thing in his whole mind; and it becomes diffused over everything else, and is especially apt to become displaced on to what is most insignificant and small. A man who doubts his own love may, or rather *must*, doubt every lesser thing. (Freud, 1909d, p. 241)

Freud's explanation of the patient's neurosis is that it is due to the repression of his oedipal aggression. However, the explanation for why one person might develop such a serious disturbance and another might not surely depends on the preceding conflicts that block oedipal development. Freud's idea that doubt of one's own love *must* imply a doubt of everything, of the whole world and everything in it, is central to pathological doubt across a spectrum from neurotic doubt through to the chronic doubt that is at the heart of more severe personality disorders.

In her paper "A contribution to the psychogenesis of manic-depressive states", Klein (1935) discusses an early sense of doubt linked to feelings of unworthiness. Due to splitting there is within the infant's mind, alongside the attacked and damaged maternal object, a compensatory *"beautiful picture"* of the mother (p. 270). Klein says that the child "knows" this is only a picture. The actual mother is experienced as dangerous, damaged, or damaging. The infant doubts its capacity to repair and restore the maternal object damaged by its attacks. Anxieties created by this doubt are defended against by means of manic omnipotence, which assures control and mastery of the dangerous doubt and dangerous objects. The infant uses the beautiful picture of the idealised, intact mother as a replacement for the anxiety-inducing, attacked, and damaged object. In so doing, the infant becomes at one with the beautiful object. I see this as a description of a chain of psychic events. Failure and unworthiness first induce shame. This creates acute or chronic doubt, which in turn induces various defences. Klein's paper is suffused with the idea of doubt. This chain of cause and effect, as I have suggested elsewhere, places shame and doubt at the absolute centre of manic-depression in adult patients (Archer, 2005). Such patients try to abolish chronic unconscious doubt. They must not fail in any enterprise. They drive themselves to over-achieve, and erect a vast, ramshackle dam against self-doubt and shame. The slightest failure, any actual or imagined setback, causes the dam to fail and a torrent of traumatic self-doubt to crash in. Klein's idea about the early origin of doubt is useful whether or not one agrees with her cataclysmic view of the early internal world of the infant. Klein asserts that guilt develops very early. I see the struggles with success, failure, shame, and doubt as preceding later guilt. Nevertheless, Klein's template helps us understand both ordinary, neurotic states of doubt and more severe forms of disturbance found in adults.

Doubt and its link with shame

In Freud's writing the word shame occurs more often than the word guilt but he did not incorporate shame into his theories despite referring to it more than once in his early writing as a cause of neurotic distress:

> In traumatic neuroses the operative cause of the illness is not the tri-fling physical injury but the affect of fright—the psychical trauma. In an analogous manner, our investigations reveal, for many, if not for most, hysterical symptoms, precipitating causes which can only be described as psychical traumas. Any experience which calls up distressing affects—such as those of fright, anxiety, shame or physi-cal pain—may operate as a trauma of this kind. (1895d, pp. 5–6)

Freud moved away from the seduction-trauma theory of neurosis, and so, in conformity with psychoanalytic orthodoxy, other psychoanalysts did not take up his early thoughts about shame as a traumatising affect. The subject of shame became for the most part neglected. In his book *Childhood and Society*, Erikson (1950) took up shame and doubt as impor-tant developmental issues but his work was regarded as marginal. Rycroft, in his *Critical Dictionary of Psychoanalysis* (1968), tried unsuc-cessfully to draw attention to the continuing neglect of shame. In the 1980s Warren Kinston published three important papers on shame and narcissism, but as with Erikson's work they did not attract the atten-tion they deserved (Kinston, 1980, 1982, 1983). In *Childhood and Society*, Erikson described a phase of development, "autonomy versus shame and doubt", in which the child struggles with dependency and help-lessness. Erikson's thinking was rooted in Freudian orthodoxy:

> Doubt is the brother of shame. Where shame is dependent on the consciousness of being upright and exposed, doubt, so clinical observation leads me to believe, has much to do with a conscious-ness of having a front and a back—and especially a "behind". For this reverse area of the body, with its aggressive and libidinal focus in the sphincters and in the buttocks, cannot be seen by the child, and yet it can be dominated by the will of Mothers. The "behind" is the small being's dark continent, an area of the body which can be magically dominated and effectively invaded by those who would attack one's power of autonomy and who would designate as evil those products of the bowels which were felt to be all right when they were being passed. This basic sense of doubt in whatever one has left behind forms a substratum for later and more verbal forms

of compulsive doubting; this finds its adult expression in paranoiac fears concerning hidden persecutors and secret persecutions threatening from behind (and from within the behind). (Erikson, 1950, p. 245)

Echoing Freud's paper on Schreber's paranoia (1911c), Erikson places the origin of the shame/doubt phase in the anal phase. He linked the characteristics arising out of the shame/doubt stage with muscular development and bowel control, and associated this phase with experiences of success and failure, helplessness and mastery, potency and impotence. This view was in keeping with Freud's idea that shame appears during the anal phase as a defence against exhibitionism, as a "dam against sexual excess" (1905d, p. 191). However, there are several places in Freud's writing where he describes shame not as a defence but as a signal of anxiety due to a sense of deficiency or failure. For example, in his study "Femininity" (1933a) he describes the shame associated with penis envy as being due to a sense of lack or deficiency. In his account of the Wolf Man, Freud does not use the word shame but he describes the patient's seduction as "offensive to the patient's masculine self-esteem" (1918b, p. 20), and proposes that his aggressive fantasies about his sister are a passive into active compensation designed to efface shameful memory traces. Shame here is not a defence but an anxiety state, giving rise to secondary, defensive aggression. A feeling of inferiority is an emotional response, not a defence. Feelings of inferiority and shame go together. Freud noticed that, "A child feels inferior if he notices that he is not loved, and so does an adult" (1933a, p. 65). Notably, in the same lecture Freud discusses the two mental states of inferiority and guilt: "Little attention has been given in psycho-analysis to the question of the delimitation of the two concepts" (ibid., p. 66). Like Freud's, Erikson's discussion of shame hovers between the two ideas of defence and anxiety signal. He describes shame as a defence against anal preoccupations but the following also depicts shame as an emotional state signalling acute anxiety about dislocated narcissism:

> Shame is an emotion insufficiently studied, because in our civilisation it is so early and easily absorbed by guilt. Shame supposes that one is completely exposed and conscious of being looked at: in one word, self-conscious. One is visible and not ready to be visible; which is why we dream of shame as a situation in which

we are stared at in a condition of incomplete dress, in night attire, "with one's pants down". Shame is early expressed in an impulse to bury one's face, or to sink, right then and there, into the ground. But this, I think, is essentially rage turned against the self. He who is ashamed would like to force the world not to look at him, not to notice his exposure. He would like to destroy the eyes of the world. Instead he must wish for his own invisibility. (Erikson, 1950, p. 244)

Erikson's ideas, ignored for several decades, are important. He drew attention to a subject that struggled until the 1980s to find a place within psychoanalysis. He proposed that shame is obscured by guilt; he linked shame with doubt; he described the way that the resolution (or not) of the autonomy-shame/doubt conflict leaves an imprint within the person's character. He made a crucial link with the mother and her manner of handling the shame/doubt/autonomy conflict.

Shame, doubt, and failure are inextricably linked. Doubt threatens infantile omnipotence and provokes a sense of failure. Failure provokes shame. Excessive shame is intertwined with excessive doubt. This combination may then become a powerful component of a negative self-image. Shame is obvious in connection with the anal phase, which is why Freud and Erikson attributed its origins to that period. This supposition was not derived from infant or child observation but from the analysis of adults who, like the Rat Man, exhibited anal preoccupations. We need to look to earlier development for the origins of doubt and shame. Where, or when, do shame and doubt arise? Some researchers into infant development began to propose that shame arises early and before guilt in the form of "proto" shame as an evolutionary, instinctual response. I have outlined elsewhere ideas about shame arising out of an inevitable sense of failure that is "built in" to the human brain, and subsequently the mind, from the start and is there well before guilt (Archer, 1993, 2002, 2005; Demos, 1995; Nathanson, 1987, 1992; Trevarthen, 2004. See also Edelman, 1992). Shame is a sign of a disrupted sense of narcissistic balance and has its origins long before the anal phase.

Erikson's link to the influence of the parental environment led him to be regarded, like Ferenczi, as less than purely analytic because his views of development were not in keeping with Freud's turning away from the seduction/trauma theory. Ferenczi (1949) had tried to revive the idea of traumatic abuse but this was only partially accepted when it was revisited by Michael Balint (1979). Ferenczi's paper discusses the identity-confusion and self-doubt instilled by parents who rely on the child to contain their projections. Balint reinforced Ferenczi's assertion that interpretations that do not take account of the identification with an intrusive parental object will only repeat the early traumatic situation. Many of my patients suffering from chronic or acute doubt seemed to carry within them a sense of an early maternal object that dispensed love and care in a manner experienced as highly conditional upon the infant bolstering the mother's self-esteem. This creates a matrix of shameful doubt. This "original" doubt seems in these cases to have led to great difficulty negotiating later developmental stages, particularly the oedipal phase when it is quite normal for the child to face readjustment of a hitherto "magisterial" position in relation to the mother.

Doubt and the maternal environment

Analytic work in the transference and countertransference may reflect the way that the maternal environment mediates the phenomenon of universal doubt. The mother–infant matrix determines whether or not doubt becomes ordinary and useful or chronic and pathological. Because my office is near to a university, I have seen for analysis or psychoanalytic psychotherapy a number of young, very bright undergraduate and postgraduate women. They have shared certain characteristics. Each had become unable to study and all were besieged by grave self-doubt. All of them described their fathers in idealised terms, but also as needy and broken, and their mothers as arbitrary and demanding. These patients were very bright academically and reminded me of Freud's clever Anna O (1895d), the dedicated nurse of her ill father. (I believe it likely that the same kind of unconscious dynamics are present in some male cases, and indeed I have found this to be so, but of course the ways these dynamics are played out is different.)

One patient, Bianca, falls into the group who do not present with conscious, chronic self-doubt. Chronic self-doubt is unconscious and emerges into consciousness only after a period of analytic work. Its emergence may depend upon the analyst's capacity to detect it via monitoring it in the countertransference as it is projected. Bianca had disabling panic attacks during which she would speak rapidly, hyperventilate, and thrash around on the couch. She had periods of being unable to study or complete assignments due to what emerged as a fear of shameful failure and chronic self-doubt. She reported that her moody mother needed constant reassurance. Father was described as a sort of genius—a "broken man" who had sacrificed himself for her—but the picture of him in my mind was of an unreliable, self-centred figure. Bianca's early infancy seems to have been a time of poor attunement with a mother who needed baby Bianca's affection as a means of fending off her own self-doubts. The family atmosphere was one in which feelings were barely contained, processed, and understood. Instead they would erupt in the form of dramatic scenes.

In the early stages of treatment Bianca would often arrive in a dreadful state, excited or speaking inaudibly and rapidly. These dramatic, histrionic scenes would induce uncomfortable responses in me: I would imagine slapping her to bring her to her senses. I would then feel uncertain and doubt my ability to contain and help her. Once I had assimilated these difficult countertransference feelings it became possible to interpret her fear that I would not be able to cope with her. She immediately linked this with her basic belief that her mother could not cope. The indications were that as a baby her infant ego-needs had been unmet or only partially met. In this situation the baby's primitive, unprocessed affects are barely contained by the mother and are not transformed into potentially coherent, nameable emotions. The discharge of id wishes, *for both mother and baby*, becomes paramount. Bianca described repeated histrionic scenes at home in which family members became distraught, running from room to room pursued anxiously by others. No one seemed able to be alone. No one seemed to know how to deal with feelings without creating a scene and projecting anxiety into others. Bianca used compulsive text messaging in this way, a means of communication tailor-made for someone who cannot hold on, even for a few seconds, to unbearable feelings.

In Bianca's situation the infant becomes a vehicle or container for the mother's projected id needs. The necessity of being mother's soother creates a false intimacy between mother and child. The child learns that to avoid rejection she must falsify herself in order to please mother. The earliest aspects of this are not remembered but exist as later childhood memories of compliantly listening to mother's lamentations about her situation. This dynamic played itself out in the transference. While desperate for me to help her, Bianca did exactly the same to me. She would often talk non-stop without any apparent expectation that I would say anything useful. Identified with the mother, she described that she expected me to passively listen to her own lament. Her chronic doubt about my and her mother's ability to help ran in parallel with her idealised longing for someone to rescue her.

As a child Bianca thought of herself as mother's saviour and her younger sister's helper and rescuer—innocent and devoid of hostile thoughts. This is a saintly "false self". All hostile feelings towards mother or sister would be repressed and disavowed because they were confusing and frightening. From as far back as she could remember she had "adored" her father. Having experienced from the start a frustrating, highly conditional sort of care, dependent on the baby pleasing the mother, the pre-oedipal little girl makes a desperate switch. She turns precociously towards the father as an alternative source of satisfaction. Father makes himself available for this idealisation. As she developed into puberty, Bianca said there was "too much information", including sexual information from mother. She reported being both excited and disgusted by this. From the time she had her first menstrual period she became constantly preoccupied with sexual and romantic daydreams. At this point Bianca turned again to father. She threw herself into schoolwork as an escape from self-doubt. Top of the class at school, she became intellectually precocious but lacked any wisdom. Like Anna O, she was:

> … markedly intelligent, with an astonishingly quick grasp of things and penetrating intuition. She possessed a powerful intellect which would have been capable of digesting solid mental pabulum and which stood in need of it—though without receiving it after she had left school. She had great poetic and imaginative gifts, which were under the control of a sharp and critical common sense. Owing to this latter quality she was *completely unsuggestible*; she was only influenced by arguments, never by mere assertions. Her willpower was energetic, tenacious and persistent; sometimes it reached the pitch of an obstinacy which only gave way out of kindness and regard for other people. (Freud, 1895d, p. 21)

In patients such as Bianca this dogmatic cleverness has several purposes. It is aimed at pleasing the father, for whom the daughter is convinced she is very special. Father seems to go along with this by setting high academic targets for her and lavishing his approval upon her. The daughter believes that father values her above mother, who exacerbates this fantasy by providing derogatory information about the father. This misfires because it encourages the daughter to think that if mother does not really want father then she can have him. Her cleverness defeats all sibling rivals at school. It generates praise from teachers, and she is top of the class in everything. Crucially, it helps her triumph over self-doubt.

With Bianca these oedipal aspects emerged in the form of her wish to occupy the dominant place in my mind above all other rival patients. It became essential at various times for me to interpret her ruthless wish to make me worry about her and doubt her commitment when she would "forget" to arrive for a session. She might make a histrionic scene when she arrived, or attempt to punish me by making me jealous via suddenly arranging a meeting with an alternative professional. The most important aspect of this was her chronic underlying doubt that I had her in my mind in any meaningful way. In this frame of mind the only way the patient can ensure that she exists in the mind of the analyst is to force her way in by generating excitement and anxiety. The reassurance gained is fleeting because nagging doubt returns in the form of thoughts such as, "He is only paying attention because I made him do so." Bianca is attractive and has "no doubt" about her capacity to seduce any man but, as described by Khan, her relationships are a "cemetery of refusals" (1983, p. 34), each one starting with idealisation and rapidly ending in disappointment. Successful seduction temporarily triumphs over underlying doubt about the ability to get what is really needed, but this doubt soon forces its way back into consciousness. The persistent bedrock of unconscious doubt periodically breaks through, creating confusion and panic, which must be discharged immediately in the form of a dramatic scene.

From infancy, patients like Bianca have attempted over and over again to get what they require from mother but experience serious inconsistency so that too much of the time they fail to get what they need. Physical care is adequate. The baby resigns itself to failed attempts to get emotional containment and constructs an internal world which is self-referential and, of course, narcissistic. All these patients reported excessive masturbation from an early age continuing into adulthood. Proto-feeling can be dealt with only by some form of erotic fantasy or orgasmic discharge. This is what seems to drive sexual acting-out. Repeated attempts to obtain ordinary emotional care lead to a particular sort of splitting. The element of splitting emerges when the patient reports being both excited and disgusted by mother. Fairbairn describes this as a powerful attachment to an exciting and rejecting object:

> Two aspects of the internalised object, viz. its exciting and its frustrating aspects, are split off from the main core of the object and repressed by the ego ... Thus there come to be constituted two repressed internal objects, viz. the exciting (or libidinal) object and the rejecting (or antilibidinal) object. (1963, p. 224)

The baby in this situation does not experience a sudden collapse of its idealisation of the mother. Instead she constructs an idealised version of herself in which her special task is to keep mother happy, which is impossible. The first internal split is carried over into the oedipal stage, but with the *father* becoming the alluring, idealised object—a substitute mother. This accounts for the way in which these patients seem to want a heterosexual relationship while unconsciously seeking a satisfying relationship with a mother. All of this is built upon a bedrock of self-doubt. Overtly asserting her sexuality, Bianca soon expressed doubt and confusion about her sexual identity. She had occasionally experimented with lesbian relationships. Consciously seeking sex with men, her underlying need was for maternal care. The patient's ability to seduce men is based on profound doubt about whether she is cherished in a meaningful way. After the seduction disappointment sets in, because the patient does not believe in herself, she feels once again let down by her object. In this repetition compulsion "The new love object has also failed to distinguish between id-wishes and ego needs in them" (Khan, 1983, p. 34). Bianca told me she was worried that during psychotherapy she would make me alter my usual boundaries because this had happened in other situations. (She had seduced more than one university lecturer.)

Doubt in the countertransference

Contrary to the girl's illusory, wishful fantasy, the fathers of the patients in the group represented by Bianca do not actually relinquish mother (or vice versa). All attempts to solve an impossible oedipal conundrum fail. The girl profoundly doubts her capacity both to truly love and to be truly loved. A way out of the predicament is to construct the idea that father is a "broken man" who needs to be cared for. She creates the conscious idea that everything father does is for her. How does the patient's unconscious doubt manifest itself in the countertransference? It is possible or perhaps inevitable that at some point the analyst will come to doubt his ability to help the patient. The patient will be stuck in a conundrum: with a male analyst she will automatically assume that she will alter the analytic frame and seduce him. For the patient this is both alluring and frightening. Some of the pressures on the analyst are obvious, such as the patient arriving scantily dressed. There are also more subtle manoeuvres, such as hints that the analyst should make special allowances over fees and times. It is the truly unconscious communications that induce real doubt in the mind of the analyst who may, without at first being aware of it, change his way of working so that he begins to "teach" or "instruct" the naive, clever but unwise patient about life in a "nice" way. He may subtly begin to abandon his preferred abstinence in favour of a modified technique. He may tell himself that it is better for this patient that he is not so "strict". It is just as likely that the patient, initially compliant and seductive, will eventually begin to irritate the analyst so that he acts out by giving the hysterical patient a verbal slap. These countertransference reactions will excite the patient and induce shame and doubt in the analyst (as well as guilt). In these ways the analyst begins to be affected by the same doubt that the patient feels. His doubt about his template of abstinence mirrors the patient's self-doubt about her ability to be understood. If it is contained by the analyst and interpreted as a projection of the patient's doubt, this induced self-doubt in the analyst can lead to insight.

The analyst as doubtful baby or broken father

With patients like Bianca the encroaching doubt and the shame that may be activated in the analyst mirrors the early relationship between the mother and baby. All of us contain a residue of early doubt and this may be activated in the analyst. In a reversed transference the analyst may become the doubtful, failing baby trying to please a desperate maternal object. When the analyst-as-baby becomes doubtful about his method and acts this out by modifying his technique, the patient is gratified in the same way that the doubtful mother is gratified by her misuse of her baby. However, the patient becomes increasingly anxious because the shift increases her doubts about ever getting help. The patient may then switch objects from mother to father just as she did in childhood. The analyst becomes, in the mind of the patient, a "broken man". The patient begins to "notice" that the analyst looks tired, seems ill, his eyes are red—a sign that he is upset—and so on. The analyst may feel a pressure to declare that he is okay. In fact he is not okay because, from the patient's point of view, he is "broken". The patient knows this because she is perceptive and highly attuned to any changes in the attitude of the analyst. The analyst has become the broken, needy father with whom the patient can have a special relationship. The patient will care for him better than any other patient. She believes that this relationship is exclusive and reciprocated.

The patient says that her father is a wonderful man, while the image of him she creates in the analyst's mind is of a hopeless, inadequate figure. At first it is only the analyst who entertains doubt about the idealised father. Idealisation of an object is narcissistic and is always a manifestation of self-idealisation. The patient rekindles a martyr fantasy of herself as the sole, dedicated carer of her father-analyst who is seen as helpless. There is for a long time no conscious contradiction in the patient's mind between her idealisation of her father and the view, now projected into the analyst, that he is broken and helpless.

Armstrong-Perlman (1991) writes that such patients:

> … have functioned as a resource for others. They are often acutely perceptive and adaptive to the needs of others and have done well in careers where the use of these skills is maximised. The currently lost, or about to be lost, other has been an object of desire. They had felt "real" in the relationship. But when they give a history of the relationship, one wonders at their blindness. Their object choice seems pathological or perverse. There had been indications that the other was incapable of reciprocating, or loving, or accepting them in the way they desire. They had been pursuing an alluring but rejecting object; an exciting yet frustrating object. The object initially may have offered the conditions of hope but it failed to satisfy. It had awakened an intensity of yearning but it is essentially the elusive object of desire, seemingly there but just out of reach. (p. 345)

The link with shameful doubt is made clear when Armstrong-Perlman writes:

> In the older child this experience is one of intense humiliation over the depreciation of his love, which seems to be involved. At a

> somewhat deeper level (or at an earlier stage) the experience is one
> of shame over the display of needs that are disregarded or belittled.
> (Ibid., p. 349)

Previously an alluring and rejecting maternal object, the analyst may
become a mutually gratifying paternal one. The analysis of this dynamic
within the analyst and the patient may help shift the patient out of a
previously unsolved and incomprehensible oedipal maze. At the centre of this maze is the alluring, rejecting maternal object. The patient's
chronic self-doubt is obscured by pseudo-heterosexuality and intellectual precocity.

Obsessive doubt

Lara represents a group of patients who are conscious of their doubt. She
was a young woman assailed by conscious, obsessive doubt. Attractive
and successful in her work, she described acute anxiety and an inability
to concentrate on her work, along with obsessive-compulsive behaviour. She did not seem to know the cause. She had tried many forms of
therapy. She compulsively checked and re-checked her boyfriend's text
messages, diary, online bank accounts, wallet, and so on, in order to
"make sure" he was not seeing another woman. She knew this behaviour was "crazy". Lara's background was similar to Bianca's except for
a crucial difference in regard to the father. Like Bianca, she had switched
early on from mother to father. Like Bianca, she had repeated this at
puberty, but her father at this time had an affair. He had lied about it
and the parents had divorced. Lara attributed her difficulties to this
single event, which had left her utterly confused. It had re-activated her
repressed, early, and chronic doubt. She felt betrayed and abandoned,
alone with her "needy mother". She had hated her father's subsequent
string of sexual partners. She clung to the idea that only she herself
could truly look after father even though she depicted him as selfish,
pathetic, and childish. She believed that one day she could win him
over. In her paper "Obsessional certainty and obsessional doubt", Ignês
Sodré (1994) suggests that:

> … obsessional defenses that involve rigid adherence to sameness,
> with the need for rituals against contamination and disorder, belong
> to a schizoid way of functioning, in which splitting mechanisms are

used not only against the experience of ambivalence, but also for the preservation of an exclusively two-person relationship with the object. (p. 379)

Sodré proposes that in this state the person has abolished the oedipal third party and has no real involvement with it:

> When tormenting obsessional doubt predominates, on the other hand, the underlying conflict is due not only to ambivalence and to the difficulty of making a choice between objects, but also to the presence in the patient's mind of the parental couple with whom the patient is, unconsciously, excessively involved. The triangular situation is not avoided; on the contrary, it is omnipresent, to the extent that it seems impossible to establish a peaceful undisturbed coupling of any sort; tormenting doubt, therefore, seems to belong to a state where oedipal conflicts are extremely intense and seemingly unresolvable. (p. 379)

During the analytic sessions Lara seemed gradually to understand that her pathological doubt of her boyfriend was really self-doubt, and her anxiety level began to decrease. However, outside the sessions she found it impossible to think coherently. She would "forget" everything I had said and would revert to obsessional checking. In one part of her mind she knew her behaviour was irrational. In another part of her mind she had an equal conviction that her behaviour made perfect sense because she was convinced her boyfriend was unfaithful. Although in the sessions she seemed to understand that she attributed her own "unfaithful" sexual fantasies about other men to her boyfriend, she could not think this through outside the sessions. I continued to interpret along these lines, but some months into her treatment I began to have doubts about my ability to help her, exacerbated by her repeated declarations of hopelessness. I interpreted this countertransference as a manifestation of *her* doubt about my abilities. However, I think I failed to appreciate the strength of her cynicism about the loyalty of her objects. Retrospectively, I think she was complying with my interpretations in a repetition of her compliant maternal object relationship. She began to insist on urgent, concrete help because she was planning a trip away with her boyfriend. She asked repeatedly for me to give her an instruction book or a "technique" to cope with her problem.

The countertransference problem then became one in which I needed to resist acting out my irritation about her resistance by dogmatically lecturing her or "force-feeding" her. She terminated treatment, disappointed and dissatisfied.

Retrospectively, what interested me was the powerful doubt I felt in the first consultation about my ability to help her. This was a warning and an important piece of countertransference. Usually I am sceptically realistic, believing I can probably help. I had shelved and denied my initial sense of doubt in favour of defensive omnipotence. Perhaps, if I had contained and made use of this projected doubt in the initial consultation there might have been two possibilities. She or I might have decided not to proceed, or we might have established a better understanding of the analytic task in terms of the splitting of her objects into two—a longed-for, idealised, totally faithful object about which she could be doubtless, and a persecuting, utterly faithless, cynical object.

Cynicism and the emergence of a fundamentalist object

The presence of cynicism was clear from the start with Cassandra, a borderline patient. Borderline patients and those with personality disorder have developed a psychic structure based upon the conviction that there is little or no hope of ever being cherished or understood. Of course, the two states are different. Borderline patients are unstable. They lurch between false hope and cynicism, fluctuating between idealisation in which all reasonable doubt is abolished, and cynical despair in which feelings of wrongness, badness, and filthiness return. The developmental order of these latter self-beliefs is important. The earliest ones are a sense of wrongness and failure. Badness and filthiness belong to later phases. In an idealised state of mind the patient is in a state of high expectation. The analyst is good and right and will provide what is needed. The other frame of mind is a fundamentalist one in which the patient has *no doubt* that the analyst is bad and wrong. These individuals have not developed a middle position of useful scepticism. Personality disordered patients are much more stable than borderline patients. They maintain a constant state of cynical self-narcissism (Kinston, 1980) in which all hope of a caring object has long been abandoned. Borderline patients wage a constant battle with persecutory doubt, whereas individuals with personality disorder have won a pyrrhic victory by obliterating doubt. They exist in a state of profound, isolated cynicism. They have no doubt that the world is no good and that there is no hope.

Cassandra painted a grim picture: her mother was depicted as lacking any capacity to understand or care for her children. She said that her mother complained self-righteously about everything and everyone and took no responsibility for anything. It seemed her mother projected negative material about sexuality and life into Cassandra, constantly warning her (before she was able to understand what mother meant) about the perils of men and sex. She allegedly repeatedly told Cassandra not to trust men or anyone outside the family. Whenever Cassandra told her mother about any difficulty, she felt her mother would trump this with dire reports of her own childhood. She believed her mother regarded her as a mistake, telling her it would have been better if she had not been born. The maternal figure is a rejecting, self-righteous, and cynical internal object with which Cassandra was identified. As with Bianca, there was evidence that Cassandra had attempted to turn early on to her father, but he was not available for idealisation. Cassandra had a partner who occasionally hit her and she had also been raped. Father emerged as a self-preoccupied alcoholic, often violent and cynical about any interests that Cassandra showed, available only as the basis of a perverse, destructive object-relationship. The apparent lack of an alternative affirming paternal object is a crucial difference between hysterical and borderline patients. With borderline patients the original and profound self-doubt is *confirmed* by the father, who has no interest, unlike Bianca's father, in being seduced by his daughter. Like Bianca, Cassandra had thrown herself into schoolwork. Unlike her, Cassandra would occasionally collapse into catastrophic states of fear in which she would feel shamefully filthy and full of doubt. She was bright at school and, as with Bianca, this provided a longed-for source of praise, but her self-image was so fragile that her underlying doubt broke through and she dropped out of university. On the surface Cassandra was heterosexual. She would turn to men, but in a hopeless kind of way, saying, "A man is better than nothing—but I don't really believe anything will come of it." The same applies to the analyst, who at the start is "better than nothing".

Patients like Cassandra struggle consciously with a mixture of idealisation and cynicism but unconsciously have internalised a *fundamentalist* object. This is a doubt-free and shameless object. This object has *no doubt whatsoever about its own self-righteousness*. Paradoxically, the patient is at the same time unconsciously persecuted by doubt. Consciously this doubt has been abolished. A split object is projected into anyone she encounters so that they may suddenly change from a good and right, idealised object into a frightening, bad and wrong, self-righteous one. This is the disturbed baby that Klein (1935) describes. The *beautiful picture* of the mother is there inside the patient's mind but is absolutely unobtainable. The patient's secondary rage, due to the constant, shameful doubt over her ability to get what she needs, destroys any relationship with any real, inevitably faulty person. Whenever Cassandra was able to make a sexual relationship with a man it was always "because he wanted sex". Soon after sexual intercourse she felt insulted and enraged by the man's inability to understand her.

The analyst as hopeful baby or doubtless object

It is very difficult to form a treatment alliance with a patient like Cassandra. She would lure me into thinking that we were making progress. I would lose hold of my ordinary, doubtful scepticism. She would smash my unrealistic optimism in a triumphant way and accuse me of being idiotic and useless. She was correct. By losing my useful scepticism I had idealised my own abilities. A way of understanding this is to think of the analyst taking the position of a baby full of innate hope that is repeatedly dashed against the rock of an impervious patient/mother. In this situation the analyst may be assailed by profound, shameful doubt about his effectiveness and even about his training. Moments of cynicism may start to occupy the analyst's mind. This may lead to one of two countertransference responses. In reaction to doubtful and shameful helplessness, the analyst may abolish uncertainty and resort to doubt-free dogma by means of relentless interpretations about envy and aggression. This is (correctly) registered by the patient as a sadistic revenge attack, and the patient may be gratified by it. By acting in this way the analyst abolishes his own doubt and becomes an aggressively self-righteous, dogmatic object. The patient has rid herself, via projection, of her own persecutory, shameless, and dogmatic object. The patient is then able to become righteously certain about the *analyst's* righteousness! Alternatively, the analyst may become too full of paralysing doubt—silent and depressively hopeless. The patient is highly attuned to the evidence of either of these two states of mind in the analyst. Either of them will confirm what the patient has always believed: both mother and analyst are too self-righteous or too depressed to help. Eventually, after several years of analysis, Cassandra was able to begin to manage her destructive cynicism and move into a more sceptical state, one in which she learned to be sceptical of her cynicism.

I have come to think that it is crucial, particularly with this kind of patient, to make interpretations from a position of ordinary doubt. These patients do not have a sense of ordinary scepticism but rather are persecuted by doubt-free cynicism. The internal, fundamentalist object dominates because they seem to have no experience of a primary object that has been able, sceptically and hopefully, to try out responses to the baby's distress. A good enough mother will run through, perhaps out loud, a series of responses: "Is baby hungry? Is baby cold? Does baby need a nappy change?" This is "scientific scepticism", and it is in this spirit that interpretations need to be given to patients besieged by cynical doubt. Interpretations given in this way help all patients to internalise a sceptical, curious, and concerned object. The analysis of varieties of doubt that can be projected into the analyst can be a key to therapeutic progress. The task for patient and analyst may be to move from an unrealistic state of splitting and idealisation—the ideal object does not exist in reality and must always fail—towards a position of realistic, ordinary scepticism in which there is "reasonable doubt" of the self and of the object.

In our analytic work and in our lives we are constantly struggling with doubt. We are no different from any other profession in that we are susceptible to doubt in all its forms. We may institutionally protect ourselves from doubt so that what are in reality only psychoanalytic *theories* about the mind become fundamentalist, dogmatic *facts* that we blandish inside and (just as lamentably) outside the consulting room. This tendency makes our profession unappealing. Without scepticism we sink into dogma. Diderot wrote (1746), "Scepticism is the first step towards truth. It should be general, for it is the touchstone" (p. 32).

References

Archer, S. (1993). Shame, guilt and counterfeiting. *Journal of the British Association of Psychotherapists, 24*: 50–69.

Archer, S. (2002). Violence and hostility from a sense of unconscious shame: Shame in the transference and counter-transference. In: H. Alfillé & J. Cooper (Eds.), *Dilemmas in the Consulting Room* (pp. 137–152). London: Karnac.

Archer, S. (2005). Shame, doubt and the shameless object. *Journal of the British Association of Psychotherapists, 43*: 93–107.

Armstrong-Perlman, E. M. (1991). The allure of the bad object. *Free Associations, 2*: 343–356.

Balint, M. (1979). *The Basic Fault.* London: Tavistock.

Demos, E. V. (1995). *Exploring Affect: The Selected Writings of Silvan S. Tomkins (Studies in Emotion and Social Interaction).* Cambridge: Cambridge University Press.

Diderot, D. (1746). *Philosophical Thoughts* (Amazon Kindle e-book edition, Trans. K. Watson, 2013).

Edelman, G. (1992). *Bright Air, Brilliant Fire: On the Matter of the Mind.* London: Penguin.

Erikson, E. H. (1950). *Childhood and Society.* New York: Norton.

Fairbairn, W. R. D. (1963). Synopsis of an object-relations theory of the personality. *International Journal of Psychoanalysis, 44*: 224–225.

Ferenczi, S. (1949). Confusion of the tongues between the adults and the child (the language of tenderness and of passion). *International Journal of Psychoanalysis, 30*: 225–230.

Freud, S. (1895d). *Studies on Hysteria. S. E., 2*: 1–306. London: Hogarth.

Freud, S. (1905d). *Three Essays on the Theory of Sexuality. S. E., 7*: 1–230. London: Hogarth.

Freud, S. (1909d). Notes upon a case of obsessional neurosis. *S. E., 10*: 153–257. London: Hogarth.

Freud, S. (1911c). Psycho-analytic notes on an autobiographical account of a case of paranoia (dementia paranoides). *S. E., 12*: 3–82. London: Hogarth.

Freud, S. (1917e). Mourning and melancholia. *S. E., 14*: 237–260. London: Hogarth.

Freud, S. (1918b). From the history of an infantile neurosis. *S. E., 17*: 3–123. London: Hogarth.

Freud, S. (1933a). Femininity (pp. 112–135). In: *New Introductory Lectures On Psycho-Analysis. S. E., 22*: 3–182. London: Hogarth.

Khan, M. M. R. (1983). *Hidden Selves.* London: Hogarth.

Kinston, W. (1980). A theoretical and technical approach to narcissistic disturbance. *International Journal of Psychoanalysis, 61*: 383–394.

Kinston, W. (1982). An intrapsychic developmental schema for narcissistic disturbance. *International Review of Psychoanalysis, 9*: 253–261.

Kinston, W. (1983). A theoretical context for shame. *International Journal of Psychoanalysis, 64*: 213–226.

Klein, M. (1935). A contribution to the psychogenesis of manic-depressive states. *International Journal of Psychoanalysis, 16*: 145–174.

Nathanson, D. L. (1987). *The Many Faces of Shame.* New York: Guilford.

Nathanson, D. L. (1992). *Shame and Pride: Affect, Sex and the Birth of the Self.* New York: W. W. Norton.

Russell, B. (1931). The triumph of stupidity. In: H. Ruja (Ed.), *Mortals and Others: Bertrand Russell's American Essays, Volume 2, 1931–1935* (pp. 27–28). London: Routledge, 1998.

Rycroft, C. (1968). *A Critical Dictionary of Psychoanalysis.* New York: Basic Books [reprinted London: Penguin Reference Books, 1972].

Sodré, I. (1994). Obsessional certainty versus obsessional doubt: From two to three. *Psychoanalytic Inquiry, 14*: 379–392.

Trevarthen, C. (2004). Learning about ourselves, from children: Why a growing human brain needs interesting companions. In: *Research and Clinical Centre for Child Development, Annual Report 2002–2003* (Number 26) (pp. 9–44). Hokkaido, Japan: Graduate School of Education, Hakkaido University.

CHAPTER EIGHT

Interpreting two kinds of love*

Joscelyn Richards

Introduction to two kinds of love and the concept of internal cohabitation

In this chapter I am going to describe the psychoanalytic work with a young woman who had a diagnosis of severe borderline personality at the time of the referral. She quickly formed an erotic and idealising transference, which caused considerable difficulties in undertaking the analytic work. Despite this we were gradually able to identify two kinds of love: one that could be described as passionate and unrealistic, and the other as companionate and realistic (Tallis, 2005). I was assisted in differentiating these two kinds of love by using the clinical concept of "internal cohabitation", which was introduced into the psychoanalytic literature in 1993 by my colleague Michael Sinason. This concept involves a dual-track analysis of two coexisting selves, each with a mind of its own. With this patient I was able to help her to differentiate each self from the other and to link the two different types of love with the

---

* A version of this paper was given at the Annual Conference of the John Macmurray Fellowship LOVE AND FEAR: Aspects of John Macmurray's Philosophy Concerning Emotional Maturity, 11 & 12 October 2002, Woodbrooke College, Birmingham.

two different selves. The challenge for me as the analyst was to hold an analytic stance under pressure and offer interpretations which neither colluded with the passionate love felt by the self we identified as "the other", nor made the patient feel that her growing capacity for appropriate companionate (or object) love was being rejected.

In thinking about this patient and the nature of love, I was reminded that over the years I have observed, as I am sure other analysts have, that most of my patients have expressed considerable distress and bewilderment at their difficulties in forming and sustaining good and loving relationships with others. These difficulties are inevitably re-experienced in the analytic relationship. Early on in my psychoanalytic work I became particularly curious about the tendency in patients to switch, sometimes very quickly, from one mode of being and relating to a very different mode, and have written a number of papers about my observations (Richards, 1993, 1999, 2007). The following is a quote from one of these papers (Richards, 1999, quoted here with the kind permission of Karnac Books):

> With several patients I had the dislocating experience that the person I was with last session—or even two minutes, or seconds ago—had gone and been replaced by another person with the same face, body and clothes but whose whole demeanour, facial expression, tone of voice and language were different. One moment there was a capacity and interest in appraising our interactions and a perception of me as a helpful partner whilst the next there was resentment of the whole therapeutic enterprise, a wish to obstruct it at every turn, and behaviour suggesting attitudes of suspicion, antagonism, superiority, or indifference towards me as the therapist. There was either hostility or a pseudo-cooperation at any attempt to explore the basis of these changes. (p. 28)

I observed over the years that the shifts from one mode to another could happen very quickly, both between and within sessions. I particularly noticed that a good session, in the sense that the patient and I would feel linked up and be able to work together, would often be followed at the next session by a dismissal of all the previous work. Similarly, I noticed that within a session a useful exchange between the patient and myself would suddenly be interrupted by a mocking comment about our communication.

In the 1999 paper I wrote:

> When I first started observing and experiencing these dislocating phenomena, I was not sure what conceptualisations to employ to make sense of them. Initially I thought the sudden change towards the therapist and the therapeutic exploration was a negative therapeutic reaction due to innate destructiveness or hatred of dependence, or a reaction to a wrong or insensitive interpretation on my part. I understood the patient's bewilderment to be the result of mechanisms of splitting and projection or those of denial and disavowal. It seemed that the ego or self split off or disowned unwanted parts or feelings. Thus I would think of the patient as disowning his destructiveness or his hatred of me or the therapy, and that the purpose of the therapy was to help him recognise and own these aspects.
>
> However, there was something about the bewilderment and distress of patients who felt driven to think, feel and see things in ways that … did not make sense to them that led me to consider that these concepts did not do justice to their experience. Alternative concepts, such as the re-emergence of repressed memories or perverse internalised object relationships were also unsatisfactory, as they did not fit with the histories of these patients or with the range of situations and interactions where these experiences of being taken over occurred. I therefore came to the conclusion that I would have to take seriously the patients' statements that they experienced themselves as being in two minds or being two people with different perceptions and attitudes.
>
> It meant taking seriously, for example, a patient who responded to my comment that she was always feeling torn between two points of view as to what sort of person she was by saying, "I am two people". She then spoke of the difficulty of living with this inner division: "Most people don't see two sides, they only see one—it feels ridiculous to say to someone, 'I've got this other person', it sounds bizarre …" Acknowledging this, however, seemed to give her much relief and led to her exploring and illustrating how she could not do or think anything without feeling sneered at and told off by someone else inside her head. (Ibid., p. 31)
>
> It also meant taking seriously my repeated observations that this supposedly split-off subordinate part was, in fact, behaving like an independent person and objecting, often strongly, either to

the patient's plans or to the working alliance established between therapist and patient. I had particularly noticed that patients often used a language that implied that a part was perceived to have a personal motive—for example, the patient who said "... the converse side *will insist* ... [on doing the opposite]" or the patient who said, "... the other side *is always jumping in accusing me of having no right to my feelings* ...". In addition, this part, rather than being subordinate, often behaved like *the senior partner*—for example, the patient who explained that he had felt driven all his life by someone in his head who gave orders like a sergeant-major; or the patient who said "this part of me seems to have a mind of its own". (Ibid., p. 32)

[However, it was my analytic] work for many years with a manic-depressive patient that particularly led me to question the concepts I was using. We had reached something of an impasse, and initially I thought that the difficulties were due to my inadequacies as a therapist and/or the severity of the patient's pathology; but gradually I had begun to think that they might be due more to the inadequacies of my conceptual framework. The concept of "internal cohabitation" ... of two minds in one body offered a useful alternative ... To move from ... familiar concepts ... seemed initially a large step. However, an examination of the literature indicated that many clinicians in the psychoanalytic field have accepted the possibility of more than one internal agency ... whilst others have struggled to make sense of clinical material that points to the possibility of a patient's intentions and autonomy being taken over by another [internally coexisting] mind (Sinason, 1993). (Ibid., p. 32)

In our paper "The internal cohabitation model" (2014), Michael Sinason and I briefly present some of the main authors whose concepts overlap with internal cohabitation. We mention Bion's (1967) differentiation of "coexisting psychotic and non-psychotic personalities" (p. 317), and Rosenfeld's (1987) concept of a "narcissistic organisation within the ego that holds the ego to ransom by functioning like an internal mafia" (p. 318) especially when the libidinal self begins to become attached to the analyst and take an interest in what he/she says. We also mention that some features are shared with Sohn's concept of the "identificate" (1985), as well as with the concept of an "ego destructive superego"

(p. 318) as initially described by Bion and subsequently developed by O'Shaughnessy and Britton (O'Shaughnessy, 1999; Britton, 2003). We go on to say:

> These authors all recognise the influence of an internal agency that sees itself as a superior self to that of the patient ... and has total contempt for the notion of mutual-interdependence. However, these conceptualisations do not afford this other entity the status of having a mind that is sentient and autonomous. Instead, these authors see such an agency as a pathological development of the ego or the superego ... (Sinason & Richards, p. 318)

Winnicott, perhaps, comes closest to the concept of internal cohabitation in his paper "Communicating and not communicating leading to a study of certain opposites" (1963). He addresses what seems a similar differentiation to the one that we have found operative across the diagnostic spectrum. He describes both a self that genuinely wants to communicate and a "secret self" that is an isolate and reacts to the threat of being found or communicated with by a further hiding of itself. Grotstein further suggests that the secret non-communicating self "prefers privacy to the point of never being known, yet it desires not to be forgotten, abandoned or taken for granted. Its desires are paradoxical; it desires privacy *and* attention" (Grotstein, 1998, p. 51).

Freud describes the possibility of two minds coexisting in both his early and later writings. For example, in his early studies in hysteria, Freud described "a duality" that occurred not only in hypnosis but "spontaneously", which he called a "double conscience" (Freud, 1910a). Breuer was even more explicit, and in describing his patient, Anna 0, he wrote: "It is hard to avoid expressing the situation [of two entirely distinct states of consciousness] by saying that the patient was split into two personalities of which one was mentally normal and the other insane" (Freud with Breuer, 1895d, p. 45).

As we know, Freud changed the concept of a horizontal mental structure consisting of a double conscience to a vertical structure in his structural model of the mind (1923b), and developed the concept of repression, conceptualising this as the primary defence mechanism of the ego. Nevertheless, he remained interested in the possibility of a divided ego (Freud, 1924b). He returned more fully to the phenomenon of two states of mind in his work on fetishism (Freud, 1927e), where he developed the concept of disavowal. He finally concluded, near the end of his working life, that the splitting into two contradictory states of mind "which exist alongside of each other ... one normal and the other abnormal ... was not only a feature of fetishism but also of the psychoses and neuroses" (Freud, 1940a [1938], p. 202).

For Freud, the division into two contradictory states of mind occurs through a splitting process of the ego, whilst the concept of internal cohabitation conceives of two selves existing from birth. It is impossible to prove which hypothesis is true (if either), but the analytic technique and aims stemming from each model will be different, as the former suggests working towards integration of a split ego and the latter towards differentiation of two different mental structures.

Over the years I have continued to find the application of the concept of internal cohabitation particularly useful in making sense of a patient's shift from a mode of engagement with the analytic work to one of hostility and rejection. Application of the concept has also been particularly useful in understanding and resolving impasses, and in helping patients to understand the reasons and triggers for sabotaging and undermining processes that, prior to analysis, they could neither contain nor understand. What patients seem to find particularly helpful is recognising that the thoughts they find in their minds are not necessarily their own thoughts. Instead, they belong to another self with a mind that has very different mental capacities and a very different relationship with reality, and which, because of these differences, needs to be recognised and understood (Richards, 1993). In our recent paper (Sinason & Richards, 2014) we have summarised the main differences between the two selves as follows:

> A socially relating self seeks and develops emotional attachments with others. This self experiences grief if these are lost and has the capacity for [empathy and] concern for both self and others and is interested in the analytic work as this assists with thinking about self and others.
>
> In contrast, a radically unilateral self is concerned only with its own desires and so deals with the world in what seems from the relational point of view to be a ruthless way. This self distrusts the analytic enterprise and views the world as governed by power relations and its thinking is dominated by simple oppositions such as: good/bad; superior/inferior; right/wrong; useful/useless, etc. This self is paranoid and does not understand any other way of

being and therefore expects to be viewed and treated by others in the same way. Although this self has no capacity for interdependence it can experience terror, resourcelessness and outrage if actually rejected or if he/she perceives rejection or abandonment. (p. 316)

No terminology quite does justice to the complexity of two selves co-existing internally, but in recent years we have tended to use the terms "relational" or "social self" for the self who can relate to the analyst and engage in the analytic explorations, and to use the terms "other self" or "internal other" for the self that is dominated by unilateralism and all-or-nothing thinking.

The idealising and erotic transference in the literature

The tendency towards an idealising and erotic transference has been known in analytic literature since the publication of *Studies on Hysteria* (Freud with Breuer, 1895d) and "Observations on transference-love" (Freud, 1915a). Many papers have been written since, and most focus, as Freud's did, on erotic dynamics between female patients and male analysts (Freud, 1915a; Blum, 1994; Person, 1985; Welles & Wrye, 1991). Most authors consider the technical challenge of the erotic transference to be considerable, and because of this Hill (1994) suggests that "the erotic transference has been a resource for the discovery and development of central ideas in psychoanalytic theory and technique" (p. 483).

When analysts do write about the erotic transference and countertransference experienced with a female patient and female analyst pairing (e.g., Siegel, 1994 & Slochower, 1999) they do not differentiate, as I do, between two different selves with differing attitudes and aims towards love and the analysis. Both these papers suggest, though, that the intense sexual longings of the patients are often an expression of a pre-oedipal maternal or maternal erotic transference in which sensitive use of the countertransference is crucial in bringing about understanding of the sexual aspect and facilitating genuine change.

Perhaps Tallis (2005), as already mentioned, comes closest to such differentiation when he recognises the difference between "passionate and companionate love", and suggests that passionate love can be thought of as "mad love or lovesickness". He points out that the similarities between lovesickness and mental illness have been noted since classical times, and that when people fall in love they frequently exhibit symptom clusters that are very similar to diagnostic categories such as mania, depression, obsessive compulsive, and delusional disorders.

For Tallis, passionate love or lovesickness is "a state of intense longing for the [idealised] beloved" (p. 72), and is a form of love that is so out of touch with reality that it can cause very difficult problems for the person gripped by it. "When reciprocated it is associated with joy, euphoria and ecstasy; however, these feelings are almost invariably shadowed by darker emotions such as anxiety, jealousy and sadness … when unrequited, passionate love will reliably engender a sense of emptiness—and even despair" (ibid.).

Gabbard and Lester, when writing about boundary violations in psychoanalysis (1995), also use the concept of lovesickness to describe the category that the majority of analysts and therapists who violate the sexual boundary with patients fall into. They report that when discussing their transgression, analysts and therapists describe themselves in the lovesick state as being "intoxicated". Two ego functions in particular are frequently impaired: judgement (i.e., the ability to anticipate consequences of one's actions), and reality testing (i.e., an inability to distinguish a countertransference wish from the reality of the situation). Another category that some analysts fall into is that of "masochistic surrender": in this situation the analyst gives in to the patient's persuasions because of unresolved guilt. Gabbard and Lester's work indicates that it is not only patients that can be taken over and derailed from the analytic task by an eroticised and idealising lovesickness (though this has to be expected and worked with), but also analysts and therapists.

Lovesickness and internal cohabitation

In ordinary life outside the consulting room it can be very difficult for relational selves to negotiate and keep their bearings when both selves feel they love the same external figure or object. The two different loves of the two selves—lovesickness and companionate—can become entangled and difficult to sort out. We have probably all observed that a distinction can be made between "mad love" and "sane love". It is well known that when people fall in love they idealise the other, become blind to faults, and are convinced that it is true love and will last forever. If people insist on getting married in that state, before they have had time to get to know the loved object better, thoughtful friends and relatives are usually worried and try to persuade the said people to wait. I would suggest that if people thought in terms of living internally with another self who always responded in an all-or-nothing way and with absolute certainty, they might recognise that they had been taken over by that self when they found themselves intoxicated and obsessed with an external object. The period of passionate (or romantic) love can be very enjoyable for relational selves, but can become very distressing and destructive for all parties when the internal other's love dominates and becomes ruthlessly controlling and possessive towards the supposedly loved object.

Clinical illustration: Zoey

In the analytic relationship it can also be very difficult for relational selves to negotiate and keep their bearings when both selves feel they love the analyst. Equally, it can also be difficult for analysts and therapists to keep their bearings and sustain an analytic stance when the patient's internal other forms a powerful erotic idealising transference that leaves little room for any other attitudes towards the analyst. I would like to illustrate, through six years of analytic work with a female patient, some of the difficulties and challenges for both patient and analyst when this occurred. The patient, whom I shall call "Zoey", and her "internal other" both believed they loved me, and the concept of internal cohabitation was a useful tool in understanding, differentiating, and containing the pressures resulting from this situation.

Zoey was twenty-six when referred by a male psychiatrist to the psychotherapy clinic in the NHS where I was working at the time. He described her as having "major and long-standing personality problems". She had been treated in psychiatric services for most of her adult life, starting with in-patient treatment in an adolescent unit.

She completed a "Self-report questionnaire", described her difficulties as "depression and anger outbursts", and stated that these problems were preventing her "from going out and facing people". She also wrote that she felt "anxious and frightened" if she saw women when with her (male) partner, and that she hoped talking treatment would help her get over her difficulties and enable her to become her "quiet self again".

She indicated that she had been unemployed since giving up work as a nursery nurse when twenty-one because of a "breakdown", and at that time had made a suicide attempt and begun cutting her arms.

Zoey was initially assessed by an experienced male colleague, who summarised her presenting problems as "self-mutilation, uncontrollable anger, fear of social situations, despondency, and suicidal thoughts". During the interview she said she did not feel close to her family, had always felt her six years younger brother was the parents' favourite, and that generally he had got on better in school and in life than she had. Her main memory was of: "crying and crying when I was little, especially after my brother was born, and the more I cried the more my father hit me. My mother never stopped him—she seemed fed up with me too".

The assessor formed the view that Zoey had a severe borderline psychotic personality organisation. He offered two further assessment interviews, but she did not keep them.

Some months later, the original referring psychiatrist wrote again to say: "Since she was last seen at your centre she has been a victim of a sexual assault which, not surprisingly, has compounded her difficulties. She is keen to be reassessed again for your help but asked if it would be possible to see a woman this time (preferably someone older rather than younger) and I wonder if you would be good enough to see if this is possible."

In the case discussion we agreed that, as I appeared to fit the bill, I would offer to see her. We were not sure what to think about her request other than that she may be seeking a maternal figure because of her bleak childhood, though we noted that there was also anxiety about being in the presence of a woman. I decided not to speculate too much at this stage.

Zoey came to the appointment with her elderly partner, Thomas, who stayed in the waiting room. She was an attractive looking young woman with long blond hair, and was stylishly dressed. I noted that Thomas looked old enough to be her father, and seemed introverted and somewhat unkempt. They seemed an odd couple.

Zoey seemed pleased to come with me into the consulting room for an exploratory interview, but then became anxious and could not speak. She seemed very uncomfortable the moment there was a silence and wanted to leave the session early. I said it seemed that she had wanted to speak to me, but that now she was here a blockage had occurred in her mind that was stopping her from speaking. She managed to say that this often happened and she thought she was stupid. I said that perhaps she was worried that I would jump to that conclusion too, rather than try to work out with her why her mind goes blank at points when she would like to speak. She seemed relieved at the idea of being understood instead of judged. She said very little about the sexual assault, but managed to explore in a minimal way the fact that she found communication difficult because she was afraid that "it will come out all wrong and this puts me off".

I suggested that we meet for three more sessions and then think together as to what she might need in terms of therapy. However, she cancelled the second appointment and did not request another. I closed the episode.

Zoey was re-referred about nine months later, as she had become agitated about the sexual assault and the pending court case. We decided that I would offer to see her as before.

She kept the appointment and again came with Thomas, whom she again left in the waiting room. This time she was more forthcoming, and spoke first about the court case against the man who had assaulted her. It had taken place a few days before the appointment and she was upset because the accused had been found "not guilty" as there was not enough evidence. However, she seemed much more concerned to speak about how troubled she was about Thomas. It seemed that they did not live together but had apartments next to each other in the same house, run by a mental health aftercare housing association. She spoke about feeling responsible for him, as he did not look after himself very well. She said two social workers were going to visit the following week to assess the situation and she was worried that they might send him to a hostel. She conveyed that not only would she feel lost and isolated without him, but also that if they were separated—either by his transfer to a hostel or because he might get ill and die any moment—she would not be able to manage.

This led us to explore how negative thoughts came into her mind and insisted the worst was going to happen, particularly about Thomas. Near the end of the session I asked if she would like to meet weekly for psychotherapy to see if we could understand and help her deal better with these recurring negative thoughts. She seemed keen to do this. When I suggested starting in three weeks time, she was immediately upset at the idea of waiting. It seemed that the terror of separating from

Thomas was immediately transferred to me. Nevertheless, she agreed to wait.

Zoey brought Thomas to the first psychotherapy session three weeks later and to my surprise asked if she could bring him into the consulting room. When I suggested Thomas wait in the waiting room, she said "No!" With a panic-stricken look on her face she said she couldn't come in without him. I decided to go along with this request—on the principle of starting where the patient can start (within reason)—though I did say that perhaps next time Thomas could wait in the waiting room.

Zoey could not speak in the session; the most she could do was to look at Thomas intensely, giggle nervously and say, "Thomas, you speak". Thomas was equally tongue-tied and looked at me helplessly. We had about six sessions like this. Zoey was in considerable discomfort, and when Thomas did not speak she would either leave early or look at me and say, "You speak". I tried to help by saying what I thought was going on, for example, that Zoey had hoped to speak to me but found she had many fears about saying what was on her mind and that she hoped or feared I knew what they were without her telling me. She could not respond verbally when I spoke, but seemed to become calmer. Occasionally, I also said that she and Thomas were not used to being apart, and so perhaps it felt difficult to leave him in the waiting room and yet perhaps she needed to do that so she could begin to talk about her worries in private.

During this time she found the gap between the sessions very difficult and would panic and cut herself. She tended to ring the crisis intervention team and have long sessions on the phone with one of their workers, who would then leave me long messages, which Zoey knew about. Through these messages I realised that there was an intense attachment to me combined with a belief that I forgot her completely the moment the session ended. After discussion with colleagues, we decided that I would offer her two further sessions a week as soon as I had a vacancy (some time into the work we were able to increase to four sessions a week). We thought this would provide a better opportunity to assist Zoey in thinking about the meaning of separations and how she was convinced that I completely dropped her out of my mind. I began to form the idea that in her internal world there was a separate self who feared and hated separations, a self who needed to be identified and understood. We also thought the reduction in the waiting time between sessions would perhaps make the waiting more manageable. As soon as we started the three times weekly sessions Zoey seemed calmer, and so I said that perhaps at the next session Thomas could wait in the waiting room.

At the next session Thomas got up to come, but Zoey asked him to wait, which he did. For some years he accompanied her to sessions but he never came into the consulting room again and eventually, though they remained close, he ceased to accompany her.

At the following session Zoey handed me a piece of paper with "I like you" written on it. Although it was early on in the treatment, because of my experience of working with the concept of two selves I wondered if the writer was "Zoey" trying to bypass the censorship of the "internal other" and let me know that she thought she could trust me and we could do some work together. Perhaps she could not say this out loud because the internal other would hear and be jealous and angry with her? Or could it be the internal other sending me a love letter that expressed her passionate feelings? Or was it both of these? I decided that if more letters were brought we could find out, and also that they might serve as a springboard for Zoey to speak about the thoughts in her head. I suggested that she might like to write down during the week things she wanted to say. I then received what I can only call love letters, which I thought were probably from the internal other because they had phrases that reminded me of pop songs and were full of declarations of true and undying love: "I will love you forever," "I wouldn't ever want to part from you," "I will always be yours." They addressed a "me" I did not recognise, as they seemed to be addressed to someone who reciprocated these feelings and who had secretly agreed that we were destined for each other. There were also statements about not liking men in "that" way, but always liking women and never being able to tell anyone before.

For a long time—months—if I tried to talk about these letters in any way or talk about the person writing them, "someone" in the room would say "shhh" to shut me up. The patient, seemingly under the influence of the internal other, would say that someone might hear, and sometimes she would ask what I did with the letters because she was worried that someone else might read them and stop her from seeing me. I took this to mean, "would interfere with the path of true love", though I did not say this at the time. If she heard any footsteps in the corridor she would look around startled and worried and say suspiciously,

"Who is that?" This "secret love" was clearly threatened by coming out into the open.

I felt I was mostly in the presence of the internal other because there was no interest in the analytic task of exploring any aspect of "Zoey's" life, let alone exploring what was going on internally and why or whose thoughts and perceptions these were. There was only an interest in declaring her love and wanting reassurance that I loved her too. She urgently wanted to know how I felt and wanted the analysis to hurry up and end so we could be together, but worried that maybe I did not want the same thing or "had gone off her". Many of the letters were about the longing the internal other had to speak her love out loud, but there was always a sentence about how dangerous this would be in case her love was rejected. She could not read the letters to me and could not let me read them out loud; I had to read them to myself. Although the content of the letters seemed to express almost entirely the beliefs of a ruthlessly self-serving internal other, occasionally there were one or two sentences that seemed to be written by a more thoughtful person. These hinted at the possibility of a Zoey who wanted to explore herself and me: "I keep thinking you forget me—is that right, do you?" or "Why am I so worried—do I have to be?" I realised quite early that in my countertransference I felt cornered much of the time: I felt that I was either going to say something that would be heard as brutally rejecting or as colluding with the idea of a mutual lovesickness. I realised I had to deal with these reactions thoughtfully so as to use them to understand the patient's inner world rather than act them out.

When, eventually, I was permitted to read the letters out loud, I used this as an opportunity to identify that there seemed to be two authors to them: one who was sure she loved me passionately and who was preoccupied with worry about being rejected by me and a fear "that it would all end in tears" (something her mother had always said); and another—Zoey—who wanted to understand why there was such fear of being rejected and why she got so worried about my state of mind. For quite some time Zoey was very quickly taken over between and in sessions by the internal other, and so went blank or could not understand a word I was saying, or agreed with the questioning that implied I had forgotten her completely. Gradually, however, she began to realise that the powerful persuasion in her head that I had forgotten her did not match her perception of me. It began to make sense to her that there was another person in her head who had an all-or-nothing mind that either expected the worst to happen or believed we were going to live together forever. Thus, slowly Zoey, as someone who could think and have a view separate from the other self, began to emerge.

For a long time, however, the self who was sure she was in love with me, but was also sure that I would reject her, dominated sessions and began to find her voice and to speak instead of writing letters, possibly because that self had mistakenly assumed I had signalled my special love, first by offering extra sessions and then by accepting and showing an interest in the first and subsequent "love letters". The emergence of the voice of the internal other provided an opportunity for myself, and eventually Zoey, to discover that she could observe and recognise the internal other as separate and different from herself, and that these capacities would lead her to know and understand the internal other and the ways in which this self dominated Zoey's thinking. Zoey gradually came to realise that using her mind in this way led to her growing and changing whilst the internal other remained the same. The other not only wanted to reiterate how much she loved me but also voiced the expectation of being rejected and forgotten, as if I would find her love bad and unacceptable. The belief that we were meant to be lovers but it could go wrong was very concrete and real. There was no "as if" dimension: "I love you not just as a therapist but because you are you, Joscelyn—when you love someone you never want to part, do you?" Thus, the internal other behaved, as I saw it, like a jealous and possessive lover, and kept asking me in a demanding way a series of questions that implied complete lack of trust and made me feel cornered and controlled: "Did you miss me?" "Did you remember me?" "What were you doing in the weekend?" "Did you talk to anyone else?" "Do you love me?"

The repetitive declarations of love brought to mind the thought that "the lady doth protest too much". It seemed that the protestations covered an opposite feeling that was more like rage. I did not feel I was being treated very lovingly when vigorously accused of being unfaithful or forgetting her. In a similar vein, although she declared undying love, she was also quick to drop me when she thought I had dropped her. For example, after breaks there would often be a number of missed sessions, and she would subsequently tell me about being driven to cut her arms and legs and to stab cushions with a knife. However, for a long time, under the influence of the internal other's fear of retaliation, Zoey could not acknowledge that there was any anger or rage towards me.

Even though Zoey was developing her observational capacities and could understand that it was not *her* but the *other* who believed in our exclusive love and was angry at my perceived unfaithfulness, she very easily became entangled with the internal other. Because of this she was always quick to join in, covering up the anger in case I retaliated: "No, I don't feel anything like that. I love you." On one occasion I said: "Well, perhaps the other person in your head has such a strong reaction that it is hard for you to hold onto your way of seeing me and trust that I would be interested in understanding the reasons for the anger rather than be angry back. Perhaps the other is very angry with me because she is jealous of our relationship and fears I would reject her if I knew she was angry with me." Zoey could only respond by saying, "But I love you". I understood by that response that the internal other had taken over and that no other point of view was possible at this stage.

The other's anger, rage, and jealousy finally emerged into the open when I was seen outside of our sessions talking to a male colleague. Despite attempts to hold back the rage at my assumed unfaithfulness, it slipped out in the session: "Who was that person you were with? Why were you talking to him?" (She looked both hurt and accusing.) It became an opportunity to recognise very clearly that the internal other held a conviction that she and I had a special and exclusive relationship that would lead to us being together, and whenever it seemed that I was betraying that commitment there was an extreme reaction of jealousy and rage toward me. This time I said: "I think you, Zoey, get quickly persuaded by that other person in your head that your love for me is the same as hers, and when she thinks that I am betraying her by speaking to Dr X, she undermines your trust in me that however many people I speak to I still remember you and want to help you understand the thoughts that the internal other has that upset you." Zoey said: "You mean you haven't gone off me like the other person says you have?" I said: "I wonder if you are beginning to think that I don't suddenly go off you like the other person says because you are noticing that in every session I remain steadily interested in remembering you and talking with you about all those things that the internal other worries about." Zoey looked thoughtful and then said, "I know really that you don't suddenly change. You are always kind to me, though I worry that I drive you crazy with all my questions," and we both laughed.

It seemed to me that I had an extraordinarily delicate and challenging task on my hands. I did not want to say anything that would sound brutally rejecting to either self; nor did I want to say anything that colluded with the idea that I had sworn undying love and that we were going to live together. I also wanted to help the patient find and develop her capacities for appropriate love and trust. Sometimes she would say, "I have never felt loved or really loved someone." It seemed to me that this was true for both selves—each in her own way felt she had never loved or been loved, and it was probably true that Zoey's relationship with her parents had been so difficult that she had not experienced a relationship where she felt appropriately loved and understood. Thus it seemed essential, in helping Zoey to disentangle her companionate love for me from the other's lovesickness, that I was careful not to undermine her capacity to experience appropriate object or companionate love.

In sorting out my understanding of Zoey's internal situation, there was a period where I was nearly derailed by pressures from my internal other to give in to Zoey's internal other rather than process and think about the demands being made on me. I experienced insistent advice within my own head that I had to do and say what Zoey's internal other wanted; otherwise Zoey would seriously harm herself (cut herself badly or kill herself). For example, at the end of a Thursday session, when she said she couldn't leave and that she was going to worry all weekend, there was an internal pressure to reassure her that I loved her too, would be thinking of her all the time, and agree that we would never part. I then had to differentiate this ill advice from my "sane" view, and realise where the pressure was coming from (my internal other). I could then see that Zoey was capable, however minimally, of understanding that she has different perceptions and capabilities from her internal other. I had to hold onto my view that the analytic aim was to help her understand her inner world rather than collude with the fantasies of the other self and give false reassurance. I had to think all the time of how to help her trust her experience that I was the sort of person who held her in mind between sessions without using phrases that would lend themselves to being heard as confirmation that I held her in mind only because I was passionately in love with her too.

On the whole, Zoey seemed to be able to leave the session in a calmer state of mind if I referred to the internal other and said something like:

> "I think the internal other is certain that parting now is the same as
> parting forever and can persuade you that I am going to forget you

as soon as you leave the session and that we will never meet again. That other self doesn't believe what you know, which is that we will have another session next Monday and can then talk further about these matters."

Sometimes this interpretation enabled her to leave saying: "All right, we'll talk again. I'll see you next Monday."

By repeatedly differentiating the two minds, the self (Zoey) who was capable of and interested in understanding her inner world began to emerge more fully and to think about the possibility that another mind coexisted in her head whose love was very different from hers. As we mapped out the existence of the other self and all its mistaken assumptions, we discovered Zoey's capacities to see situations differently from that self, and that she had the capacity to understand that I was not abandoning her (or the other one for that matter) between sessions. When she realised that she could hold me in mind and that I could hold her in mind, and that this enabled us to get on with other aspects of our lives when we were apart without forgetting each other, she was delighted and said: "It's taken so long for the penny to drop but I can now see that we can remain connected when I don't see you. I've been listening to that other mind too long; she's always been persuading me that you forget me but it's her that feels forgotten, not me." She went on to say that she was appreciative of the work we did together because for the first time in her life she could recognise the existence of another mind that had always negatively influenced her. She said she had always listened to the thoughts of the other and thought they were her own thoughts and that she had to believe and act on them.

One of the issues that we explored again and again was the assumption of the internal cohabitant that my love was the same as hers, that is, passionate, exclusive, and forever, but ready to be switched off at any moment because, "You could go off me". Zoey, however, began to realise that I did not love her in that way and thus would not suddenly switch my love off or on, nor suddenly switch off my concern and interest in helping her. She began to get an idea that she and I loved each other in a steadier, more reliable and concerned way, which involved getting to know each other during sessions and holding each other in mind between sessions. Thus, we began to talk in more detail about the two sorts of love and their differences, and I would say something like: "I think you have grown to love me over the time we've been meeting because I listen to you and do my best to help you understand the difference between yourself and the other person in your head, whereas the other self fell in love with me immediately before knowing what I was like."

Sometimes Zoey was able to respond thoughtfully and indicate that she understood, but at other times the internal other would jump in and ask, "But have you grown to love me?" On one occasion I said: "I think the internal other gets jealous of the solid love that you and I have, which has developed over time between us as we have talked more and more about important things in your life and how to differentiate yourself from the internal other. That one always feels insecure and feels jealous of the security you are able to feel and quickly tells you that I haven't grown to love you in that solid, thoughtful way." She nodded thoughtfully.

On another occasion I said: "I think what we are learning is that the other person never changes her view of love or of me. That other is certain that we should be lovers and live together, and when that internal other realises that you and I have a different sort of love—based on getting to know each other and working together—she is angry with me and wants to attack me."

Zoey responded by saying: "And me, she wants to attack me too. When I love you my way she comes straight back into my head and says awful things like you don't love me." The development of both Zoey's understanding of the difference between herself and the internal other, and of her capacity to articulate her own thoughts was, of course, a considerable achievement, which we both acknowledged.

However, this did not mean that the internal other had disappeared. In fact, we often noted that as soon as Zoey had a new thought that she wanted to share with me the other one would feel provoked to speak up. For example, on one occasion, soon after she had grasped that I had the sort of mind that could remember her and that gaps between sessions did not mean what the other mind thought—namely, that she was horribly abandoned—she said, "I'm really grateful. It makes so much difference." Immediately, a "voice" said, "But do you really remember me?" I said, "You know, that sounds like the other person who can't believe that I can hold her in mind too." The same voice said, "No, it's me that feels you don't hold me in mind." I said, "I think it can feel difficult to work out who feels I can't remember her and who feels I can when there is someone who is absolutely certain that I forget her." In a thoughtful way Zoey now responded, "I know you can remember me—I do know that—so it must be her. She's so quick to get back into my mind again. Perhaps she feels left out when I feel connected to you."

I was impressed with Zoey's observation that she had realised that when she could relate to me in her way by sharing her ideas with me the internal other would feel jealous and left out and immediately ask if I remembered her. In fact, this led to Zoey realising that if she was going to live better with the other self she needed to understand how quickly that self could feel excluded and dropped. Zoey began to realise that if she forgot about the existence of the internal other she was vulnerable to believing the other's persuasion not to trust her own perceptions and knowledge.

One of the most vivid ways that the internal other demonstrated the belief of being excluded and dropped was in asking questions or making a statement about not smelling nice: "Do I smell?" or "Do I smell of smoke? It's horrible isn't it!" or "I know you can smell me—you can, can't you!" Questions or statements like these would come in an intrusive and insistent way, either during a session when Zoey and I had been able to have a meaningful dialogue or at the beginning of a session following one that had gone well. Zoey was puzzled at these outbursts and would say, "I don't know why I asked that because I haven't been smoking recently but I feel I have to ask you; I can't help it." We came to understand that when the internal other believed that Zoey and I got on well together this could only mean that I preferred Zoey and saw the other as a horrible, smelly person who I did not want to have anything to do with.

In later sessions, Zoey made it clear that when she could identify and separate her own thoughts from those of the internal other she did not suffer such terrible anxiety and fears as previously, and was not in a constant state of worry that I was going to behave as the other one said and suddenly fall in love with someone else and "go off her". Thus, she no longer felt compelled, under the influence of the other, to "torture" me with questions about my state of mind. She understood that the love she and I had for each other was not that of being in love and having an exclusive relationship, but was a form of love in which we enjoyed working together and holding each other in mind however many other people we might know. She also understood, unlike the other self, that the aim of the analysis was to help her to live in the world better, rather than to live with me.

It took about five years for Zoey to get to the point where she had sufficient understanding of the internal other to have a reasonable chance of recognising when she was getting caught up with the other's mistaken beliefs. Once she could recognise this, she was more able to differentiate her thoughts from those of the other self.

We eventually began thinking and talking about ending, and noted the two reactions to the idea of it. Zoey was sad at the prospect of ending, but began to feel hopeful about the possibility, and was able to negotiate and plan an ending date that she could manage, whilst the other inevitably felt betrayed and insisted, "When you love someone you never want to part." As the end approached, although it was not easy for Zoey because of attacks on her thinking by the internal other, she was able to hold onto the knowledge and understanding she had gained over the years of our analytic work, and was thus able to attend the last session, recognise that we had both enjoyed working together, and leave in a dignified and contained manner.

Concluding comments

In this clinical case the patient, Zoey, had difficulty from the start in forming a working relationship with me—or finding and developing her capacity for companionate love—because the internal other formed an instant idealising erotic transference which for a long time dominated the clinical situation. From the point of view of internal cohabitation, the other self fell in love with me almost immediately and experienced all the symptoms of passionate lovesickness. Zoey thought the internal other's lovesickness was all there was, and therefore that the internal other's belief in our true and undying love, and the consequent feelings of betrayal and anger with me when I did not live up to my role as a reciprocating lover, were also her beliefs and feelings. She was always being internally influenced to believe that either I loved her back passionately and we would live together forever, or that I had completely dropped her out of my mind between sessions. The belief in being so absolutely dropped caused considerable anguish to Zoey but enraged the other self, though this could not be communicated directly for fear of my rejection and retaliation. Instead, there would be a reporting of stabbing a knife into cushions or cutting her arms and showing me the wounds, but also a firm denial that this had anything to do with a perception of me.

The main problem for me as the analyst was that the person in love with me did not believe or have any interest in exploring or understanding anything—which, of course, is what Freud discovered many years ago and called "transference resistance" (Freud, 1912b). The self in love with me only wanted to say "I love you", and wanted me to say the same thing back, and was either broken-hearted or intensely accusatory when I did not.

I thus felt very much challenged as the analyst to find ways with Zoey to think about and explore these convictions rather than reject or collude with them. Without the concept of two selves, who had very different attitudes to and capacities for love, I think I would have had even more difficulty than I had, both in keeping an analytic stance and in helping Zoey find her capacity for more balanced thinking rather than being gripped by the all-or-nothing views of the internal other. In my countertransference I never felt in danger of falling in love with the patient, but I did feel under intense internal pressure to give in and agree with the insistent, recurring, and unrealistic demands and wishes of the patient's internal other, especially at the end of sessions when she could not leave.

By using the clinical concept of internal cohabitation, I was able to keep my analytic bearings and gradually help Zoey to differentiate her thoughts and feelings from the all-or-nothing thinking of the internal other. As the analytic process unfolded and I made more and more interpretations that differentiated the different loves and perceptions of the two selves, Zoey began to emerge more fully and to think about the possibility that another self coexisted in her head whose love was of a very different kind. Whereas at the beginning of the analysis she was too dominated by the internal other to be interested in or capable of analytic explorations of her inner world, she was gradually able to form a working relationship with me in which she could explore her inner world and experience the relationship as one that we both enjoyed and that was an expression of her growing capacity for realistic and companionate love.

References

Bion, W. R. (1957). Differentiation of the psychotic from the non-psychotic personalities. *International Journal of Psychoanalysis, 38*: 266–275 [reprinted in: *Second Thoughts: Selected Papers on Psycho-Analysis*. London: Heinemann Medical, 1967; reprinted London: Karnac, 1984].

Blum, H. P. (1994). Discussion on the erotic transference: Contemporary perspectives. *Psychoanalytic Inquiry, 14*: 622–635.

Britton, R. (2003). *Sex, Death, and the Superego: Experiences in Psychoanalysis.* London: Karnac.

Freud, S., with Breuer, J. (1895d). *Studies on Hysteria. S. E., 2*: 1–306. London: Hogarth.

Freud, S. (1910a). Five lectures on psycho-analysis. *S. E., 11*: 3–56. London: Hogarth.

Freud, S. (1912b). The dynamics of transference. *S. E., 12*: 97–108. London: Hogarth.

Freud, S. (1915a). Observations on transference-love. *S. E., 12*: 157–168. London: Hogarth.

Freud, S. (1923b). *The Ego and the Id. S. E., 19*: 1–59. London: Hogarth.

Freud, S. (1924b). Neurosis and psychosis. *S. E., 19*: 149–153. London: Hogarth.

Freud, S. (1927e). Fetishism. *S. E., 21*: 149–157. London: Hogarth.

Freud, S. (1940e [1938]). Splitting of the ego in the process of defence. *S. E., 23*: 275–278. London: Hogarth.

Gabbard, G. O., & Lester, E. (1995). *Boundaries and Boundary Violations in Psychoanalysis.* New York: Basic.

Grotstein, J. S. (1998). The numinous and immanent nature of the psycho-analytic subject. *Journal of Analytical Psychology, 43*: 41–68.

Hill, D. (1994). The special place of the erotic transference in psychoanalysis. *Psychoanalytic Inquiry, 14*: 483–498.

O'Shaughnessy, E. (1999). Relating to the superego. *International Journal of Psychoanalysis, 80*: 861–870.

Person, E. S. (1985). The erotic transference in women and in men: Differences and consequences. *Journal of the American Psychoanalytic Association, 13*: 159–180.

Richards, J. (1993). Cohabitation and the negative therapeutic reaction. *Psychoanalytic Psychotherapy, 7*: 223–229.

Richards, J. (1999). The concept of internal cohabitation. In: S. Johnson & S. Ruszczynski, (Eds.), *Psychoanalytic Psychotherapy in the Independent Tradition* (pp. 27–52). London: Karnac.

Richards, J. (2007). Psychosis and the concept of internal cohabitation [Special issue: Internal cohabitation]. *Psychodynamic Practice, 13*: 25–42.

Rosenfeld, H. (1987). *Impasse and Interpretation*. London: Tavistock.

Siegel, E. V. (1994). Clinical observations of sexual and sensual aspects of the transference in women. *Psychoanalytic Inquiry, 14*: 591–603.

Sinason, M. (1993). Who is the mad voice inside? *Psychoanalytic Psychotherapy, 7*: 207–221.

Sinason, M. (2007). The discovery of an internal other—in everyday life, in illness and in art [Special issue: Internal cohabitation]. *Psychodynamic Practice, 13*: 7–24.

Sinason, M., & Richards, J. (2014). The internal cohabitation model. *British Journal of Psychotherapy, 30*: 314–327.

Slochower, J. (1999). Erotic complications. *International Journal of Psychoanalysis, 80*: 1119–1130.

Sohn, L. (1985). Narcissistic organisation, projective identification and the formation of the identificate. *International Journal of Psychoanalysis, 66*: 201–214.

Tallis, F. (2005). Crazy for you. *The Psychologist, 18*: 72–74.

Welles, J. K., & Wrye, H. K. (1991). The maternal erotic transference. *International Journal of Psychoanalysis, 72*: 93–106.

Winnicott, D. W. (1963). Communicating and not communicating leading to a study of certain opposites. In: *The Maturational Process and the Facilitating Environment*. London: Hogarth.

CHAPTER NINE

Destroying the knowledge of the need for love

David Morgan

"Autobiography" by Louis MacNeice

In my childhood trees were green
And there was plenty to be seen.
Come back early or never come.

My father made the walls resound,
He wore his collar the wrong way round.
Come back early or never come.

My mother wore a yellow dress,
Gentle, gently, gentleness.
Come back early or never come.

When I was five the black dreams came;
Nothing after was quite the same.
Come back early or never come.

The dark was talking to the dead;
The lamp was dark beside my bed.
Come back early or never come.

When I woke they did not care;
Nobody, nobody was there.
Come back early or never come.

When my silent terror cried,
Nobody, nobody replied.
Come back early or never come.

I got up; the chilly sun
Saw me walk away alone.
Come back early or never come.

(Kind permission for the reproduction
of this poem granted from the publisher Faber & Faber)

This poem demonstrates how the wakeful child makes a song out of frightening abandonment in the night. The refrain, "Come back early or never come", is one of wounded ultimatum. In this way, it is a lullaby thrown into reverse and represents the resignation that a child might feel when faced with overwhelming trauma occurring too early for its level of cognitive development and understanding. At these times a turning away from a knowledge of the need for the other in the face of life and death anxieties is a reasonable solution.

I am going to write about the difficulties of managing countertransference manifestations when working with patients whose grasp on life is tenuous, and who unconsciously enact their trauma and provoke enormous concerns within themselves, their families, and in their analyst, about whether it is possible or worthwhile to live in the shadow of death. In discussing and presenting some clinical work with two examples of such patients, I draw on and discuss the three "facts of life" as originally proposed and developed by Roger Money-Kyrle. He wrote in 1969 that he has found it useful to consider three core facts of life: "the recognition of the breast as a supremely good object, the recognition of the parents' intercourse as a supremely creative act, and the recognition of the inevitability of time and ultimately death" (Money-Kyrle, 1969,

p. 30). He went on to say about this third "fact" that "to fear death is not the same as to recognise its inevitability, which is a fact forced on us much against our will by the repeated experience that no good (or bad) experience can ever last forever—a fact perhaps never fully accepted" (ibid., p. 62). In my experience I have found, as Money-Kyrle argues, that we all work unconsciously to distort or blunt our acceptance of these profound human experiences. However, I argue in addition that traumatic events may destine some patients unconsciously to devote all their efforts to subvert the recognition of these facts as an activity in place of living.

As fundamental schematics of the human experience, these "facts" belong to us all, not just our patients. My work leads me to believe that it is the process of the analyst bearing to face these facts afresh for themselves whilst bombarded with death, fear, and resistance in the transference that may begin to allow inklings of digested realisation to be taken in by the patient. As analysts we too are defended against the painful recognition of these facts, which, as Money-Kyrle argues, are interrelated. However poor our experiences may have been, we must all have had some experience of nurturing and we are all the products of a procreative union that made us but inevitably excluded us. We have lost the breast and struggle to re-find it and we all fear exclusion and, ultimately, the exclusion that comes through death. It is only perhaps as we grope our way to understanding that good and nurturing experiences are all transient in reality, but must be kept alive psychically, that any of us are able to experience hope for ourselves and others.

The patients about whom I will be writing both had traumatic experiences in the realm of death that left their capacity to manage the fear of loss of love and death disabled. In turn, in my countertransference, I felt myself also to be disabled at times, and I was forced to live as they had done with visions of the chasm. I try to show how I think my countertransference developed and how understanding it in consideration of my patients' unconscious phantasies played its part in enabling me to provide a more or less adequate container for my patients' shattered projections, which enabled them to begin to think and feel about these facts of life as they had not dared to before. In the beginning this struggle to conceptualise precedes interpretation and is, I believe, an exploration of the analyst's ability to bear what has never been born before. It is a close to the bone experience, a concrete manifestation of the transference, looking for authenticity in the analyst but not expecting to find it.

Concrete transference sounds like a contradiction—transference is usually understood as a symbolic concept. I understand concrete transference, however, as transference in action. Unlike enactment, a concrete transference is the beginning of a search for symbolic understanding in the mind of the analyst. To begin with, however, the analyst will feel pushed to respond in a concrete manner, will feel at sea and unable at times to find the words or thoughts to symbolise the experience.

The patient sees the analyst as a concrete figure and this inability to conceive of the analyst symbolically manifests itself in the patient's actions toward the analyst. This poses interesting questions about the state of the internal object world which gives rise to a concrete transference. In the concrete transference there seems to be no experience of internal object permanency; it is the analyst's job to supply the setting where this can be discovered. The analyst has to live with the threat of loss and breakdown before this occurs.

These patients, in the early parts of treatment, act on the analyst in such a way that they are unable to experience the analyst as an object separate from themselves. Only when the patient feels that she is acting upon the analyst and feeling the impact on him does she experience the analyst as existing. In extreme cases, there are moments when the patient experiences no internal object, and the analyst stops existing. This is a terrifying return to the original trauma, perhaps a reflection of losing the belief that one exists in the mind of the other: "Come back early or never come".

When this happens, the patient experiences extreme anxiety. These patients exhibit a concrete transference to the analyst that depends on his physical presence in the consulting room, exhibiting in the beginning a lack of any internal space. This space has to be demonstrated through the analyst giving the patient their first experience of a mind that can think about what has heretofore been believed to be unthinkable. This exploration of the analyst as object will often be a repeated attempt to locate in the analyst a thoughtless, uncaring lovelessness or deathliness.

I think this dynamic is a part of working with patients who fill up the black holes in their psyche through destroying any need for the other by creating triangular relationships with substances or perversions, creating loss and pain in their human objects. They pursue activities and preoccupations that fill their minds and bodies with desire, whilst the real person, the other, is excluded and diminished. These patients enact their defences against their need for love and their need for the other, having given up hope of finding a mind that's capable of bearing their projections of vulnerability. Interpretation is therefore aimed at demonstrating to the patient that anxieties around life and death, and the facts of life may be able to be symbolised in the mind of the analyst, thus eventually in the mind of the patient.

Clinical example: Dr L

Dr L was a bright and reasonably successful doctor who was referred from a local teaching hospital to which she had taken herself with self-diagnosed ME. She had become depressed and incapacitated in her work, socially isolated within the confines of her flat, and she was very lonely. She had tried to cope with this situation by attempting to become more involved with her work but felt unable to continue without help. The intellectual defences that she had employed to get on and be successful in her life so far, including migrating from another country, speaking another language, and excelling in exams, were beginning to fail her. She had also begun to seriously lose weight. My first thought when I saw her was that she looked like death warmed up. She informed me that she had recently begun to frighten herself whilst alone in her flat at night by attacking her mind in such a way that she was having frightening hallucinations. This felt both genuine and heartfelt, but was accompanied by a memory of wanting to jump into her mother's grave after her premature death. In this melodramatic account of her state of mind it was possible to see both real feelings of pain and loneliness but also some evidence of her exciting herself with florid morbid imagery. I felt an inner deathliness was in danger of taking her over. Despite my instant reaction of alarm about her weakened state and a countertransference of hopelessness about her, we began analysis.

Dr L was the fourth child in a family of seven. Her mother developed breast cancer around the patient's fifth birthday and this had involved her being away for extensive treatments in a city some distance from the family home. Dr L remembered her mother coming home without her hair after chemotherapy and radiation therapy. Her mother's anxiety for her children apparently led her to emphasise the need for the children to make the most of their academic abilities and to get on in life. There was a strong family history of cancer and there had been several deaths.

It was a feature of the early months that Dr L had many colds and flu that she seemed to catch easily and hold onto. She always looked cold and weak, as if she needed to wear more clothes, which evoked in me an interesting state of mind, one of exasperation and rage at her helplessness rather than concern about her self-neglect, which might more ordinarily have affected me. I often felt like telling her briskly that she seemed to be deliberately making herself appear to be helpless to get me to look after her but that this wouldn't work. In time I came to understand these early countertransference feelings of mine were projective identifications of her relationship with a mother who simply had no capacity to take care of her and who wanted her to take care of herself. I found Dr L's sessions draining as, presumably, Dr L's mother had found looking after her family draining when she needed to be looked after herself.

At the age of eleven, Dr L was sent to a religious boarding school, following in the footsteps of her three older sisters. Throughout her time there she did well academically whilst at the same time managing to be rebellious. She would often adopt the mannerisms of a tomboy. I later discovered that she had also suffered from nocturnal enuresis and, although I did not know this, her fear of incontinence, both real and imagined, continued well into adult life and through the beginning of her analysis, becoming confused with her sexuality. This was one of the reasons that led her originally to come for help, although unspoken at the time.

Her mother eventually succumbed to a very painful version of cancer when Dr L was twenty. This was closely followed by her father's death only six months later of liver cancer. My understanding of the father's role in the family was fairly sketchy but apparently he couldn't survive the mother's death, his cancer developing quite suddenly afterwards. Dr L had responded to the death of her parents by working hard academically and training as a doctor. She had tried to find sexual partners but no serious relationship had materialised.

Dr L's history showed very considerable emotional privation and there had clearly been a divorce between her work-self and her emotions. It was significant that her enuresis began at boarding school, where it is likely that the sense of emotional isolation by having been sent away from home led to a regression to incontinence.

In her second session, she told me that in her view she would be unable to conceive of getting help from me and continuing to work as a doctor. Instead she had been looking at advertisements to become a street cleaner for her local borough. I felt this phantasy of cleaning up other peoples' effluvia in the middle of a very cold winter evolved from an unconscious phantasy that she could revive her dead parents by becoming closer to a deathlike state herself. She posed a dilemma, as I did think it was reasonable for her to consider not working in medicine whilst she was clearly in such a vulnerable state. On the other hand, she had no financial cushion to fall back on. Her alternative job choice was evidently dangerous as her current physical health was very fragile.

I was confronted immediately by my reactions to her depleted mental and physical states. At this time I was torn between being furious at having to try to sort out this immediate dilemma, reluctant pity for her, and a sense that I didn't want to have to think about any of this. I gradually began to realise that she was insistently bringing versions of death and deadly states into my room, and that I did not want to think about these any more than she did. To manage this dilemma of life and death, I could only fall back on my theory and the structure of the setting to feel some permanence in and continuity within my own world.

Therefore, as I was in no position to make decisions for Dr L, my task was to try and see how she responded to our working together. I said to her that she seemed to find it difficult to conceive of both getting help and helping herself; it seemed that it had to be one or the other. Again, I came to see this as a re-enactment of being with a mother who could not help. Dr L was forever tempted to regress to infantile dependency in order, I think, to try to find an object to depend on. With great difficulty she continued to work. The pattern of her employment reflected her internal state, that is, feeling over-burdened and expected to do too much, often near the edge of collapse. In the first two years of her analysis, it was harrowing to feel on this edge as I existed within the anxiety that she might die. She was deeply depressed, always with a cold, had very little money, and was without any apparent social or family contacts.

The first dream she ever brought to her analysis seemed to be a fairly accurate representation of her internal state:

> I am standing on a stage and I am overlooking a swimming pool full of dead male bodies. They had all died due to some myste-rious disease like AIDS and seemed to be floating in a urine-like

substance. In the distance a little boat is coming toward me that is picking up the dead bodies.

Dr L's only association was that it was deeply disturbing to be the only one alive in this sea of deadness. She was unable to think or say more about this powerful dream but I was able to use it to help me understand more about her. I kept in mind that her urine seemed to be a negative version of "the waters of the unconscious", dangerous waters in which you don't swim. I saw the male corpses as symbols of her dead, frozen, dissociated emotions, especially her sexual feelings, which seemed to have been annihilated by deadly AIDS viruses. That they were men seemed significant, given that I am a man. I felt her identification with her dying mother had left her with the sense that she had a womb filled with amniotic poison and urine that could only produce dead babies. The boat I thought might be seen as an ego, or the hope of a thinking ego that might develop in analysis, and that might "pick up", that is, understand, her dead, frozen self. I wondered if I might be partly represented by the boat, but I felt daunted and exhausted by the floating male corpses. This "aid" clearly came with the price of a risk of very severe contamination.

At the time, I interpreted to her that the dream seemed to indicate her fear that her mind and thoughts would be lethal to anyone who came into contact with her, particularly men and including me. One aspect of all Dr L's dream presentations (and let us remember her initial morbid death wish to jump into mother's grave) was that there often seemed to be some excitement in telling me the dreams. Her dramatic presentations could easily distract me and I would from time to time get involved in what seemed to be lively and creative depictions. I knew Dr L felt a great deal of sensitivity to what I and others thought about her and that she had a wish to impress me. It would sometimes come as a dramatic shock to realise just how preoccupied, unconsciously, she was with her own and my death. Her excited phantasies and dreams, I discovered later, were accompanied by involuntary urination into her bed, and this act seemed to demonstrate in her a frightened sexualisation of deathly states as some attempt at staying alive, a very concrete manifestation of her dilemma. She lived in fear of repelling me and the men she began to meet and while I was not actively repelled, it is true that I found it hard to register Dr L as a woman.

Another dream later in our work shows, I think, how Dr L was beginning to use our work.

> I am lying on a bed on one side of a partition, on the other side of which is an old nun on a trampoline who is jumping up and down, trying to see me over the top of the partition.

By this time we were able to think together about this view of a rather frustrated, possibly celibate person excitedly trying to reach her. The nun seemed to me clearly to be a reference to her own celibate, perhaps childlike, self, but it could also have been an unflattering attack on me, her analyst, as a celibate, impotent person, which in this phase I often felt myself to be. But we could not ignore the manifest shape of the dream in which someone was jumping up and down to see something. In the manner of dreams, this was, I felt, Dr L becoming excited about being close to a man who seemed to be interested to see her, even if she had to turn this man into an old nun or herself into a sexless being.

Over time and with Dr L's confession of her urinary incontinence, her internal conception of herself as a lethal being began to emerge. I thought about how she brought her deathly pee in a deeply regressed state for the first time to someone whom she hoped might convert it into thought. It was both aggressive and deeply defensive, with the belief that no one would wish to be with an incontinent child.

As the analysis developed, a frightening cervical smear result forced Dr L to confront her mortal (as well as now sexual) body, and after considerable work this led her to engage with her own and my mortality as real things to be thought about. This in turn brought grief for her mother's and father's deaths. This seemed to me to come from a recognition of Money-Kyrle's facts of life, namely that her life was the result of a supremely procreative act and that she had somewhere inside her knowledge of a supremely good breast.

This later work urged upon us as an analytic couple the awareness of her body and the difficulty she had had in moving from an androgynous place where male and female are confused, to the beginnings of sexuality. In my countertransference I had to negotiate not just the usual oedipal feelings of recognising Dr L's physical presence but also to respond to her increasingly desperate terror about losing me. At times her fear for me joined with my own fear for myself and us, and I would mirror Dr L in finding thought about our mortality overwhelming. Again, I depended on the setting and my own analytic perspective to help us.

At times, Dr L experienced real terror that talking about death would actually bring it about in a concrete way—the magical power of words. It was of vital importance at these times that I was prepared to entertain the uncomfortable idea of my own death and my own limitations. It was an exploration of my capacity to cope with the thought of death and dying without defensively interpreting this fear away, or reassuring her, or expiring on the spot.

This question about life and death became the focus for my patient of a great deal of exploration with me. She would pose the question, of how I, an older man, lived with the knowledge of my own mortality, a reasonable question for someone whose own objects had been dogged by such fears or who had succumbed to death all through her life. This exploration of my capacity to cope with her streams of urine-like emotion about my death was an important ongoing aspect of her analysis. As Dr L's ambivalence towards life abated, her fear that I would die or reject her increased. We could see this perhaps, to reference early Freud, as hysterical misery turned to common unhappiness.

Clinical example: Mr D

With the second patient I wish to discuss, Money-Kyrle's facts of life continue to be relevant, particularly if we understand depression as a form of death in life which has to be vigorously defended against. Mr D's defences were directed towards vigorously rejecting any idea of a procreative couple and, in so doing, to project his dependent child states into another where they could be contemptuously beaten whilst he used transvestitism to comfort himself. One understanding of the transvestite wish to get inside the object is that it contains experience of an unreliable primary object, which experience is reversed by the expedience of climbing inside and outside the female clothing. Added to this, the real woman is marginalised in the process, carrying split-off, denigrated aspects of the self. Working with perverse and violent patients brings a particular problem of distaste, sometimes revulsion, in the countertransference, and there is the ever-present fear that the work might exacerbate violence rather than contain it.

Mr D came into treatment feeling confused and depressed because his wife refused to continue to participate in his transvestite activity and was threatening to leave. He wanted to be a writer but he only wrote articles for women's magazines that were rejected. He lived on a trust fund left to him by his mother's father, which also paid for his house.

Mr D's father had left the family when he was three, leaving his mother depressed and unavailable. Mr D was left lonely in his early childhood and he remembered having a rubber sheet that comforted him. This attachment to materials intensified later into a secret wish to dress up in his mother's clothes in identification with her as a substitute for being close to her. He described a sense of calm that would descend on him at these times. He found the experience of putting on and taking off his mother's clothes extremely gratifying, relieving him from confusion and need in relation to an unreliable or unavailable object. He thus avoided his need for a mother's love by asset-stripping her and putting his desire into a substitute skin into which he can climb whenever he desires. It is a container over which he has control. It avoids the fear of a dependence on a claustrophobic relationship with a depressed mother, both facing the abyss left by his father.

After university Mr D married a student from abroad who became very dependent on him. She had been sexually abused by her father. Together they regressed to an isolated world. He drew her into his transvestite activities, dressing up as a woman and masturbating in front of her. He felt this gave him power over her that comforted him through projecting his needy infantile self into her whilst he became the provider with his trust fund. His wife's subsequent refusal to participate in this arrangement distressed him. His fragile world was collapsing. He described feeling almost catatonic with depression, raising himself from this torpor only to eat or evacuate.

In frustration, he berated his wife, often violently, for being stupid and lazy. He kept her financially and threatened her with eviction. Ever since they had married their sexual relationship was minimal, except for the transvestite activity. She seemed at first willing to play the voyeur to his exhibitionism, presumably re-enacting her own abuse by her father. She again carried the need whilst he treated her cruelly and retained the power.

Mr D told me this story with little sense of shame, but with rage that his wife could wish to depart. In my countertransference, I felt the pricklings of disgust towards this baby man, who hadn't had to work for money whilst I had to work hard, and whose sexual practices were both infantile and, at face value, silly. As he described his aggressive and contemptuous feelings towards his wife and others in the sessions, I had to manage my own urges towards violent expulsion of him from my mind and to struggle to find some productive way of thinking about him.

I was particularly struck by the visceral strength of my emotional reaction to Mr D's presentation. I was shocked to find the depth of my contempt for Mr D, for his false-guru-self who bullied his wife, while he was at the same time "stuck" inside his mummy, in a house that had been bought for him, with a trust fund provided, trying to get further inside his mummy with his articles for women's magazines. I had the unpleasant feeling that I was sadistically kicking someone who was desperate and abject. It took me some time to realise how difficult it was to feel the plight of this infant who was so deprived. He managed his terror by clinging to the rubber sheet that was the precursor of his cross-dressing, his attempt, I take it, to get inside his mother's skin. I was taken aback by this lack of feeling in me and reflected eventually that it corresponded perhaps to the "numbness" that seems to have accompanied his consciously "putting away childish things at the age of three" and also the numbness that his abandoning father must have utilised to leave his family in such need.

At the beginning and throughout my work with Mr D, I would at times shockingly feel that I was in the room with a turd on my couch and, while I disliked myself for this fleeting idea, it came to help me get hold of what I believe Mr D's mother must have felt towards her two dependent boys with their nappies and infantile needs, whilst she was abandoned and depressed. There was in reality, at that time in M. D's early life, little sense of any procreative coupling, and it took time for any sense of coupling to emerge between us in our work.

My early understanding was that Mr D projected his infantile self into his wife and she had to stay in that position, keeping all dependency and fear away from him, whilst he retained the power to look after her or abandon her as his father had abandoned him. His own experiences were reversed and projected into his wife, who was always frightened that he would leave. He reversed earlier experiences of deprivation through putting them physically and psychologically into the body and mind of the other. His wife's experience of abuse made her an available recipient of his projections. There was then no need for love or dependence, killing his knowledge of the need for love, as she had nothing loveable in her that he might need.

In the first year of analysis Mr D was increasingly fearful about his needy self surfacing. He became enormously anxious about becoming addicted to his analysis, which he said was an arrangement that would rob him of his autonomy. He felt that I was intent on seducing him into a relationship with me so that I could use him entirely for my own ends without considering him. He was convinced of the accuracy of his perceptions and oblivious to the irony that they contained a mirror image of how he used his wife. I interpreted these anxieties, saying that he feared a rather empty analyst whose own life was so devoid of any real substance that I derived my only comfort by seducing and controlling my patients into providing me with the feelings of power lacking in my impoverished life. He was interested in these observations and curious at my willingness to be explored as such an unattractive figure. This was the beginning of his willingness to think about rather than enact his early experiences.

But as Mr D became more aware of his dependence on me, by now perhaps a father in the transference, his fury with his wife increased. After a bank holiday weekend he felt enraged with her, calling her a bloodsucker, as if she was a parasite that he felt like killing to protect himself. He comforted himself through compulsively dressing up and masturbating. Thus, he seemed to evacuate any awareness of his own emerging dependency on me into his wife, whilst he, in phantasy, could feel self-sufficient. As with many Portman Clinic patients, both the real threat of violence and the distastefulness of the defences produced in me the feeling that he was the bloodsucking parasite that I would like to get rid of in a violent manner.

As I encouraged him to think about, rather than enact his feelings of frustration and rage, he became very critical of me. I was a man dressed up in the clothing of psychoanalysis, a discredited theory, used as a way to control him. I thought he was searching for a mind that could contain and understand his evacuated feelings of abandonment and loss rather than become identified with them, like his mother and wife, or reject him by walking out, like his father. I knew both through theory and experience that Mr D had to feel towards me the contempt that he felt towards others and feared from me. If I could bear these feelings he might be able to have some sense of what a relationship with a paternal figure could be, in order to be able to begin to renounce his infantile omnipotence and to accept that there might be the possibility that there were couples who could come together to be creative.

After the third year there was an important development. His need to project the unwanted aspects of himself into his wife, who was becoming stronger, abated. Faced with the prospect of owning these unwanted aspects, he became terrified that he was going to slip into a massive depression. He dreamed of falling, of losing his grip, of being lost at sea with a lighthouse in the distance, of losing himself in the underground. These dreams suggest original fears of disintegration, of the overwhelming mother and the distant unavailable father who could not throw light on his predicament and save him. His fears of being engulfed by a void felt palpable and we were confronted by the possibility that he might break down. I was mindful of the attacks that he might make on his wife, as she could become the recipient of his breaking-down self. This manifested as a powerful wish to impregnate her, despite her wishes, thinking this would provide relief from his own feelings. I said to him that he wished to get rid of his childlike feelings in his analysis by putting them physically into his wife, impregnating her with his split-off self, enacting the transvestite's wish to occupy mother. This interpretation made sense to him, and for the first time I began to feel that there were two minds in the room and that we were doing creative work together.

At this time, he had a dream confirming his emerging baby-like feelings and his fear of them. He was living in a flat on the set of *Eldorado*, the soap opera that flopped. He was with his wife. He thought it was wonderful but a child looked into the window of the flat and he felt terrified that it would get in and take over. Then the flat was taken over by lots of children and he and his wife were overwhelmed. I said that his dependency on me frightened him because he feared that we together might not be able to cope with the extent of his baby feelings. I noted that although he and his wife shared feelings of terror, they had become a couple in his unconscious.

A week later he reported a second dream. He was again in a flat in *Eldorado* with his wife but this time he was aware of being frightened. The whole set was on fire. He realised this was just a superficial film set and, as it was about to collapse, the Prince of Wales rescued him and then left him. I thought that although Mr D was beginning to feel rescued by me, he felt I quickly abandoned him, like father. Around this time he discovered where his father lived and, amidst great pain and sadness, found he was remarried with two children.

As with Dr L, when she became aware of the importance of life when it was endangered in the face of her medical treatment, this intervention by the reality of his father's life came at a point in Mr D's analysis when he was able to begin thinking and ultimately to beginning mourning, rather than simply to project and deny. By this time, my own violent and infantile feelings of needing to reject and feel contempt for Mr D had correspondingly abated. It seemed to me crucial that with Mr D, some recognition of a procreative internal couple needed to be restored in order for him to grow up. Painful though it was, the re-finding of Mr D's father and Mr D's acknowledgement of help from his stepfather led to more mature defences and a relationship with his wife that relied less on infantile projections.

For both these patients, these elemental facts of life were intolerable, as they had never experienced a mind with which they could think about them rather than succumbing to the power of their infantile defences. This left them in a world where they could only deal with their terrors by enacting or evacuating into others, in the case of Dr L in the concrete form of urine and with Mr D through the violent insistence on his wife's dependence, enacted through his perversion, dressing up, and projecting his helplessness. It was essential with both patients that I was eventually able to manage my own countertransference terrors around the fear of death and disintegration so that these frightening thoughts could become symbolised in the patients' own material.

As a human I know that I struggle too at times to accept the three facts of life that Money-Kyrle sketched out forty years ago. The tool that I make use of is my belief in the analytic method and the need to have some theory to make sense of violent and frightening countertransference experiences. We do not need to reify these facts of life but perhaps we can make use of them with particularly challenging patients. They have often had good reason to attack and asset strip any object that threatened awareness of the need for love, and the terror of the abyss, something we all have to deal with. As Nietzsche said, "One can look into the abyss and the abyss looks straight back" (1872).

These patients have been exposed early on to living in the world with objects that do not provide the equipment necessary for facing these fears. I think it's the analysts' capacity to bear these anxieties in themselves that can allow patients to gradually begin to internalise a relationship that can allow for love as well as hate. Despite the painful reality exposed to early in life, they can begin to discover that all relationships are finite but still worth having.

According to Hannah Arendt (1958), the world, as opposed to the Earth, is something manmade. It is planned out with the ideas from our heads and composed of the work of our hands. But without deep human relatedness, it is but a static "heap of things", a hardened reality that we run around while remaining in the same place. What lends pliability to reality, she claims, as Freud did decades earlier, is taking the time to talk with one another without any predetermined purpose, without hurrying from one topic to another, without seeking solutions, and without skirting the real difficulty of actually communicating with one another. It is here that the continuing value of Freud's discovery asserts itself.

* * *

Afterword

There are so many distractions from our internal world, that turning away from deep involvement has reached epidemic proportions in a market economy providing a multitude of entertainments, where the commodification of human experience is fast replacing human attachment.

This often manifests itself in the consulting room as traumatised patients, looking for quick fixes and short term treatments, putting unrealistic pressure on the therapist to collude with current fashionable treatments, rather than to provide the first frightening experiences of unstructured thought in what might have been a world dedicated to avoidance.

Some experiences have been so painful that human contact and love is a real threat to whatever defences and structures people have been able to develop. The terror of the abyss is always with them and analysis can threaten exposure to this frightening place.

References

Arendt, H. (1958). *The Human Condition*. Chicago: University of Chicago Press.

MacNeice, Louis (2007). Autobiography. *Collected Poems of Louis MacNeice*. London: Faber and Faber.

Money-Kyrle, R. (1969). Cognitive development. In: R. Money-Kyrle & E. O'Shaughnessy (Eds.), *The Collected of Papers Roger Money-Kyrle* (p. 92). Perthshire: Clunie, 1971.

Nietzsche, F. (1872) (Aphorism 146, p. 230). *On Yon Side of Good and Evil*, section 146, entire. London: Random House, 2012.

CHAPTER TEN

"Holding and Interpretation": Winnicott at work*

Lesley Caldwell

Introduction

Holding and Interpretation: Fragment of an Analysis is the record of an analysis begun in the early 1940s, continued in the 1950s, and published posthumously (Winnicott, 1986) with an introduction by Masud Khan (1989). An earlier version of the same material, with a clinical commentary from the American psychiatrist and analyst Alfred Flarsheim, had been published in 1972. *Holding and Interpretation* is an account of an analytic treatment by a senior clinician committed to researching some of the features this analysis brought into prominence. Its elaborate interpretations, together with detailed notes mostly taken during the sessions themselves, question the stereotype of Winnicott as an analyst wary of interpretation, while, more generally, they illuminate how specific to a particular time and place are the interventions clinicians make every day, and how, implicitly or explicitly, all interpretations contain basic theoretical assumptions. In this work two emphases stand

---

*Extracts from *Holding and Interpretation* are included in this chapter by the kind permission of The Marsh Agency Ltd on behalf of The Winnicott Trust.

out: Winnicott's thorough insertion in Freud and the centrality of the Oedipus complex, and his concern with the much earlier establishment of a self able to confront the impulses deriving from infantile sexuality and aggression. Winnicott is known for his interest in early emotional development and an apparently lesser concern with the drives, but both arenas are present throughout *Holding and Interpretation*.

"Holding" and "interpretation" are concepts that may be approached as alternatives, sequentially, or with each having a place from moment to moment in the work of any analysis. While "holding" might lead towards a priority being ascribed to the preverbal and its modalities, "interpretation" would seem to locate the treatment in a more classical framework of words. Winnicott makes the case for their being regarded as two, always linked forms of the analytic process, so that the words, the concepts, and the density of the language employed in this analysis are to be considered as illustrations of a particular form of analytic holding of the patient by the analyst and, in a different temporality, of the patient's holding of himself. The case history is introduced as "An illustration of the depressive position as it can appear in an analysis" (Winnicott, 1986, p. 19), and Winnicott judged it a success in his clinical diary. Although much of it contains a focus on explicitly oedipal material, the patient's early infantile situation is seen as forming and shaping him and the trajectory of the analysis.

The analysand had been in analysis with Winnicott as an adolescent in 1940–1941, in wartime conditions. When, years later, he was hospitalised for a breakdown after his qualification as a doctor, Winnicott sought him out, having been informed by his doctor of his presence at the Cassel hospital. The case and his decisions about treatment are strongly influenced by his original assessment and that first analysis, perhaps also by his interest in working with patients whose psychopathology is seen as originating in early deprivation. In the analysis presented in *Holding and Interpretation*, the patient's and his mother's fantasies of perfection, and their consequences, which had been a major focus in the earlier treatment, are further elaborated through the relationship between the parents and the son's relationship with his father. The material I have selected gives some opportunity to see the constant interaction in the transference between different developmental levels and the defences the patient had developed from a very young age to cope with early failures in the establishment of a self that could relate to others, be spontaneous, and develop the capacity for reflecting on his own behaviour and his life.

Though he left before Winnicott considered him to be really ready, Dr A's analysis is recorded as successful in that Winnicott seems to have believed that his patient had progressed enough in being aware of his dependence and his wish for independence. This appeared in the beginnings of making decisions for himself and his awareness that he owed such a capacity to his analysis. His analyst made his position clear, but accepted the patient's decision and was not concerned by it.

The analysis

The earlier months of Dr A's second analysis are the subject of "Withdrawal and regression", a paper published in 1954, and included in *Holding and Interpretation* as an appendix. In that paper Winnicott said:

> The main thing that keeps this patient consciously seeking analysis is his inability to be impulsive and to make original remarks although he can join very intelligently in serious conversation originated by other people. Over a long period his free associations were in the form of a rhetorical report of a conversation that was going on all the time inside, his free associations being carefully arranged and presented in a way that he felt would make the material interesting to the analyst. (1986, p. 187)

The verbatim record in *Holding and Interpretation* covers the last six months of the second analysis (January to July 1955). "The patient spoke slowly and deliberately … and what he said could be easily recorded" (Winnicott, 1986, p. 7). Winnicott recorded it in great detail.

Dr A thought of himself as boring, and in his introduction Khan (1986) discusses the boring patient as a patient actively involved in doing something, that is, being boring. In his view, and also in Winnicott's, this is a patient who still has hope, despite the hopelessness that forms the background affect that Winnicott's interpretations consistently address. The patient uses the concepts of psychoanalysis knowingly and easily, and he talks extensively to and with Winnicott, but both recognise a barrier. Winnicott does not believe that Dr A is primarily set on destructiveness. Rather, his quasi-dissociative state is what he can bring; it is what he does/is. Winnicott accepts his talk and the frequent sleeping that accompanies it, and goes on analysing. He listens, he stays awake, he takes notes, he comments, he makes reference to the patient's external world, and when he interprets, often in quite complicated ways, he assumes the patient's capacity to understand him. When he realises he has made a mistake, or said something the patient is not ready for, he says so.

Dr A also goes to sleep, sometimes several times in a session. From the beginning, Winnicott notes the patient's sleepiness, but his first explicit mention of it is in response to the patient's anxiety as to whether Winnicott could tolerate "his need for an extreme dependence such as his living with me" (1986, p. 24). He describes Dr A speaking "of his own negativity and how it bores him, it makes him depressed. It leaves him high and dry. This negativity is a challenge. Sometimes speech is not worth the effort. He feels literally dried up. Sleep means lack of emotion. Nothing presents itself" (ibid., p. 24). Speech and sleep and what each means for this patient become increasingly important as the analysis continues. Words, silence, sleep, and the analyst's note-taking comprise the framework of the analysis.

Khan suggests that Winnicott's patient could be thought of as "a patient for whom nothing existed but his thoughts" (ibid., p. 14), and it is the establishment of the beginnings of a person in his analysand that seems to guide Winnicott's positive assessment of this analysis. This description takes up a particular quality of Dr A to propose that being a person, psychoanalytically speaking, involves more than having thoughts. The terms "holding", "being", "illusion", and "disillusion" form the foundations for Winnicott's consistent challenge to a one-person psychology approach in understanding human development and, in the course of these recorded sessions, Dr A begins to bring himself as a person. He becomes aware of his dependence and, therefore, of his potential *independence* from his analyst. Through the analytic work that has facilitated the beginnings of a person finally able to have "real" thoughts and feelings about himself, he also becomes aware of what he lacks.

In his paper "Mind and its relation to the psyche-soma" (1949), Winnicott gives his account of the ontological origins of thinking, grounded both in the Freudian assumption of the ego as first a bodily ego, and in his own exploration of it through the primacy of the bodily relationship of the baby with the mother as fundamental to the emergence of mind. He outlines the development of mind and the development of thinking in the neonate from two perspectives: healthy development and pathology. In the case of healthy development, he seems to suggest, we can take the mind for granted, assuming its primacy in a person's location of self in body as a facet of integration. He writes:

> Given the necessary environmental conditions the mind is a specialized part of the overall organization of the infant's integration of psyche and soma. As such it does not exist separately but is the imaginative elaboration of somatic parts, feelings, and functions, that is physical aliveness. It depends on a healthy brain but is not necessarily localised there (or anywhere). (1949, p. 244)

If the necessary environmental conditions are not there, the mind is an unintegrated phenomenon, reflecting splitting, dissociation, and fragmentation. It arises as a kind of false entity with a false localisation. Thinking in these terms provides a way of understanding certain dimensions of certain patients. Where the infant has to deal with environmental failure beyond his capacities, he has to adapt to impingements. "Thinking as a mother substitute, a sitter-in, with the mind being exploited in defence" (Winnicott, 1965, p. 155) describes a function called upon to be exercised prematurely, and the processes of dissociation between psyche and soma can give rise to the mind as a split-off phenomenon. Several possibilities in which one or other entity is excluded and not integrated can result in distorted development: (a) over-activity in mental functioning, where psyche-soma is in opposition to mind and "thinking" results in a precociously self-sufficient child; (b) a "without mind" state, where the self affects stupidity; (c) a "without psyche" self, where the imagination is curtailed (Winnicott, 1949); (d) a "false self" acting as a carapace to protect the hidden true self (Winnicott, 1960).

Dr A presents a highly intellectualised persona, which, towards the end of the analysis, Winnicott describes as his "false self", a combination of the first and last possibilities noted above:

> At first it can be said that he came to analysis and talked. His speech was deliberate and rhetorical. Gradually it became clear that he was listening to conversations that were going on within and reporting

any parts of these conversations that he thought might interest me. In time it could be said that he brought himself to analysis and talked about himself as a mother or father might bring a child to me and talk about him. In these early phases (six months) I had no chance of direct conversation with the child himself.

In the next stage I could deal with the child directly, which was the patient. There was a rather definite end to this phase and the patient himself said he *now came himself* for treatment (and for the first time he *felt hopeful*). (1986, p. 20)

Holding and Interpretation begins with Winnicott recording his patient approaching feelings of excitement with decided ambivalence. "This excitement was not experienced but it led to the work described in detail in the case notes that follow. The case notes refer to the work done between the excitement that arrived in the transference but which was not felt and the *experience* of the excitement" (ibid., p. 20).

Dr A had mentioned something quite new, love for his baby daughter, which he felt and described as "excitement". Although this theme continued, the patient became more and more "damped down". In a lengthy speech on 9 February, he described how much easier it now was to be excited. He paused and then added, "I do not want to talk about excitement" (1986, p. 22). Winnicott replied, "The point of excitement is being excited." The patient thought this risky, "You look silly. People might laugh if you prattle ... And then you are left holding the baby (meaning excitement)" (p. 25). Winnicott then brought together in the transference "prattling" (a reference to family descriptions of Dr A as a small child), and "holding the baby", but the patient distanced his adult self from "prattling": "The danger is that if you are excited you lose it. You have it taken away or undermined." Winnicott responded, "'If you show excitement it gets bagged.' (I might have interpreted the castration anxiety here but refrained)" (p. 26).

Winnicott describes making a rather general interpretation linking the patient's feeling for his daughter and his crying at the cinema (another unexpected act) to what the patient had himself missed as an infant, and with what he was needing his analyst to provide in the analysis by "the holding of a situation in time, so that the dependence phenomena could be tested in relation to the instinctual moments and ideas" (1986, p. 28). The interpretation brings together Winnicott's assessment of Dr A with his account of ego development as preceding awareness of the drives, and the need for a period of dependence as the condition for the establishment of a self that can experience and manage impulses and desires (the excitement).

The patient begins to think about a future where he is less afraid of being excited: "In the past it seemed I had difficulties in the present with no solution, as well as no prospect for the future. There was no hope of living an ordinary life ever. My depression was something to do with looking for dependence. I could say that in the dependence and therefore in the depression I was claiming my birthright" (ibid., p. 27). Earlier in that session Winnicott had commented, "It appears you have lived most of your life at a level below par in regard to excitement, and now when you come even to ordinary excitability you feel conscious of it" (p. 26).

Winnicott accepts the patient's ponderous elaborations, clearly derived from his own previous interpretations, and meets him in them; he accepts Dr A's defensive use of his intellect which makes him such a "boring" patient, but this never forms his own focus. As their exchanges highlight, for Winnicott there is very little point in interpreting the way this man uses his mind until the patient himself recognises this affectively and can begin to articulate the absence in himself of some of the attributes of personhood. Until Dr A himself begins to be interested in how and why he talks, his analyst accepts it as their shared analytic terrain. He continues to interpret Dr A's hopelessness about present and future as a past hopelessness, and he states, "What you are looking for is your capacity to love and, without our knowing all the details, we can say that some failure in your early life made you doubt your capacity to love … it is this that the analysis has to provide so that dependence and the instinctual excitement could be experienced there" (1986, pp. 27–28).

When (5 April) the patient (long-windedly) reports *feeling* things, even jealousy, which, his analyst agrees, is "uncomfortable but preferable to the former lack of feeling" (p. 84), Winnicott introduces a link between the verboseness and the frequent sleeping: "The sleepiness may be about searching for ideas that are not available by direct intellectual effort," or, "defending yourself against an anxiety when you do not know what it is about" (ibid., p. 84).

The patient sleeps on a further fourteen occasions, sometimes several times in a session, but on 31 May a different dimension is introduced when he says, "the only emotional experience [here] is going to sleep 'which is going away'" (Winnicott, 1986, p. 123). Later in that session, when Winnicott speaks of "my loving you", Dr A sleeps again. A week later, the patient talks of his intellectual approach as a barrier and sleep as the alternative. The following exchange sees Winnicott maintaining a particular view of his patient's actions, based in his own assessment of the patient's early development and his conviction of the value of establishing an authentic self as the primary task of this analysis.

WINNICOTT: "Going to sleep is really you."
  PATIENT: "But it blots out everything else. If I were to sleep for the whole hour …"
WINNICOTT: "Even that would be something. You would not sleep anywhere. It is because you are here … You cannot take it for granted that I am here unless your intellect is active." (Ibid., p. 136)

The patient slept, snored, then suddenly awoke.

  PATIENT: "It does seem not only guilt, also a challenge to you expressing contempt."
WINNICOTT: "That is you and is real." (Ibid., p. 136)

After this, sleep is more directly referred to. Winnicott (1986) observes that sleep protects Dr A from rage (10 June), that "talking is killing" (p. 142), that sleep is a way of getting round his dilemma about the environment and his relation to it (p. 157). When the patient asks, "How is it possible to deal with absence of feeling?" (p. 158) Winnicott replies, "What you are fearing here is being awake while feeling no hope about contact with me here …" (p. 158). In a later session Dr A insists, "I insult you by sleeping" (1 July, p. 168). Soon, Winnicott interprets "… the whole of this [sleep] is the continued expression of your hopelessness about our meeting in a way in which there is a subtle interchange" (p. 172).

Winnicott's interpretations link Dr A's talking and lack of affect with his going to sleep—an extreme form of being silent. He emphasises its difference from "intellectual effort", from the patient's proficiency in explaining his experiences in words, proposing it represents his anxiety when he does not know, his fear of feeling, his wish to feel. While Dr A agrees that, for him, the emotional area is going away, he insists his behaviour is negative and denigrating, whereas Winnicott sees the shifts between discourse and sleep as impelled by something very different: the patient can bring a part of himself only through going away in sleep. It is because Dr A is aware of his intellectual competence but lack of emotional contact that he acts to grasp a part of himself that, albeit negatively, is potentially more alive. It is not only Dr A's incapacity, his lack, but his anxiety that it is *only* via the intellect that a contact with the other, in this case Winnicott, can be guaranteed or, indeed, would be wanted. He fears not only his own inability to be in touch, but his analyst's losing interest if he cannot show he is intelligent and capable.

Winnicott notes two other physical actions, initially without interpreting. First, the patient puts his foot onto the floor (six times in the middle of this period). When he does interpret, he describes this movement as a new relation to external reality, the gathering together of feeling, a movement towards spontaneity, an impulse towards life through motility (1986, p. 84). Second, towards the end of June, Dr A puts his hand to his face three times and Winnicott, in linking this to a baby's wanting contact and the sensitive mother realising this and giving it, explicitly aligns it with interpretation: "a correct interpretation well timed is a physical contact of a kind" (ibid., p. 160).

In a way that might well be questioned now, the analyst's interpretations frequently refer both to the patient's anxiety about loving and being loved, and his analyst's love for him: "looking for your capacity to love", "you doubt your capacity to love" (Winnicott, 1986, p. 27), "the perfection and hopelessness is about being loved" (p. 44), "after intercourse you feel free to love and be loved which is what you are always looking for" (p. 50), "the barrier is between you and me and one of the things it avoids is the idea of my loving you" (patient asleep) (p. 144), "being loved with no santions, (p. 149) without any ifs" (p. 151). On 5 July Winnicott says, "The word love means lot of things but it has to include this experience of subtle interplay, and we could say you are experiencing love and loving in this session" (p. 172).

Although Winnicott (1986) is often associated with ideas of regression or, to use his own term, "regression to dependence", the clinical material in this case study is organised around the patient's "withdrawal", a "momentary detachment from a waking relationship with external reality, this being sometimes of the nature of brief sleep" (p. 187). Where regression is understood as a state in the transference when an infantile dependence is established, a stage Winnicott regards as central in some analyses and which may provide the basis for development, Dr A did not become clinically regressed; instead, "his regressions were localised in momentary withdrawal states" (p. 187). Through Winnicott's understanding and acceptance of the relation between these states, and his talking, the patient comes alive enough to generate a curiosity about his own behaviour, to wonder about it and think about it with his analyst.

The difference between the sexes and rivalry

In mid-February Winnicott had interpreted the patient's anxiety in moving towards a triangular situation and his resort to sleepiness as an attempt to deal with it (Winnicott, 1986, p. 41). He had linked it to Dr A's confusion about the difference between the sexes and who has the penis—Dr A himself, his girlfriend, his wife, his analyst. These anxieties circle through the material and the patient's associations. The dominant theme of the first analysis, the patient's wish for perfection and his belief that his own satisfaction amounted to the annihilation of the object, continued alongside themes deriving from recollections of his adolescent dreams of girls with a penis and the currency of this fantasy in his present relations with his wife, his girlfriend, and his analyst. Winnicott interprets that Dr A cannot get to his hatred of the man in the triangular situation (p. 15), a theme that is increasingly analysed throughout the rest of the analysis. The patient's difficulties in his relations with both women and men are explored with each of these key figures as they appear in the transference, and are linked with their origins in early relations with and between mother and father. They highlight the impoverishment of Dr A's emotional life, bringing him to a devastating realisation about himself: "I never became human. I have missed it" (p. 96).

In late March the patient speaks about the changes in himself and his problems through analysis, and how his current problems relate to personal and sexual matters. Winnicott responds, "You couldn't show a more specific symptom at the start because you weren't there as a person to be having sexual difficulties. It is a part of your emergence as a person that you now come with personal symptoms" (1986, p. 71). With this shift, Dr A also begins to see men as rivals, as he "becomes conscious of the fantasy of the girl with the penis and vagina" (p. 71).

For Winnicott, Dr A's general inability to choose derives from an early experience of a combined parent figure that resulted in "this being used by you eventually in your difficulty in dealing with him, father, as a man" (1986, p. 73). He develops these themes through Dr A's different ways of using him, which involve competition and aggression, the beginnings of a negative transference, and the patient's anxiety about Winnicott's jealousy. Winnicott links this to recent material about the dentist that had directly related to Dr A's fear of castration:

> You had some work to do about the mouth excitements and the idea of a dentist punishing in a direct way. Only gradually have you come to be able to deal with me as a human being rival. It would seem at first as if you are in a position to triumph but this is only true if we consider the girl. I suggest that in regard to the wife it is different ... you have accepted in regard to your wife the complete absence of a sexual future. In other words, you have accepted a one hundred per cent ban on sex as if giving me the triumph. (1986, p. 74)

The patient describes his wife and Winnicott as rivals, saying he "can only come to analysis at the expense of her not allowing it ... In this case you are a woman, a mother figure from my wife's point of view". Winnicott agrees: "Here your mother claims you and so your wife has no chance" (ibid., p. 74).

In the following session Winnicott returns to Dr A's problem of dissatisfaction with finding his mother in his women, and his fear of both rivalry and friendship with men. The patient reports listening to some Elgar and being excited by it, noting that the variations were written about friends. Winnicott observes that Elgar was capable of love and warm friendship. The patient describes his girlfriend as uninterested in music, interested only in sex and medicine, and he fears Winnicott might not only forbid sex with his wife but also with the girlfriend. Winnicott says that Dr A can only see him as either "prohibiting or permitting ... You never met your father as a man to hate, a rival, someone you feared. Whether because of him or yourself or both you missed this and so you never felt mature" (1986, p. 76). He links this to the patient's incapacity at fifteen to mourn his father's death. In the following session, when the patient reports being annoyed with the girlfriend, Winnicott responds, "In the imaginative situation I am the person who has prohibited you from visiting the girl. In the previous session you half said you were expecting me to tell you to keep off her ... You are all the time looking for a man who will say 'No' at the right moment ... you are just a little bit allowing me to be in that position" (ibid., p. 83).

After a three-week break, Dr A reports things are happening and he feels involved in his emotional contact with Winnicott, who interprets the rivalry, which had been so difficult for the patient to feel until then, coming more directly into the transference: "The patient felt impotent, he had seen himself as 'cut off in midstream' so that in fantasy the idea had been introduced of two men, one of whom maims the other. Previously there had been only killing and this meant that the rivalry situation was not worth taking up" (1986, p. 100). Dr A's open rivalry means he now regards Winnicott as dangerous: "... it was the word impotent that you used ... a few days ago to describe the state I brought about in you ... if you yourself come and get into contact with me here, you will be maimed" (ibid., pp. 103–104).

When Dr A associates to ending his affair and leaving analysis, Winnicott says, "Soon the end of the hour will come and then I shall be quite literally in the position of someone who is maiming you ... I think the holiday was experienced by you as a serious maiming" (1986, p. 104). Dr A responds, "Today is quite exceptional in this matter of going to sleep. It must have something to do with the topic of father being perfect and my not being able to compete and all that" (p. 104). Winnicott writes that it was as if the patient had not heard his interpretation. Nonetheless, he replies, "Yes, father and you in rivalry brings dangers, especially if you include actively making love. I am not sure if you feel father could make love?" (p. 104). The patient replies that his father being dead makes it all seem futile, to which Winnicott says, "It seems a funny thing to say but at this moment I think you are forgetting that in fact I am alive. And now it's time" (p. 105).

Winnicott's grounding in Freud and his attention to the shifts in the transference led him to bring together the patient's earlier lack of awareness of a third position and what its acceptance both allows and enables, that is, the need for rivalry with an actual person, his analyst. The patient's realisation of his murderousness could then be interpreted directly.

At the end of May, Dr A describes his daughter's spontaneity, comparing it with his own experience:

PATIENT: "No one had any time for me when I talked and so it was best not to say anything."

WINNICOTT: "I am reminding you of the changeover from prattling to your need to think first so that the content would be appreciated and people would not laugh and you would not feel ashamed. It is rather like a stammer this deliberate talk of yours which holds people."

PATIENT: "'Even now there seems to be hidden excitement. It is touch and go. Will the barrier break through when I am safely out of sight?' (Here the patient put his foot on the floor.)"

WINNICOTT: "You put your foot on the floor and I think that you feel at this moment that you could act, for instance, walk away. That is an expression of your true self" (1986, p. 125)

Later Winnicott adds that, for Dr A, the intellectual is his false self (ibid., p. 126).

Uses of talking and sleeping

At the beginning of the next session (Wednesday 1 June), Dr A says, "For the first time I feel that I am here myself. That means that I was unaware of time at the end of last session. I got carried away" (Winnicott, 1986, p. 129). Winnicott compares the place of talk earlier in the analysis—as a confirmation for the patient to himself—with its place in the present: "At the start when you talked, this talking had its own importance, as I have said, apart altogether from content, it meant you were alive, awake, eager" (ibid., p. 129).

After a pause, the patient contributes an important insight: "I felt anxious then. One difficulty is that a breakthrough might release so much and then I would become changeable with each emotional facet as it presents, so I keep busy talking, and this gives no time for me to take in what you say. I have a vision of being careful not to do all the talking so that you might not bother to listen" (ibid., p. 129). Subsequently, the patient continues to explore not coming, and having thoughts he does not have to tell his analyst:

> PATIENT: "In the relationship with the girl every detail came into the analysis. It always felt to me that it all belonged to Winnicott. Now I seem to want something for myself. Talking about things here is a deterrent to freedom outside."
>
> WINNICOTT: "So this is really what you mean about not coming. It is part of your wish to find out what you are like."
>
> PATIENT: "Previously everything was talked out and I had no desire for privacy."
>
> WINNICOTT: "I think the point was that you had nowhere to put it."
>
> PATIENT: "The intellectual was simply an area for discussion not a place where anything could be hidden."
>
> WINNICOTT: "So it seems you have turned up and you have an inside and an outside." (1986, p. 134).

Winnicott's response here anticipates his paper "The location of cultural experience" (1967), where he discusses having a place to put what is found. Dr A's awareness of an inside and an outside, and the sense of difference on which it depends, have developed in the analysis.

In the following sessions they discuss all the uses of Dr A's talking and its links with his emotional states, the limits he feels are imposed on his spontaneity by there being only three sessions, its relation to whether he speaks or not, and his fear he may not talk at all as a protest:

> PATIENT: "If I am operating emotionally then I must have the right to come when I want, so that to be expected to start right off is an adjustment to try to meet an unsatisfactory time-table. What I fear is that I will protest by not talking for the whole hour."
>
> WINNICOTT: "It is like letting me know that you want to be away but coming in order to let me know."
>
> PATIENT: "If I do not start I have a definite fear that I won't be able to begin. Each second provides a mounting difficulty and I also talk because I cannot bear time wasted though of course trivialities may be a waste too ... I would like a relationship in which it was not necessary to talk or there

could be a jumble of words and phrases and that would be no use. This happens with my wife. I try to say what comes, try to be natural, but there is nothing but a jumble of ideas. This seems artificial, glib. I am talkative trying to be lighthearted but the result is confusion. This is why people lose interest in me. At times that could happen here and you would not be able to take in what I was saying because it would be too confused. This is why I edit everything." (Winnicott, 1986, p. 135)

When Dr A wishes he could talk like his daughter without regard for whether it makes sense, Winnicott wonders if anyone allowed for his being incomprehensible as a child. Dr A replies, "Possibly I was rebuked for nonsense, probably by father, who would call me longwinded" (ibid., p. 136). When Winnicott takes up his anxiety in the transference about having to avoid speaking like a child, the patient explains that he wants to get away from the intellectual approach, but his only way of doing it is to fall asleep. Winnicott replies, "Going to sleep, however, is really you" (p. 136). Here the interpretive choice is not on the object, Winnicott, and its effect on him, but rather on the only way at this time the patient can allow himself to be a subject. The analyst emphasises the patient's moves towards an expression of himself, and the need for the existence of a private, internal space in which to do that. For Winnicott, this is a valuable, fundamental acquisition that Dr A is in the process of acquiring.

The ending of the analysis

The patient decides to apply for a job that would involve either his finishing or his reorganising his analysis, a decision that Winnicott sees and interprets, in part, as a move towards independence and the beginnings of the patient's capacity to decide something for himself. The sessions increasingly demonstrate the patient's growing interest in exploring his own presentation: his talking/not talking, coming/not coming, and the meanings of his frequent sleeping in sessions.

The idea of who is responsible for starting sessions is one area Dr A raises. This is again linked by Winnicott with early infantile states where the mother anticipates the baby's needs, without the baby needing to signal them. This second analysis has brought about the patient's recognition of his own hopelessness, but as a result it also enables the beginnings of a capacity to bring, however anxiously, an emerging self, one emerging precisely through the analytic process. This "self" begins to take some interest in his symptoms and behaviour towards himself and his analyst and the feelings that accompany them.

The various meanings of talking and the kinds of talking in which Dr A has engaged are linked with an inner world where one form of speaking—intellectual, cognitive, without affect—was developed precociously as a defensive response to the lack of reception of an earlier state. To assert a self at odds with this false, intellectual self, Dr A goes to sleep. Winnicott interprets his protecting everyone, thus saving the world: "If you do not go away everyone will die" (1986, p. 140). Dr A's very young self, his adolescent self, and the patient in the session who goes to sleep, are linked in the unconscious. Winnicott makes the affective connection: "Not talking is equivalent to killing" (ibid., p. 141). These patterns also involve Dr A's established ways of trying to make contact, but not too much contact, with the other, initially because of fear of the other's indifference, but increasingly because of his awareness of his own inexperience and lack of knowledge about how to talk to someone spontaneously, without constant editing of content and feeling accepted or rejected. Behind all these fears lies the patient's hopelessness about being loved for himself and his growing awareness of his assumption and cultivation of an intellectual self to deal defensively with this fear. He imagines that from about the age of five his wish was to become an adult as quickly as possible.

Winnicott identifies the birth of Dr A's sister and his attendance at his first school, run by his mother in their house, as significant contributions to his withdrawals. Dr A adds running away or the wish to run away, both as a child and in his sessions, and in those moments when he is silent. When he again expresses a wish to be able to talk like his daughter who doesn't have to make sense, Winnicott picks up how driven is his continuing need to make sense, to be clear, originating probably in his not having had what his daughter enjoys. The constant flow of words is interpreted as a way of controlling unacceptable feelings, of keeping his analyst and everyone else at a distance, of his enactment of what is expected of him, of an external expectation that was internalised and became rigidified.

The patient increasingly begins to recognise irritation and anger, and this anger becomes linked with its alternative, hopelessness, and his fear of his capacity for destruction. When he expresses a wish to turn over on his face in the session, Winnicott comments that his presumption is that he, Winnicott, is forbidding it (1986, p. 137). The patient remembers his fears, aged about twelve, of lying on his back as "like being in his coffin" (ibid., p. 138). The analyst reminds him that in the first analysis one major symptom that was overcome was his inability to lie down and tolerate the anxiety it produced. At the time the symptom had been interpreted around his fears of annihilation through satisfaction of a feed from a perfect mother. These fears had prevented him from realising that, with waiting, both desire and the object would return.

Winnicott comments on the patient's increased capacity to be aware of these conflicts. Dr A responds by saying that the first analysis had been closer in time to his twelve-year old self, and therefore was more frightening. His father had developed the illness that would kill him soon after. Winnicott outlines the patient's need to protect his father from his rage and fury, characteristics of any normal adolescent but in this instance blocked because of his father's condition. Although the patient's father had died before he began the analysis, he had not accepted that death. Winnicott interprets, "It is impossible to accept the death of your father unless you are able to encompass your anger with him and the death of him in the dreams in which you kill him. He, being ill, had to be protected and your protection of him has kept him alive all this time" (1986, p. 139).

Where to be

Dr A's silence enacts his dilemma: "There is no way of bringing not coming" (Winnicott, 1986, p. 141). On 4 March he had discussed a fantasy of not coming, which Winnicott had interpreted as material for the session, precisely because he actually came. Dr A had said, "Not coming would be really wasting it all. Also, I was reluctant to make the break bigger still by not coming. That would not be taking the analysis seriously. It would be unprofessional" (ibid., p. 50).

Winnicott was unimpressed by this dutiful account, and concentrated instead on the search for spontaneity and feeling: "But what you seek is the impulse and by not coming you would be making coming more real. If it is a professional matter, you come for other than reasons of impulse" (1986, p. 50). In this exchange many possible interpretations present themselves around the patient's apparent awareness and his sense of a break, but Winnicott is more attuned to a deeper level; it is the desire the patient is seeking that is central.

In the June session the patient has realised something more:

PATIENT: "Part of silence is a need to keep some feelings away from here" (p. 141). "I am beginning to discover what is behind the not-talking of the past, I have always thought of this symptom as just a nuisance though you have spoken of it as potentially valuable. I believe that it was concealing something, only now I mean what I am saying, that the silence itself is the significant thing." (p. 142)
            [After a pause]
PATIENT: "I was silent then because I recognised it is a good thing in itself sometimes not to talk. Not to talk for talking's sake. In the past I made too big an effort to try and say everything". [Pause] "I feel that if I don't talk there is a danger of never talking at all, and then going to sleep. I can't trust silence."
WINNICOTT: "There is something real here in your silence, that it is you yourself, whereas talking for talking's sake means you are not sure you exist, or me." (p. 143)

Towards the end of this session Dr A says, "It seems very difficult this not talking, it's dangerous, nothing happens. Can you make use of it? It's only too easy never to talk. I remember now as I left yesterday I wondered if it is worthwhile to carry on if not talking is life." Winnicott replies, "'This connects with the idea of being loved with sanctions, or being loved meaning having your existence valued" (1986, p. 144).

In the following sessions fury or hopelessness continue to appear as alternatives, but Winnicott links fury with deprivation, claiming that the patient has actually reached deprivation in recent sessions. When Dr A says, "Anger is more productive than hopelessness which is negative" (ibid., p. 148), Winnicott replies that anger is preferable because he feels more real, although it is dangerous to his analyst. The patient replies, "Anger involves an object but hopelessness well, there's nothing to pursue" (p. 148). He goes on to say that he should be pursuing new things: "The next stage, making use of these discoveries etc." (p. 148). Instead of interpreting this as an evasion, Winnicott takes it up more positively. The patient can think of a next stage because he is aware "that to some extent here and now I have love for you … I mean love with no ifs and no sanctions, nothing more nor less than my capacity to be identified with you" (p. 149).

A further exchange leads Winnicott to say, "So we come to a positive meaning for silence—the expression of the idea that the start must come from me" (1986, p. 149). The patient agrees he often wants Winnicott to produce something first. But Winnicott says, "If you like me to start it is already no good for me to start because in doing so I only follow your wish. To make adaptation to your need I must come to you with love before you know about the need" (p. 149). In this material Winnicott returns to Dr A's earlier emotional development and his own theory of the mother's being there for the baby both before and as a condition of the baby then being there for himself. Again this case history conveys the experience of the psychic movement between developmental stages that constitutes the analytic process.

The patient says that women always approach him first, which Winnicott links to his mother's inability at the start to identify fully with her infant. Winnicott follows this up in the transference: "In the same way I am caught up with you in the process of your analysis and of your going back to infantile dependence and your emotional growth forward again. Only if I am caught up in these processes as you are can you start to exist" (ibid. p. 150).

In the last weeks of the analysis these themes are enlarged, along with the patient's rivalry towards other men and killing them in fantasy. Dr A questions Winnicott persistently about leaving, and Winnicott finally says it would be useful to continue to explore these themes further, but he also insists that the decision must be the patient's and that making a decision in itself represents an advance. Dr A did not return. He wrote to Winnicott the following April to bring him briefly up to date and to thank him. At the end of the sixties, Winnicott made contact with this patient, who is recorded as replying at some length (ibid. p. 13).

Through Dr A's deepening awareness of his sense of self through his growing recognition of both its absence and the profound hopelessness at its roots, the analytic exchanges in the last weeks became more concentrated on oedipal themes. Dr A's early relations with his father and the parental couple had been further frozen in adolescence by his father's illness and death. His realisation of the severely impoverished quality of his actual relationships, and his ways of handling internal conflict by evasion and avoidance, were increasingly brought home to him by his developing curiosity about how he behaved with his analyst: either constant talking or going to sleep. Winnicott's acceptance of these extremes displayed both an acute sensitivity to his patient and a very clear set of ideas about technique.

Discussion

Interpretation is a strong feature of this treatment and the course of the sessions appears determined both by a secure clinical assessment and by the analyst's willingness to proceed at the patient's pace: "The analyst follows the basic principle of psychoanalysis, that the patient's unconscious leads and is alone to be pursued" (Winnicott, 1955, p. 297). Before analysis of defences, for instance against anxiety, can take place, the patient's ego has to be sufficiently developed to "experience id impulses and feel real in so doing" (ibid., p. 298).

Holding and Intrepretation provides fertile ground for thinking about an analysis and how it proceeds, just how much is said, how much each session may have to offer, what kind of relationship is set up by the transference illusion, what is enabled, and, as importantly, what is not. The title immediately draws attention to the different contributions that "being" and "doing" play in an analysis, and the very different weights they are to be assigned in different kinds of analyses with different patients. It also suggests that the interpretation/not interpretation dichotomy may be a false one in terms of how work proceeds and how Winnicott, who became more and more hesitant about the use of interpretations, himself worked. A close reading of this text highlights the space an analysis enables, even as it continually opens up questions about the analytic project, about this analysis, and about how we do analysis ourselves. It is a text from our history that deserves a place in our deliberations now.

In answer to the patient wondering why his analyst does the work he does, what is in it for him, Winnicott replies:

> In comparing the analyst and doctor's job you are noting a difference. The doctor deals with illness and if he cures the patient of the illness he has finished. The analyst, on the contrary, needs to have a positive feeling, something in his relationship with the patient that does not end with the cure of the illness. This concern for the

existence of this human being underlies any wish the analyst may have to cure the patient of his illness. (1986, p. 150)

For Winnicott it is the holding environment provided by the analysis that enables Dr A to move towards a capacity to experience an emotion rather than observe or comment on it, a shift in his capacity to live and to be alive. In this analysis the analyst's assessment of environmental failure in very early development provides a framework in which both the form and content of his interpretations, together with his interest in the patient's physical behavior—going to sleep, putting his foot on the floor, putting his hand to his face—are linked to what the patient himself says and how this is understood in the transference.

An interest in imagination and the life of the mind more generally has come to be associated with Winnicott, and finds its most elaborate expression in *Playing and Reality* (1971). But, as Schwarz proposes, "His work invites us to build up a capacity for psychoanalytic imagination" (1992, p. 171). This seems to derive from an interest in health and the attributes of the healthy individual together with a belief that psychoanalysis provides both a way of approaching them and offering a more profound understanding of them. "What is life about?" asks Winnicott towards the end of his own life. "You may cure your patient and not know what it is that makes him or her go on living. It is of first importance for us to acknowledge openly that absence of psychoneurotic illness may be health but it is not life" (1967, p. 134).

References

Flarsheim, A. (1972). Holding and interpretation. Annotated version in: P. L. Giovacchini (Ed.), *Tactics and Techniques in Psychoanalytic Psychotherapy*. New York: Science House.

Khan, M. (1989). Introduction. In: D. W. Winnicott (1986) *Holding and Interpretation: Fragment of an Analysis* (pp. 1–18). London: Karnac.

Schwarz, M. M. (1992). Introduction: D. W. Winnicott's cultural space. *Psychoanalytic Review, 79*: 169–174.

Winnicott, D. W. (1949). Mind and its relation to the psyche-soma. In: *Through Paediatrics to Psychoanalysis* (pp. 243–254). London: Tavistock, 1958 [reprinted London: Karnac, 1975].

Winnicott, D. W. (1954). Withdrawal and regression. In: *Through Paediatrics to Psychoanalysis* (pp. 255–261). London: Tavistock, 1958 [reprinted

London: Karnac, 1975. Reprinted as Appendix to *Holding and Interpretation*. London: Karnac, 1989].

Winnicott, D. W. (1955). Clinical varieties of transference. In: *Through Paediatrics to Psychoanalysis* (pp. 295–299). London: Tavistock.

Winnicott, D. W. (1960). Countertransference. In: *The Maturational Processes and the Facilitating Environment* (pp. 158–165). London: Hogarth, 1965 [reprinted London: Karnac, 1990].

Winnicott, D. W. (1965). New light on children's thinking. In: *Psychoanalytic Explorations* (pp. 152–157). London: Karnac, 1989.

Winnicott, D. W. (1967). The location of cultural experience. In: *Playing and Reality* (pp. 128–139). London: Routledge, 1971; reprinted 1991; 2006.

Winnicott, D. W. (1968). Thinking and symbol formation. In: *Psychoanalytic Explorations* (pp. 213–216). London: Karnac, 1989.

Winnicott, D. W. (1971). *Playing and Reality*. London: Tavistock [reprinted Routledge, 1991, 2006].

Winnicott, D. W. (1986). *Holding and Interpretation: Fragment of an Analysis*. London: Karnac, 1989.

INDEX